Praise for *Greening Your Small Business*

"A comprehensive, practical guide—takes small businesses by the hand and tells them all that they need to know in order to take full advantage of greening." —Jacquelyn A. Ottman, president of J. Ottman Consulting Inc. and Eco-Innovation and Green Marketing

"An essential guide for anyone interested in learning more about building a 'green' small business—from sustainable business plans to ecologically minded travel, it offers comprehensive business solutions."
—Mike Benziger, winegrower, general manager, and estate winemaker for Benziger Family Winery

"There must be a thousand and one ways that small businesses can profit from greening their operations, and Jennifer Kaplan has done a yeoman's task, researching and consolidating nearly all of them. The result is a rich collection of practical tips that harried small business owners can easily access in order not only to green but to thrive." —Byron Kennard, executive director of the Center for Small Business and the Environment

"Smart business leaders know green is now a strategic imperative. *Greening Your Small Business* is an extensive, practical guide that makes it easy to discover and prioritize the best ideas for your organization. Whether you're just getting started or well on your way, you'll find hundreds of tips and resources to help make your business more profitable and eco-friendly."
—Randy Paynter, founder and CEO of Care2.com

continued...

D1057773

GREENING
YOUR
SMALL
BUSINESS

How to Improve Your Bottom Line, Grow Your
Brand, Satisfy Your Customers—and
Save the Planet

JENNIFER KAPLAN

PRENTICE HALL PRESS

PRENTICE HALL PRESS
Published by the Penguin Group
Penguin Group (USA) Inc.
375 Hudson Street, New York, Ne~~~~
Penguin Group (Canada), 90 Eglinto~~~~2Y3, Canada
(a division of Pearson Penguin Canada Inc.)
Penguin Books Ltd., 80 Strand, London WC2R 0RL, England
Penguin Group Ireland, 25 St. Stephen's Green, Dublin 2, Ireland (a division of Penguin Books Ltd.)
Penguin Group (Australia), 250 Camberwell Road, Camberwell, Victoria 3124, Australia
(a division of Pearson Australia Group Pty. Ltd.)
Penguin Books India Pvt. Ltd., 11 Community Centre, Panchsheel Park, New Delhi—110 017, India
Penguin Group (NZ), 67 Apollo Drive, Rosedale, North Shore 0632, New Zealand
(a division of Pearson New Zealand Ltd.)
Penguin Books (South Africa) (Pty.) Ltd., 24 Sturdee Avenue, Rosebank, Johannesburg 2196, South Africa

Penguin Books Ltd., Registered Offices: 80 Strand, London WC2R 0RL, England

While the author has made every effort to provide accurate telephone numbers and Internet addresses at the time of publication, neither the publisher nor the author assumes any responsibility for errors, or for changes that occur after publication. Further, the publisher does not have any control over and does not assume any responsibility for author or third-party websites or their content.

First edition: November 2009

Library of Congress Cataloging-in-Publication Data

Kaplan, Jennifer.
    Greening your small business: how to improve your bottom line, grow your brand, satisfy your customers—and save the planet / Jennifer Kaplan.—1st ed.
        p.   cm.
    Includes bibliographical references and index.
    ISBN 978-0-7352-0446-1
    1. Small business—Environmental aspects. 2. Sustainable development. 3. Entrepreneurship—Environmental aspects. 4. Social responsibility of business. I. Title.
    HD2341.K286   2009
    658.4'083—dc22   2009033275

PRINTED IN THE UNITED STATES OF AMERICA

10 9 8 7 6 5 4 3 2 1

The products, services, and brands mentioned in this book are representative. The list is not meant to be exhaustive, and neither the author nor the publisher specifically recommends or endorses any of these products, services, or brands.

Most Prentice Hall Press books are available at special quantity discounts for bulk purchases for sales promotions, premiums, fund-raising, or educational use. Special books, or book excerpts, can also be created to fit specific needs. For details, write: Special Markets, Penguin Group (USA) Inc., 375 Hudson Street, New York, New York 10014.

To
Alexander, Helena, Natasha, and Gabriella
and
Alex
and
my mother

ACKNOWLEDGMENTS

My heartfelt thanks to those who have helped, listened to, encouraged, and tolerated me during the writing of *Greening Your Small Business*. There is no doubt that this book would never have happened without the assistance and incredible skills of Susan Dynerman. Thank you to my fabulous agent, Joelle Delbourgo, who provided early and unwavering help and support. Thanks also to Maria Gagliano at Prentice Hall Press for being a wonderful editor. I am deeply grateful to Byron Kennard of the Center for Small Business and the Environment for being an incredible mentor and also Dr. Louise Marshall at Marymount University, who first gave me the opportunity to teach.

My gratitude would not be complete without a huge shout-out to the many knowledgeable voices that helped guide me along the way. This includes Joe Fuld, Nick Aster, Dave Anderson, Maryanne Conlin, Leah Edwards, Randy Paynter, Taylor Martin, and John Friedman. And of course, to the incredible small business owners and green gurus, Jeremy Barlow, Chris Bartle, Jeannete Bitz, Omay Elphick, Ben Grossman, Jason Holstine, Mary Hutchens, Andrew Jacobs, Sue Lynn, Tim Malooly, Christine Nevers, Daniel Peacock, Chris Rankin, John Roeber, Charles Sathrum, Andrew Smith, Evan Smith, and Alex Szabo, all of whom generously gave their time and shared their stories and insights.

And finally, I especially want to thank Phyllis and Sheldon Busansky; my children—Alex, Helena, Natasha, and Gabriella—all of whom put up with my daily absences; and last but definitely not least, my husband, the incredible and supportive Alex Busansky.

CONTENTS

ONE

DEVELOPING
YOUR
GREEN PLAN

1 WHAT DOES GOING GREEN MEAN?

We can evade reality, but we cannot evade the consequences of evading reality.

—Ayn Rand

Not long after the turn of the twenty-first century, Jason Holstine, founder and president of the largest independent green building center in Maryland, started noticing that more of his customers were beginning to share his interest in green building materials. "I'd say: Check out this cool product. Isn't this great? This is a countertop made out of paper. Or here's this product that slashes your energy use," says Holstine. Then, when he'd look into how and where to get it, he'd end up telling them something like this: "Well, I don't have samples. You have to order it from the West Coast. It's really expensive because you have to order a sheet at a time. And you can't match the colors." And at one point, it became obvious to him that there was a need for actual supply of product—green product. Not long afterward, he and his colleagues started working on the model for the Amicus Green Building Center in Kensington, Maryland, which is essentially a hardware store where everything is green.

In 2006, when Wal-Mart first started talking about the concept of "grading" packaging on measures of its greenness, Matt Kistler, the company's vice president of Packaging Innovation, told *USA Today*: "A 2% reduction in a package's size is worth millions and millions of dollars. You can get more in a container, more in a boat, more in a truck. The numbers are just amazing."[1] Two years later, the company officially launched its Packaging Scorecard, which rates the packaging used by Wal-Mart suppliers on a number of variables related to environmental sustainability. The greener the packaging, the higher the scores. With a single program, the retail giant effectively changed the way the consumer product industry—from toy makers to electronics manufacturers—thinks about packaging. Fast-forward to 2009. When Mike Duke began his tenure as Wal-Mart CEO, he immediately reinforced his commitment to sustainability by declaring: "Sustainability . . . is not optional."

In 2005, TheGreenOffice.com began with the idea of offering green office supplies online—and ultimately evolved into one that stocks both green and "brown" products, featuring an elaborate product rating system that helps consumers make choices based on a range of factors, including performance, cost, and sustainability. "We wanted to design a system that would create a race to the top among manufacturers," says Alex Szabo, CEO and cofounder. "Now, more and more manufacturers are [calling], because they say: 'Hey, I notice that such and such product was ranked above mine.' The idea, over time, being to get more and more manufacturers hitting higher and higher trying to one-up each other." And it's starting to work.

A hardware store that only offers green products? Consumer product companies competing on the basis of the greenness of their packaging? Office supply manufacturers one-upping each other to find ways to produce more and better green business supplies?

There's a revolution going on in the American marketplace. Entrepreneurs like Jason Holstine and Alex Szabo are getting in on the ground floor. And to varying degrees, major corporations are stepping up to the plate. They're changing the way business operates by incorporating green practices, green products, and green objectives into their business models.

Where do small businesses fit into this new paradigm? How can you get greener? What does it mean and what will it involve? This book is designed to guide you through the green planning process, and provide you with the practical information and resources you need to go green—as well as offer insights from small businesses that have already begun to green their operations.

Maybe you want to go green because volatile energy costs are affecting your bottom line. Or because you think your customers want you to—or even expect you to. Maybe you want to stay competitive or become more competitive. Or you're just committed to doing whatever you can to reduce global warming and protect the environment. Whatever the reason, like millions of small business owners across America, you're asking yourself whether there is an economic advantage to going green. This book will help you find the answer.

The Green Mandate: A Little Background

"Sustainability"—a new name for an old concept.

—Nikki Johnson, Marketing Coordinator, FoxJet[2]

Going green isn't a new idea. In fact, awareness of environmental issues has been steadily rising for the past generation. Politically, the issue came to the forefront in the 1960s, and in 1970, the Environmental Protection Agency was established in response to growing public awareness of green issues. However, for many years, corporations resisted taking action, predicting that green practices and directives would be cost prohibitive, and hinder innovation and growth.

Interest in the environment—and the impulse to change our behavior by going green—has evolved with our growing understanding and awareness of what's at stake. "Over the last few decades," says an Infor Solutions Whitepaper, "the mounting evidence in the form of warnings and reports about global warming, toxic-product dangers and rising energy costs have pushed the green movement to the forefront of consumers' minds, and, subsequently, forced business leaders to focus on finding cost-effective and profitable solutions to these and other environmental problems."

 Global climate change (aka global warming and the greenhouse effect) refers to the buildup of man-made gases in the atmosphere that trap solar heat, causing negative changes in global weather patterns, including variable rainfall patterns, rising sea levels, droughts, and habitat loss.

The facts are compelling. Scientists now agree that recent human-induced carbon-producing activities are the root cause of the enormous global climate change issues we now face.

In February 2007, the U.N.'s Intergovernmental Panel on Climate Change (IPCC) reported that a discernable climate shift began with the Industrial Revolution. In the mid-1700s, human activities began to play the chief role in the shifting chemical composition of the atmosphere. Since then, carbon dioxide (CO_2) quantities in the atmosphere have been rising exponentially. Atmospheric loads of two other major greenhouse gases, methane (CH) and nitrous oxide (NO), were relatively constant until the nineteenth century, at which point increases began to be detected. In addition, a slew of other synthetic chemicals now found in the atmosphere did not even exist in preindustrial air. But the real wake-up call has come with the most recent scientific findings. It's now clear that the most significant damage from carbon-producing activities that cause global warming has occurred in the last decade. *The large quantities of greenhouse gases emitted during the 1990s were greater than at any time during the past one million years.*

In a 2008 lecture, Peter Orszag, who was later named the director of the Office of Management and Budget under President Obama, stated that the basic science of climate change supports these four fundamental facts:

1. Growing emissions of greenhouse gases (GHGs) are accumulating in the atmosphere.
2. These emissions are mainly from fossil fuel use and land use.
3. Growing concentration of GHGs will change and warm the global climate.
4. Global climate change represents one of our most serious long-term risks.[3]

In response to rising awareness and concerns about the impact of climate change, consumer, government, and corporate interest in going green has skyrocketed. As evidence, consider these statistics compiled in 2008 and 2009:

- 28% of Americans have made major changes in their lifestyles to protect the environment—and 55% have made minor changes (Gallup Poll).[4]
- 77% of consumers describe themselves as "green,"[5] and 57% "think or behave" green—a number that is increasing every year (Simmons Market Research Bureau).[6]
- 68% of consumers find the ENERGY STAR label to be "extremely" or "very important" (EcoAlign EcoPinion Survey).[7]
- 54% of shoppers consider environmental sustainability characteristics in their buying decisions (GMA-Deloitte Report).[8]

When it comes to actually buying green, a 2008 Havas Media survey found:

- 76% of respondents said they would buy greener products if more were available.
- 79% said they would rather buy from companies doing their best to reduce their impact on the environment.
- 89% are likely to buy more green goods in the future.
- 35% are willing to pay a premium for green goods.[9]

In terms of business activity, the GreenBiz State of Green Business 2009 reported:

- Venture capital investment in green technologies soared to a record $7.6 billion in 2008, double the previous year.[10]
- U.S. patents for clean energy technologies in 2008 were at their highest level in seven years.[11]
- The annual buying power of green consumers was estimated to be $500 billion in 2008.[12]

Today, most major corporations recognize the wisdom of eco-friendly initiatives. A survey of retail, manufacturing, and wholesale/distribution companies conducted by the Supply Chain Consortium showed that organizations are implementing sustainability initiatives throughout the supply chain not only to achieve regulatory compliance, but also to improve their brand image and customer satisfaction levels. The survey revealed that nearly two-thirds of the survey participants have at least some portion of their budget allocated to environmental initiatives.[13] It is no surprise that most leading companies across a variety of industries—from Wal-Mart and Google, to BP, Dupont, and General Electric—have major green initiatives in place.

Sustainable practices are proving to make business sense. For example, in 2008, the Aberdeen Group, a business-focused research organization, found that green practices among retailers were "essential cost control and customer service practices." On average, best-in-class retailers achieved a 20% decrease in energy costs, an 8% decrease in their overall logistics and transport costs, and a 5% decrease in merchandise costs through their green initiatives.[14]

Just as importantly, businesses increasingly recognize that they have a responsibility to help protect the environment. As Auden Schendler, executive director of Sustainability for Aspen Ski Company, says: "Ethics have to play a role . . . an economic pitch in a vacuum may not make sense to managers if there's no context, no broader environmental mission within the company." Take the example of Ricoh. A Japan-based corporation with over $17 billion in annual sales, Ricoh is a global leader in digital office solutions. The company has made a commitment to promoting sustainability. In 2007, Ricoh produced a 36-page Sustainability Report, much like an annual report. Substantial space on the company's corporate website is devoted to green issues, where they put the green movement in this historical context this way—and issue this mandate to businesses of all kinds:

> In recent years, the environmental impact of human activity has increased beyond the Earth's ability to recover, and that has led to global warming, the depletion of the ozone layer, the submersion of land due to the rising sea level, epidemic diseases making their way northward from southern regions, and an increase in the number of people suffering skin cancer caused by strong ultraviolet light. Currently, environmental conservation is a global issue, and companies, which are major economic players in society, are required to be serious in their commitment to environmental conservation.

Given that, where does your business fit in? How can you make a difference? What can you do? That's what this book is all about. But for starters, recognize that small businesses can have a big impact.

Small Business = Big Impact

When Taylor Martin started his own graphic design firm in June 2007, he knew he wanted to be as green as possible. He checked into alternative energy sources, and found that wind power was available in his Northern Virginia neighborhood—although he had to buy energy through a new provider. He purchased sustainable office equipment—shelving made from recycled content, metal file cabinets, recycled dividers, and an environmentally friendly ZODY chair. All his equipment is ENERGY STAR, and all the paper he uses is 100% post-consumer waste (PCW) recycled.

He checked online for the green office supply stores and found one FSC-certified—meaning green-certified—printer in his area to handle major print jobs. For those jobs, he uses paper from a sustainable paper company such as New Leaf Paper, a paper firm dedicated to sustainability. New Leaf provides an environmental benefits statement—a report that tells the end-user how many trees, how much water, how much energy, and how much solid waste were saved in the production of the print job. That information, in turn, can be passed on to Martin's clients—and their customers—to substantiate the greenness of the project.

Martin employs a variety of green practices. He uses computer power management strategies that, for example, force his computer to go to sleep automatically when it idles; all his lights are compact fluorescents (CFLs); he recycles his printer cartridges and his computer equipment. When he gets his utility bill, it tells him that all his energy now comes from wind power. And he's undergoing an audit to be certified carbon zero at CarbonProject.org. The costs of his green efforts: Martin estimates that he pays about 30% more for power than he did before—but he figures, the way energy prices are going up, he's soon going to have an advantage. "It cost a little more, but it won't be more for very long," he said back in the spring of 2008, before fuel prices skyrocketed the following summer. As for the research that went into it, it probably took him about 10% more time to set up his office than it would have otherwise. "But when you read about it, and look at the pros and cons," he says, "it's just the right thing to do. Eventually, green is going to be the norm. Everything you buy is going to be green at some point." Although the numbers are not yet in, as of his first anniversary, Martin estimates that he has continued to win new clients and weather the economic downturn because of his green strategy.

As a small, home-based enterprise starting from scratch, Taylor Martin Design had an advantage over businesses that are up and running. And as a graphic design firm, Martin is in a position to have a big impact through his clients—who produce thousands of printed pages each year. But every step that every small business takes can make a difference.

No matter what your industry, in order to run your business, you use power for electricity, heating, cooling, transportation, and other services. But you may be wondering how your small business can possibly play a role in managing climate change. Surely, you may be thinking, you are not in a business that actually produces greenhouse emissions. Surely your small business' individual impact is minuscule, possibly immeasurably small. But the reality is that, in aggregate, the total climate-related impact—or carbon footprint—of small businesses adds up. Although you may not be in a business that directly produces greenhouse gases, without question your business has an indirect impact on climate; the electricity, heating, cooling, transportation, and other services you use all translate into CO_2 output with global warming impact. Consider these facts:

- If every one of the 26.4 million small businesses in America replaced just one lightbulb with a compact fluorescent (CFL) or light-emitting diode (LED) bulb, the energy saved would be equivalent to taking 312,000 cars off the roads. *That's the law of large numbers—a small action multiplied by 26.4 million has a significant impact.*
- Similarly, if every employee of a small business in the United States stopped printing pages of paper that are unnecessary—

those that are printed but never used—it would save 57,000 trees a year. Every single mature tree releases oxygen back into the atmosphere, offsetting the impact of CO_2 production.

■ And if the employees of every small business in the United States recycled all of the 51 billion aluminum beverage cans they consumed every year rather than throwing them away, they would conserve the equivalent of 28 million barrels of oil or 1.3 billion gallons of gasoline.

High-efficiency lightbulbs: Energy-saving lightbulbs that can last up to ten times as long and require a quarter or less of the power of equivalent conventional incandescent bulbs. There are currently two types of high-efficiency lightbulbs commercially available: CFL (compact fluorescent lightbulb) and LED (light-emitting diode) bulbs. High-efficiency lightbulbs are not without their critics. Complaints about CFLs, which typically use about 20 percent of the energy needed for a standard bulb, include a less pleasing light quality, inability to dim, large size, and safety issues related to their mercury content. LEDs, which use about 15 percent of the energy needed for a standard bulb, are considered the future of high-efficiency lightbulbs, but are not currently in wide use because of high prices and limited applications.

What Does Going Green Mean?

Going green: All this talk about going green, but what exactly does it mean? For the purposes of this book, our working definition of going green is: the implementation of a broad range of policies and procedures focused on conserving and improving the natural environment, both for its own sake as well as to improve business strength and sustainability.

When people talk about going green, they are typically talking about efforts to reduce or mitigate carbon-producing activities that cause global warming. The primary culprits are the by-products of burning fossil fuels to provide the energy we use in the course of our daily lives. Fossil fuels are used to produce electricity in our homes and businesses, to provide our travel and transportation, and to create the food, clothes, and other products we buy and consume every day. However, ask 100 people what it means to go green and you will get 100 different answers.

While it may be hard to pinpoint exactly what going green means, we know that going green is not just an energy issue. Going green involves adopting a set of guiding principles related to sustainability and implementing practices that support those principles throughout your business. In other words, environmental sustainability becomes the lens through which you view every business decision you make — including what you purchase, the resources you use, and the products and services you provide. At its heart, going green is about changing the way you think about the impact your business can have on the environment.

 Sustainability is the capacity of a process or operation to be maintained indefinitely. When it comes to business, this typically involves three elements of the enterprise—environmental, economic, and social. Corporate social responsibility refers to the deliberate and voluntary inclusion of public interest into corporate decision making; in particular, it refers to practices a business assumes in order to manage the social and environmental costs of their operations.

What Does Going Green Mean for Your Business?

At this point you may be asking yourself: What exactly do I have to do to go green? Where do I begin? And why should I do it? Starting the process of greening your business can be as simple as following your interests. If you design your green program as an extension of what's important to you, you'll end up creating a program that fits your business and is rewarding to implement. For example, if the prospect of your computer going to sleep when it is idle doesn't faze you, then an IT power management program might be a good place to start. If you recycle at home, maybe you'll want to make a commitment to recycle in your business.

The steps outlined in this book—including a checklist for assessing your existing operations—are designed to make it easier for you to identify the green practices that are right for your business and your budget. In fact, the book is designed to arm you with the information you need to identify your green priorities—and opportunities.

As you get started, keep this in mind: The foundation of your green program lies in what you're already doing that's green. Do you recycle? Do you use high-efficiency lightbulbs? Do you have a programmable thermostat? Do you leave your PCs on all night? Depending on your answers to these and dozens of other questions, you will be able to identify the areas where your green opportunities lie. As you go through this process, you'll probably find that you've adopted a few green business practices already, and that you can implement others with no cost or change in business performance. You'll also discover green practices to implement that save time and money, but otherwise have little impact on your overall business practices. As an example, for most small businesses, changing to high-efficiency lightbulbs or using recycled copy paper will have no direct impact on your core business operations.

But that's only the beginning. As you move forward, it will be important to think strategically about greening your business. Implementing specific practices—such as recycling, power management, or sustainable food initiatives—may be necessary to be green, but in and of themselves, they're not sufficient. To maximize the benefits of going green, it's important to create a well-defined green program with a mission statement and a plan that articulates your goals, action steps, timelines, and desired outcomes. Without these, it will be difficult to fully communicate your greenness to your customers, investors, suppliers, and other stakeholders. And communicating your greenness can be as valuable as the greenness itself.

If you're still wondering why you should green your business, the answer is also pretty simple. Wasted resources increase the cost of doing business. No matter what size or type of business you run, by being proactive in your efforts to go green, you can improve your company's financial performance by reducing waste and streamlining costs. You'll also benefit from increased customer loyalty and a new competitive advantage.

An Overview of the Resources Provided in This Book

The details of your green program will depend on your industry and myriad other factors specific to your business. But regardless of the particulars of your business, you'll find easy methods on these pages for customizing an effective and workable green program that will fit *your* business. Here are a few of the elements of this book that are designed to help you along the way:

- A comprehensive guide to green business best practices. Part Two of this book features hundreds of green practices from which you can pick and choose to develop your own program. To help guide you, Part Two is organized by subject area—such as energy management, water conservation, business travel, and so forth. Again, some of these practices will make sense for your business. Others won't. Not every green practice will fit everyone's needs or budget.

- An easy-to-use Going Green checklist featuring all the green business practices outlined in the book so that you don't have to be an operations genius to implement your green program. See Appendix A.

IMPERIAL CAT: GOING GREENER

CASE STUDY

Twenty-two years ago, Bill Seliskar, an Arkansan in the corrugated cardboard business, invented the corrugated scratching pad for cats and founded Imperial Cat, a cat product manufacturing company. Made from 30% recycled and 100% recyclable materials, the scratching pads were pretty green to begin with. But in 2006, recognizing the potential marketing value of a green product, the company decided to up the ante. Says Daniel Peacock, project development coordinator at Imperial: "I said, well, our product's pretty good. Let's find out exactly how good. I did the research to find out how our products are made to see what was involved in making changes so we could be a green company." In the process, Imperial Cat made the scratching pads even greener—for example, switching to eco-salt inks for printing—and made a company-wide effort to implement green practices by purchasing ENERGY STAR equipment, changing the lighting at their facility, and finding green shipping boxes that minimize waste and are recyclable. "All the waste from making the scratchers is bailed and resold back to the recycled paper company," says Peacock. "And then we buy it back from them when it's processed." As a Certified Organic processing facility and Green Business Alliance member, the company can include green certification logos on its products, website, and collateral materials. For Imperial Cat, going green represents the opportunity to turn an existing product into a green marketing opportunity.

■ Sidebars marked by the following icons provide tips and insights into issues of particular interest:

   Case Studies: In-depth reports on how small businesses across the country have dealt with the very same challenges and opportunities you face.

Eco Chat: Information on significant issues facing businesses that are considering a green program, as well as advice from experts and knowledgeable business owners.

Definitions: Clarification of green terminology and jargon.

■ A list of fifty easy ways to make your workplace greener. If you just want to stick your toe in and test the waters, this is a good place to start. This list is a practical guide to fifty quick and easy actions you can take to help minimize the company's carbon footprint.

■ The resources section at the end of this book contains a list of useful links to websites, reports, white papers, content sites, and vendors, to help you take action on the topics discussed in the chapter.

2 GETTING STARTED

He has half the deed done who has made a beginning.
—*Horace*

Going green may seem like a daunting task, but it doesn't have to be. If you start slow and take it one step at a time, you can keep the process manageable and still build a valuable green program that yields tremendous benefits. You may find that implementing a small-scale initiative is all you want and need, or that you're just not ready to commit to implementing a full-blown green program. Even if you just want to stick your toe in the water, there are many small things you can do that can have a big impact. Here are fifty of them—all quick, easy steps any business can take to help minimize its carbon footprint. In fact, if you were to take ten of these steps, you'd be doing more than most businesses out there. If you were to implement all fifty of them, you would have created an acceptable green program. Each one of these steps appears elsewhere in this book; some of them are discussed in greater detail. Others represent elements of a more comprehensive green strategy. But this list is designed to give you a sense of what you can accomplish—even with relatively little effort.

Fifty Easy Ways to Make Your Workplace Greener

Reducing Waste and Recycling (from Chapter 7)

1. Recycle as many of your office supplies as possible.
2. Make recycling easy by providing clearly marked bins throughout the workplace.

Energy Management (from Chapter 8)

3. Get a free energy audit.
4. Go to ENERGY STAR for Small Business (www.energystar.gov/index.cfm?c=small_business.sb_index) for free information, resources, and technical advice on hundreds of cost-savings practices.
5. Turn off lights (and other equipment) when not in use (i.e., at night).
6. Turn off computers and monitors every night. Just shut them down!
7. Replace existing lightbulbs with high-efficiency bulbs.
8. Use unheated—or the least heated—water whenever possible; heating water uses a great deal of energy.
9. Install programmable thermostats and set goals to shift temperatures +/– 2 degrees.

Water Conservation (from Chapter 9)

10. Discover and repair leaks. Leaks can lead to a significant—and completely unnecessary—misuse of water.
11. Insert water displacement devices in toilets to reduce the volume of water used every time you flush.
12. Install aerators on faucets to reduce the amount of water coming from your fixtures.

13. Water lawns and flower beds between 9 p.m. and 9 a.m., when water pressure is highest, wind is lowest, and there is less evaporation.

Green Office Supplies (from Chapter 10)

14. Make use of scanners and PDF formatting to digitize hard copy data for future use and distribution. Send invoices, correspondence, and documents via email.
15. If your copier permits it, set the default to two-sided.
16. Install software that automatically eliminates wasteful pages in printouts.
17. For word processing, use the Arial Narrow font. It will reduce your printed page area by approximately 15%.
18. Add this message to your email signature: *By not printing this email, you've helped save paper, ink, and trees.*
19. Fax electronically—send and receive faxes directly from your computer(s); if you fax the old-fashioned way, eliminate cover sheets by sticking a Post-It fax cover note on the first page.
20. Opt out of unnecessary catalogs and unwanted mailings. Whenever possible, provide other businesses only your company's name, phone, and email, but no physical address.

Green Human Resources (from Chapter 11)

21. Encourage carpooling by posting sign-up lists and providing access to online rideshare sites.
22. Encourage biking by providing safe, accessible bike racks.
23. Donate leftover food to a local food bank instead of throwing it away.

Green Transportation and Shipping (from Chapter 12)

24. Reuse boxes for shipping.
25. Put a no-idling policy in place. No matter how short a stopover, drivers should turn off their engines.

26. Plan out driving routes in advance, to use the most direct route possible and avoid backtracking. Use maps and Internet sites to help determine the best routes.

27. Use the vehicle with the best gas mileage. If you have more than one car, truck, or van, use the one that gets the best gas mileage, particularly when making long trips.

Green Marketing and Communications (from Chapter 13)

28. Whenever possible, eliminate direct mail from your media mix. If you must send it, eliminate envelopes by using smaller mailers, postcards, and fold-and-mail forms.

29. Create electronic versions of materials such as media kits, press kits, reports, and other documents, and then post them to your website.

30. Update your company's mailing lists regularly to remove the undeliverable and duplicate addresses.

31. Offer customers the option of receiving communications electronically. Consider switching periodic mailings, such as invoices, reminders, and promotional pieces inserted into mailing envelopes to an electronic system to reduce the paper and postage you use.

32. Add Internet marketing to your media mix. Whenever possible, use digital media to spread your marketing messages.

Green Business Travel (from Chapter 14)

33. Take fewer, longer trips.

34. Use mass transit when out of town.

35. Walk or bike to meetings and for deliveries.

36. Carpool to business meetings.

37. Don't serve bottled water at meetings.

38. Opt out of daily sheet and towel service when staying in hotels.

39. Teleconference to conduct meetings, training programs,

demonstrations, and workshops involving multiple people in different locations.

40. Web conference if you need visual presentations or document sharing.
41. Take a train. Train travel is far more efficient than air or automobile travel.
42. Rent small cars. Most small vehicles, other than small luxury cars, get better gas mileage.

Green Purchasing (from Chapter 15)

43. Use recycled content, biodegradable, or recyclable products and materials everywhere you can. It's easy to source recycled content paper, napkins, toilet and facial tissue, and trashcan liners.
44. Buy local. Often products and materials can be sourced locally without extra cost.
45. Purchase remanufactured products whenever possible.
46. Look for eco-labels when making purchasing decisions.
47. Eliminate disposable items in the workplace.
48. Choose vendors that have environmental policies and initiatives in place.

Thinking Green (from Chapter 4)

49. Join or start a green task force within your trade association.
50. Join a national or local small business organization that has a green agenda.

Creating a Successful Green Program

Now you have a sense of what a small business can do to be greener. How can you craft a green program that's specific to your needs? This is where strategic thinking comes in. Developing and implementing a successful green program involves eight key steps. This book will guide you through these eight steps, and as you work through them, you'll discover which green practices make sense for your industry, your business, your market, and your management style. Don't let these eight steps intimidate you. They're just a framework for understanding the process. And you're free to devote as much energy to each individual step as you choose.

The Eight Key Steps to Going Green

1. **Commit.** The first step involves making a commitment. This means creating a green management team. Depending on the size of your organization, it may be one person—you. Or you may have additional staff you would like to have involved in developing and/or managing your green initiatives. In any event, you need to have a green team that is committed to the goals, strategies, and tactics of your green program. The key is to give a person or team of people the responsibility for creating a green plan and sticking to your plans.

2. **Define goals and objectives.** The first order of business for the green team is to set up a launch meeting. You may want to read Chapter 5 before the first meeting. During the launch meeting, you'll want to begin to define your overarching goals and set some specific, measurable objectives that will help you realize those goals. You'll want to ask these kinds of questions:

- Do we want to create an action plan for a full-scale green program or just investigate the viability of one course of action?
- What kind of green program can we implement now? Can we implement a program in phases?
- Who is going to be responsible for each task and what is the timeline?
- What are our goals and objectives? And what information do we need to achieve those goals and objectives?

Defining your goals early in the process is the first step in determining what you want from your green program. For example, if your overarching goal is to become more competitive, you may want to start by looking at what your competitors are doing and what they lack. Then, to establish your specific objectives, look first at steps that will set you apart. Review the practices laid out in Part Two of this book for ideas about where to focus your attention.

3. Assess your greenness. Take inventory of your greenness — or lack thereof — on a variety of measures including energy, water and materials usage, products and packaging, transportation and travel, even your marketing and communications programs. In order to develop a green plan, you'll need to know where and when you're expending resources — and where you can conserve. You'll need this information to *set priorities*. Again, use Part Two as a resource and reference to help you assess your current practices. As you work through your assessment, you'll begin to see the potential costs and benefits of going green.

4. Assess your risks. You'll need to assess the risks your business faces — the threats posed by the physical, regulatory, and economic forces associated with climate change. Proactive risk management will open up a variety of opportunities. For example, on the regulatory front, a sustainable approach to disposing of old technology will soon be mandatory for many businesses. If you're not prepared, your business will be subject to risk. Or say you're in the coin-operated laundry business. If you fail to adapt your business to inevitable increases in energy costs and the possibility of water shortages by investing in water reduction technology and energy-efficient machinery, that means you're not managing your risk. A limousine service that doesn't think strategically about ways to conserve gas is a business that's failing to manage risk. We're going to give you the tools to help you assess and manage the risks facing *your* business.

5. Assess the opportunities. At this point, you'll be in a position to assess the strategic branding and product opportunities related to greenness. Don't try to fit your identity into a green program, but rather make your green program fit your identity. For example, if you operate a diner in North Carolina, your brand may benefit from focusing on locally grown produce. If you operate a high-end restaurant in New York, your brand might benefit more from adding naturally raised grass-fed beef tenderloin to the menu. You may find that you are in a good position to capitalize on programs that are already in place. For example, a dry cleaner that just happens to be using organic chemicals in its cleaning process may discover an opportunity to market itself as an organic dry cleaner. That's a green practice that can be used to strengthen your brand's identity. If done strategically, going green will present you with a variety of opportunities to strengthen your brand and identity, and improve your product and service offerings.

6. Create a plan. Once you've completed Steps 1 through 5, you'll be in a better position to develop a plan. You'll have a clear understanding of the opportunities and challenges you face, and the costs and potential benefits. You'll be in a position to set measurable objectives — and report measurable results. This is where you formulate a concrete set of objectives and action plans designed to help you reduce energy and other resource expenses. Start by writing a green mission statement (see Chapter 3).

7. Implement your plan. As you implement your plan, you'll be putting policies and procedures in place to achieve your goals, one step at a time. We'll help guide you in finding the resources you need to execute your plan, and the tools you need to put your initiatives in place.

8. Communicate with key stakeholders. You don't have to be 100% green. In fact, no business is. Pick and choose what works for your business. Once you've decided what you're going to do, this step will help you capitalize on your plans in an honest and profitable way so you can maximize the benefits of your green initiatives. You're going to engage in a public dialogue about your green program, disclosing your assessments and plans in company communications, marketing materials, and on-site signage.

Part of your communication strategy involves engaging your customers, employees, clients, and vendors. The goal of this is to get valuable feedback and develop proactive responses to green issues. Remember, going green is an ongoing process.

Putting a Small-Scale Green Initiative in Place

One of the best places to start a greening program is through the ENERGY STAR for Small Business program. You can join the no-cost program or simply make use of the site's free information, technical support, "How-to" guides, financing resources, and public relations materials. Additional site resources include a downloadable copy of the free ENERGY STAR for Small Business Guide, "Putting Energy into Profits," and information about ENERGY STAR–labeled products. Go to www.energystar.gov/index.cfm?c=small_business.sb_index.

Not every business is ready for a full-scale green business plan. In fact, for many small businesses, starting small makes sense. When MSHC Partners, a communications firm with a staff of forty-five and four U.S. offices, decided to put a green program in place, they set up a committee (their green team) and established a set of five straightforward, easy-to-implement initiatives for their offices. They placed recycling bins throughout the workplace, asked employees to use them, and set up a system for emptying them daily. To reduce paper waste, they encouraged employees to bring real cups, dishes, and silverware from home, and stashed the disposable cups, plates, and forks behind closed cabinet doors. They also promoted the use of double-sided copies. And they implemented a program to encourage people to drive together or use public transportation for business meetings.

But in fact, MSHC Partners recognized their greatest potential for having an impact on the environment lay in leveraging their position as a service provider and implementing *external* initiatives — that is, by educating their clients about green practices. The firm produces print and direct mail jobs for its clients, and to promote sustainability, MSHC made a conscious decision to research the prices and availability of greener options for print projects — particularly green paper options, such as chlorine-free and 30–100% PCW (post-consumer waste) recycled paper — so they'd be better prepared to give their clients greener choices.

For MSHC Partners, the firm's green initiative represents an opportunity to leverage their green initiatives, play a leadership role in its industry, and promote green practices through its broad client base. Even though MSHC's green program was relatively small-scale and low-key, they still incorporated vital elements of the Eight Key Steps. In fact, MSHC was successful because the company:

1. Created a green team that included senior management and then committed to implementing a program.
2. Took the time to assess their current operations.
3. Determined which internal practices could be changed with relative ease and at low expense.
4. Identified an opportunity to make a bigger impact by counseling their clients.
5. Made sure they implemented, monitored, and communicated their plans.

Choose Ten

A great way to start small is to choose a few—let's say ten—internal business practices you want to green. Think about your priorities and look at the chapters in Part Two for examples of green practices you can choose. And remember, no matter how insignificant your efforts may seem, the law of large numbers applies: If every small business in America switched to high-efficiency lightbulbs or carpooled to business meetings or turned off computers and monitors every night, the impact would be huge. If you choose ten green practices to put into action, implement them, and then communicate them, you will be doing a lot more than most of your competitors. Of course, if you want to have an even greater impact, you can always choose fifteen or twenty!

Start with Sexy

Start with things that you will find fun to implement. Things that interest you. First, do a sexy project, advises Auden Schendler in his book *Getting Green Done*. Try something highly visible and appealing, like upgrading your company cars to a fleet of hybrids or supplying events with products from sustainable vendors. Sexy projects are more likely to get everyone engaged. Once you've done a sexy project or two, choose the ten or twenty internal practices you want to implement. Finally, determine whether there are any steps you can take to help your customers green themselves. Whatever you come up with should be considered part of your first greening steps since, once again, the impact can be huge.

The Green Planning Process

Regardless of whether you decide to implement a small-scale initiative or a full-blown one, the planning process is the same. Effective green programs don't just happen. They require planning. In fact, the steps are virtually identical regardless of the ultimate scope of your program. Like MSHC, you've got to make a genuine commitment and have a concrete plan, however simple it may be.

Once you've set a program in motion and implemented a handful of green practices, you may find that you're pleased with the results. Maybe after installing high-efficiency lightbulbs, your energy costs drop. Or your expanded commitment to recycling generates strong employee support. Or your customers respond positively to new menus printed on recycled paper. Success breeds success. Make a plan to choose five or ten more items to green next year—and the year after. You may find the entire process so rewarding that you decide to expand to a full-scale green program. Either way, you're on your way to becoming greener.

THE FIRST STEPS FOR STARTING A SMALL GREEN PROGRAM

1. Create a green team.
2. Hold a launch meeting. Set next steps and give staff members specific assignments with deadlines.
3. Define your goals and objectives.
4. Set priorities and choose the green practices you want to implement internally. (See Part Two for practices.)
5. Write a green mission statement. (See Chapter 3.) You can assign this.
6. Identify ways you can help your customers go green. (Again, see Part Two.)
7. Communicate your plans to stakeholders via meetings, emails, newsletters, and/or on-site signage.

3 GREEN OPPORTUNITIES

You don't just luck into things as much as you'd like to think you do. You build step by step, whether it's friendships or opportunities.

—*Barbara Bush*

To create a successful green strategy, it's important to step back and analyze your present situation. As part of this assessment process, you'll need to evaluate your business' current situation and determine how various greening factors will affect your success. That means assessing your strengths and weaknesses—and the opportunities and threats your business faces—before you start greening your business. Such an analysis, traditionally called a SWOT (an acronym for Strengths, Weaknesses, Opportunities, and Threats), will help you identify green opportunities, and manage and eliminate potential weaknesses and threats related to climate change. Before you start your SWOT, however, it makes sense to write a green mission statement.

A green mission statement defines your company's intentions to mitigate the environmental impacts of the business practices needed to make and get your products and services to the end consumer.

The Green Mission Statement

I spend a lot of time looking at websites of companies that sell green products and services. Most provide a wealth of information about those products and services. Many have eye-catching, green-themed graphics and lively testimonials from customers about how their products or services surpass expectations, yield cost savings, or earn them points toward a green certification. But most generally fail to do one very important thing: that is, publicly share their green mission statement. A green mission statement defines your green efforts, it clearly states your company's intention to mitigate the environmental impact of your business practices, it articulates your commitment to being green, and in some cases, it outlines the precise steps you plan to take to do so. It sets the green bar for your business. As such, your green mission statement should be at the forefront of all your communication efforts. In fact, failing to share your mission is a missed opportunity.

A green mission statement can—and should—be a critical element of a company's profile and marketing efforts. I say this because the communication of your greenness can be as valuable an asset to your company as the greenness itself. The first step to successful implementation of a green program starts with a clear statement of intentions. So your green mission statement is the first piece of tangible evidence that your business is invested in reducing its impact on the environment. It's a written expression of what you hope to achieve. You'll find it much easier to achieve those goals if all your stakeholders understand what they are, and that they're realistic and achievable. So share your green mission statement with customers, employees, investors, partners, vendors, and suppliers.

Writing Your Green Mission Statement

A green mission statement clearly defines the objectives of your green program for both internal and external audiences. The mission statement can be broad or go into detail about the range of activities you plan to implement. Its purpose is to provide information about the values behind your decision to green your business, what you plan on achieving, and how you intend to do it. At the same time a good green mission statement should reflect a holistic view of your environmental beliefs and intentions.

Here is some guidance on what to say:

- Explain the rationale for embracing green opportunities along with the underlying values.
- Describe what actions you are taking to achieve your goals.
- Make it clear and easy to understand.
- Use proactive words—such as "reduce," "promote," "provide," and "purchase."
- Address one issue at a time.
- Avoid unfamiliar technical terms or jargon.
- State your company's green intentions in ways that motivate your stakeholders to support your programs.

By clarifying your objectives, you establish clear benchmarks for success in the minds of customers, employees, and suppliers. That engages everyone in the process and helps stave off accusations of greenwashing. Explains Marketing and Strategy Consultant Leah Edwards: "I encourage my clients to be really transparent—to have a sign or a statement on their website or on-site about the choices they have to make, why they're making them, what their values are, and what they're aiming to do. Hopefully, the consumers will see whether it's a genuine commitment that an entrepreneur has made or if it's greenwashing."

Greenwash refers to efforts by companies to portray themselves as environmentally responsible in order to overstate environmental benefits or misrepresent, mislead, diminish, or divert attention from environmental wrongdoing.

You may even want to include specific benchmarks in your mission statement. The more detail you provide, the easier it will be for stakeholders to see exactly what you're trying to achieve—and how you're going to get there. That helps them stay invested in the process and helps you establish credibility. According to Jason Holstine, you want to tell people: "This is a journey we are taking. Here are the things we've started. And here are the commitments we've made to improve in the future . . . You want to create some benchmarks that you can track . . . and say within the next month, we'll do this and this and this. And within the next year, we'll do this and this and this. You don't want to say something loosely—like, we're on a journey and in the future we'll be carbon neutral. You want those benchmarks."

Here's an example of a green mission statement for a hypothetical children's clothing store—Kid's Stuff—that incorporates the specific details of the store's green program.

Kid's Stuff Green Mission Statement

Kid's Stuff is committed to reducing our impact on the environment. Toward that goal, we have assessed our store operations and pledge to implement the following sustainability initiatives within the next twelve months:

1. Reduce energy use.
    a. Replace all existing lightbulbs with high-efficiency lightbulbs.
    b. Turn off interior store lighting at night.

c. Install Smart Strip Power Strips throughout the store.

d. Implement effective PC power management strategies.

e. Install a programmable thermostat.

f. Install ceiling fans.

g. Upgrade the energy efficiency of the store whenever financially viable.

h. Institute a procurement policy favoring ENERGY STAR–rated products for future product purchases.

i. Join the ENERGY STAR Small Business network.

2. Reduce use of unsustainable materials.

a. Offer reusable totes for customers to purchase, with the cost being refunded upon the customer's next visit with the tote.

b. Offer recycled gift bags and tissue paper in lieu of traditional gift wrap and boxes.

c. Introduce organic and fair-trade products (these will be "coded" with a green ribbon).

3. Reduce waste.

a. Institute policies that will reduce consumption internally (management and employees) and externally (customers, supply chain).

b. Institute policies that promote reuse internally (e.g., reuse shipping boxes) and externally (e.g., ask for reusable delivery materials, request less wholesale packaging).

c. Institute policies that promote recycling including the introduction of a TerraCycle Cookie Wrapper end-of-life drop-off recycling program.

Here is a hypothetical example of a less detailed green mission statement that still clearly outlines the scope of the green mission for a small, local produce distributor.

Green Peas Fruits and Vegetables Green Mission Statement

Green Peas Fruits and Vegetables is committed to the health and well-being of its customers and employees, and to promoting environmental sustainability in its purchasing decisions and its business practices by:

- Buying and selling only locally grown and/or certified organic produce.
- Implementing energy-saving practices into our back office processes.
- Making shipping decisions that incorporate fuel-saving practices.
- Reducing waste through recycling and donating day-old produce to local charities.

A business can use its green mission statement to set itself apart by communicating its unique commitment to sustainability. Small businesses—such as Kid's Stuff—may want to communicate the specific details of their green program.

By sharing a detailed mission statement with your customers, employees, and supply chain partners, you engage them in the process. They gain an understanding of exactly what steps you plan to take to become greener. As a result, they can get a clear sense of your commitment and the role they play in helping you achieve your goals. It also eliminates confusion by clearly defining what you mean by going green. Of course, you may choose to provide fewer details in your mission statement and focus more broadly on the scope of your green initiatives. For example, the mission statement for the hypothetical Green Peas produce company concentrates exclusively on key elements of the supply chain—purchasing and shipping. Either way, it is important to communicate your mission statement to key stakeholders by posting it on your website and distributing it to customers, employees, and supply chain partners.

For a small business, the challenge is to craft a mission statement that reflects your commitment and key objectives. Again, make it as broad or detailed as you like. But whatever direction you take, a well-defined mission statement will help you prioritize your objectives, communicate your intentions, and ultimately, achieve your goals.

The Green Advantage

If you're like most business owners, you want to provide value to your customers in a way that gives you an edge over the competition. Fundamentally, that means being able to seize opportunities to provide offerings that deliver more value to your customers than your competitors deliver. In other words, your commitment to the environment can be a competitive advantage. By going green, you can attract customers who value your environmental efforts. Depending on whether you sell business-to-business (B2B) or business-to-consumer (B2C), the value of your greenness to your customers will be different.

In a 2006 article in *Environment* magazine, "Green Marketing Myopia," researchers concluded that consumers value green for health and safety, convenience, efficiency and the associated cost savings, performance, and (at times) status.[1] B2B customers often have green procurement guidelines that dictate green supply chain criteria for materials, products, packaging, systems, and logistics. Regardless of who your customer is, the nature of the value you provide to your customers should be at the forefront of your green mission statement. For example, if you operate a dry cleaning business that uses safe, organic cleaning solutions, communicating the safety of your service will be a key element of your mission statement. It might say: *We are committed to the health and safety of our employees and customers. We use only safe, organic products during the cleaning process.* You differentiate your business from the competition and create a competitive advantage by communicating the ways in which your green program creates value for your customers.

Understanding Green Consumers

Not all green consumers are the same. According to research on the green marketplace, only about 65% of consumers are interested in buying green products and services—for any reason. And when it comes to environmental issues, consumers have different values, different motivations, and different levels of commitment. According to the BBMG Conscience Consumer Report, there are four primary types of consumers[2]:

- **Enlighteneds** (10% of consumers): These individuals go out of their way to reward companies that align with their social goals.
- **Aspirationals** (20%): They balance their ideals with convenience and often switch between social concerns, availability, and price.
- **Practicals** (30%): This group looks for convenience and prioritizes, respectively, products based on price, quality, and energy efficiency.
- **Indifferents** (40%): These consumers are the least motivated by social concerns; they prioritize price, quality, convenience, and products made in the USA. Indifferents represent the largest segment of consumers.

Given the mixed profile of green consumers, you'll want to think carefully about what motivates consumers in your market and position your products and services accordingly. In general, some marketing messages—and some green practices—tend to be more powerful motivators than others. "I see a lot of evidence that consumers care most about the health of their families," says Consultant Leah Edwards. "You rarely will find people that say they want to hurt the environment. However, the broader environment is not necessarily a motivator for them to choose one product over another. If you really are trying to reach a mass market, the messages that have a broad appeal are about health and safety." Conversely, some people take the environment very seriously. If you're marketing to the greenest consumers, tread carefully. For example, when Sue Lynn, owner of the Confluence Bookstore, Bistro, and Business Center in Bellevue, Nebraska, began construction, she was surprised by the level of skepticism that greeted her green claims—despite the fact that she was putting a broad range of green materials, appliances, and practices in place. To diffuse the greenwashing backlash, she decided to call the store "eco-sensitive" instead of green. At the time, she was new to the market; since then, she's gotten to know her customers better and built a successful business. "I got through a kind of a minefield," she says now, looking back.

Although the mission statement is not created specifically as a marketing device, once you have a green mission statement, use it to your advantage by publicly sharing it. *At a minimum, post it on your website where people can find it.* It deserves a tab on your main navigation bar. Include a link on emails and online newsletters. Your green mission statement provides the basis of your competitive advantage in the green marketplace, so share it.

The Green SWOT

By conducting a green SWOT, you'll learn how the environment relates to every aspect of your business every day—from what you buy to your relationships with customers and vendors to every stage in the development and production of your products and services. Once you see how it all fits together, you'll discover countless opportunities for making environmentally responsible choices that can lead to business success.

Consider the example of Tayst Restaurant and Wine Bar in Nashville. For chef-owner Jeremy Barlow, going green was an evolutionary process. It started with a dedication to buying local food. "The quality was so much better, so we just kept driving to find more and more local farmers," says Barlow. "You find out why people are farming that way and what it takes to farm sustainably." The experience led Barlow to begin the step-by-step process of greening the business. "Green was becoming all the rage," he says. "And we thought, foodwise, we're basically green anyway." Some steps—such as adding aerators to the faucets to conserve water and printing menus on 100% PCW recycled paper—were relatively simple. Others—such as switching from paraffin to natural beeswax candles and implementing a full recycling program—involved greater cost and effort. At this writing, Barlow plans to add a water filtration system to eliminate bottled water altogether, and redo all the lighting. Conserving water and electricity will help offset rising utility costs. "Those are two steps that, in the long run, are going to save me money," says Barlow. The local food focus will save him money as well, because he won't be paying the long-distance shipping costs that drive up food prices. "If you look at the economy right now, the biggest thing going on is that food prices are going through the roof. And it only promises to get worse," says Barlow. "But for local guys, their price is the same this year as it was last year and the year before." For Tayst, going green means being part of a broad effort to promote sustainability; it's a way of life. But it also provides a buffer against the uncertainty of a future where energy and food costs are expected to continue to rise.

Strengths

Strengths are the positive aspects of your business. These should relate to internal factors—things over which you have control. In contrast, regulations, seasonal considerations, and competitive pressures are external factors. For example, for a restaurant like Tayst, the strengths might include a loyal customer base, an intimate atmosphere, a reputation for high-quality, locally produced food, a strong footing in the neighborhood, a great relationship with local farmers, and a reputation for innovation. Consider the factors that contribute to your business' success. You'll want to focus on the overall products or services you offer, not just those strengths that have green potential. Ask yourself:

- In what ways is your business unique?
- Does your location provide an advantage?
- Are you the only business of your type in town?
- Do you tap into an unserved niche market?
- Are you a low-cost producer?
- How do your products and services differ from the competition?
- Do you hold the exclusive rights to sell something?
- Is your customer service superior to the competition?
- Are you offering higher-quality goods?
- Do you sell well-known brands or status items?
- Are your systems better?
- Do you offer faster delivery?
- Do you have a better returns policy?
- Are you poised for growth?
- Are you diversified?
- Are you consolidated?
- Is your supply chain strong, and are there numerous good suppliers to choose from?
- Are you already in compliance with federal and state environmental, health, and safety requirements?

Now, once you've looked at your overall strengths, ask yourself: Is there a green slant to any of these strengths? Try to think about ways to leverage your strengths as part of a green program. From a marketing perspective, bundling core consumer benefits—also called core selling points—with green benefits is often the most winning combination of all. As an example, Milgard Manufacturing has been making windows and doors for fifty years. The company maintains a high level of quality control at every step of the manufacturing process by producing many of the components that go into their products. This allows for competitive pricing and high quality, including one of the industry's best warranties. In addition, Milgard has become a market leader in energy-efficient building products. How? By leveraging all of its products' core strengths, only one of which is inherently green. Milgard advertises its windows and doors as "high performance" with three selling points: superior energy efficiency (green benefit), superior protection for furniture from damaging ultraviolet rays (core benefit), and superior comfort/temperature control (core benefit). That combination of benefits—which includes energy efficiency—creates a winning package for the customer.

Write down all the ways your company meets unmet needs and provides superior value and benefits to your customers (remember to consider the complete life cycle of your products and services). These are your strengths and will be the foundation of your green program.

Opportunities

Opportunities are the positive aspects of your business that are defined by the external environment—your market, your industry, the trends and regulations that affect your business. For example, to identify general business opportunities, you might ask yourself: Am I operating in a growth industry? Are there opportunities for expansion domestically or overseas? Is new legislation opening up new markets? Are the consumer trends favorable? Now that you're implementing a green program, in addition to general business opportunities, there will be a host of new green opportunities available to you. The big question is: How can going green differentiate you from the competition? For Tayst Restaurant, one of the first restaurants in the United States to be certified by the Green Restaurant Association, going green has attracted significant media attention—including coverage on CNN and in *Martha Stewart Weddings*. It's also cemented the restaurant's reputation for quality food and innovation, and significantly increased business for the small neighborhood restaurant.

Here are some questions that will help you identify specific green opportunities:

- Are there new customer segments that you can now attract? Which customers will have a greater interest in your offerings?

Consider how your going green will be attractive to customers you don't currently serve. Can you now market to health-conscious consumers? Thrifty consumers? Enlightened consumers? Aspirational consumers? Practical consumers?

- How can you expand your products or services to meet the needs of new consumers or businesses that care about sustainability? Can you add a greater selection of green and fair-trade products? Can you offer one-stop shopping for green products such as office supplies or gardening supplies? How much do you need or want to shift your focus in order to attract each consumer segment?

- Can you increase your market share? Will your green efforts allow you to attract the competition's customers?

- What new markets will open to you? If you are a B2B business, is there a consumer market you can now tap into? If you are a B2C business, is there a business market you might now be able to attract?

- Are there new product lines you can now offer? Can you release green line extensions of existing offerings? What about green services that are not available in your area? Is your business in a position to provide these services?

- Will going green improve your bottom line? Will it reduce your expenses? Allow you to take advantage of new tax conditions? Free up capital for other investments? Generate new profit centers or improve existing profit margins? Reduce governmental oversight or paperwork requirements?

- Are there new opportunities to influence your customers or your industry? Can you reduce demand for resources by steering your clients toward sustainable behavior?

- Think about how going green creates value and think of all the opportunities it opens up. These are your new green opportunities and you will learn more about how to identify them in Chapter 5.

Weaknesses

Every business has internal weaknesses. Refer back to the list of potential strengths. Everything that can be a strength can also be a weakness if it's working against you. Here are some thought-starters to help you identify your business' general weaknesses:

- Is your location weak or about to undergo a shift in traffic patterns?
- Is there a new competitor in town?
- Are you losing an exclusive right to something?
- Have your competitors upgraded their systems?
- Do they provide faster or more personal customer service?
- Are your offerings relatively expensive?
- Is your supply chain secure or too heavily dependent on a few key vendors?
- Are you not yet in compliance with state, local, and federal environmental, health, and safety regulations?

By identifying your weaknesses, you will be in a better position to turn them into strengths. For example, if you recognize that quality control is lacking, you could choose to make improvements that would allow you to provide superior quality in the future. If your offerings are relatively expensive, you could expand your offerings to include either lower-cost alternatives or a broader range of upscale products, and then target these to a niche market.

Threats

Threats are external factors that can negatively impact your business. Again, take a look at the list of potential opportunities. Everything that can be an opportunity can also be a threat if it's working against you. Your goal in implementing a green program is to make sure you don't miss out on new green opportunities available to you. Use these questions to guide you in identifying potential threats posed by external change:

- Can you match or exceed the green capabilities of your competitors? If not, how much pressure will their green offerings put on your business?
- State, local, and federal governments will continue to introduce levies, taxes, and subsidies that encourage sustainable products and services. Is there environmental legislation on the horizon that could impact your business or the business of your suppliers? Or new local, federal, or industry-wide regulations that might affect your business?
- Are you up to speed on what's happening in your industry? At this writing, dozens of trade organizations are developing new rules and regulations that incorporate sustainability requirements. In addition, trade associations representing industries from restaurants to real estate now offer their membership everything from green certification programs to green business tools.
- What about the rising costs of fuel, food, and energy? Potential water shortages? Is your business in a position to respond to threats related to the reallocation of these crucial resources?
- Are you unable to locate products or materials that will meet the needs of consumers who care about green?
- By going green, might you alienate any segments of your existing customer base?
- What about missed opportunities? Consider whether *not* going green would inhibit your ability to be successful. Will failing to address environmental concerns mean missing the boat or falling behind your competition?

By identifying threats to your business, you will be in a better position to turn them into opportunities. For example, if your competitors have been adding innovative products or services, you could choose to follow—and outdo them—by offering more and better innovations. If your business is dependent on a specific resource that promises to become scarcer or more expensive, such as water or fuel, you can plan ahead and implement strategic conservation and procurement tactics.

The SWOT Grid

Now record your strengths, weaknesses, opportunities, and threats on this grid.

ENVIRONMENT	EVALUATION	
	Positive	Negative
Internal	Strengths	Weaknesses
External	Opportunities	Threats

You'll be using the information you gained from your SWOT when you reach Chapter 4.

At that point you will be thinking about how to use your strengths to exploit opportunities and/or avoid threats. You will also need to determine how to overcome or shift the paradigm on your weaknesses in order to exploit opportunities and/or avoid threats. The SWOT grid will help you determine the strategic directions that are likely to be most productive for your business, as well as the environmental threats you want to address through the green planning process.

4 THINKING GREEN

What's the use of running if you are not on the right road.
—German proverb

Greening your business involves not only adopting green business practices, but also adopting a greener mind-set—maybe even a greener vision. By reading this book, you've already taken a huge first step to recognizing the role you can play in mitigating the carbon-producing effects of your business activities. It means you're ready to take responsibility for finding more efficient, less wasteful, and more environmentally friendly ways to run your business—and view greening your business as a route to greater progress as well as better business practices.

Changing Workplace Attitudes

Changing workplace attitudes about going green is fundamental to this entire process. If a company can't change no-cost behaviors—by, say, shutting off computers at the end of the day or replacing paper cups with mugs—it's not going to be very successful in implementing a full-fledged green strategy. The most successful approach to changing workplace attitudes is from the top down—in other words, from you, the business owner. It's important to demonstrate your personal commitment through your words and actions. As your commitment to going green trickles down, employees will be compelled to jump on the bandwagon and new, green-minded recruits will find you.

To go green, you've got to walk the walk, as well as talk the talk. Customers and clients are wary of greenwashing—green business claims that are perceived as either inaccurate or misleading. In order to implement a green strategy, you need to establish credibility. Improving your environmental impact and mind-set is the only way to do this. Without a pervasive organizational shift to greener attitudes, most businesses will fail to reap the benefits of going green, because stakeholders will smell the greenwash from miles away.

No matter what your industry, there are actions that any and every small businesses can take to become greener, actions that involve little or no cost, and little or no planning—but speak volumes about your commitment to greenness. Many of these simple, everyday green practices are listed among the "Fifty Easy Ways to Make Your Workplace Greener," which appear in Chapter 2. Implementing these very basic practices is as good a place as any to start walking the walk—and reinforcing workplace attitudes.

Making a Difference

Changing your business practices is only one piece of the greening puzzle. Just because you can't afford to install solar panels right now doesn't mean you can't make a difference. In fact, the time you invest in making a difference may be as valuable to environmental progress as installing new lightbulbs. Get involved. Join green business organizations. Strengthen your green requirements for suppliers. Provide customers with greener alternatives.

Become an advocate for change. Small businesses can have a big impact on promoting change—not just within their businesses, but by working together to change attitudes, influence policymakers, and promote innovation. When you begin to think about getting involved, think nationally, think statewide—and think locally. Many issues related to sustainability and your business—from energy policy to recycling services—are addressed at a local or state level. Says Scott Hague, who founded Small Business California, a statewide advocacy organization: "The amazing thing is, we have incredible numbers. In San Francisco, there are over 110,000 small businesses—if you include sole proprietors. If just a very small percentage—only 10% of small businesses—would get involved and spend a half hour a month on advocacy, with the kind of numbers we've got, we would be a powerful force . . . We could own the world with those kinds of numbers." Just as importantly, when it comes to local policy and legislation, small businesses have the access to an expansive grassroots network. The key, according to Hague, is to get involved, stay informed, and be persistent. "Joining an organization and not doing anything is probably a waste of time," says Hague. "Write letters, make phones calls, meet with legislators, talk to employees, and talk to customers about your issues."

Get involved through membership organizations. As new environmental laws that affect your business are proposed and introduced, a good membership organization—which, in some cases, will be a trade association—will be a source of valuable information and guidance. Conversely, and as importantly, if the membership organizations to which you belong are not aggressively advocating for green public policy changes, let them know you think they should be. Or better yet, get involved in the organization. Small business alliances and associations can serve as a valuable platform for advocating for specific goals—such as funding for energy-efficient programs, tax credits that support small businesses, and innovations, such as on-bill financing. (See "Scott Hague: An Advocate for Small Business" on page 52.) In fact, 95% of the National Small Business Association's activities are advocacy-related.

Work to ensure that your interests are represented and that you have a venue from which to comment on proposed legislation; use your influence as a business to drive policy change from within a membership organization:

- ■ Join a green trade association and push for greater advocacy.
- ■ Join a national or local small business organization that has a green agenda.
- ■ Join or start a green task force within your trade association.
- ■ 🔗 Sign up for the National Small Business Association's Action Network advocacy email alerts that let you know how and when to send letters to your elected officials about important small business environmental issues at http://capwiz .com/nsbaonline/mlm/signup. Then mobilize others to do the same.
- ■ 🔗 Put a "Write to Congress" web sticker on your website so visitors can use the interactive banners to support small business issues, or write letters to officials and the media. For information, go to http://capwiz.com/nsbaonline/remotecontent.

Use your leverage. Look for the levers—the things you can do to move others to be greener—to make a broader impact on the environment than your own business alone can effect. In other words, look for ways to influence others. Ask yourself: Can we influence our suppliers to be more environmentally responsible? Can we influence our customers to be more environmentally responsible? The more leverage you exert, the more influential you will become. The more influential you become, the better your reputation in your industry and brand equity will become.

Auden Schendler of Aspen Skiing Company (ASC) calls this approach "asymmetric warfare." When ASC, which spends about $30,000 a year on Kleenex, banned the brand from the resort because of their unsustainable forestry practices, media outlets around the world picked up the story. Only then did the CEO of Kleenex's $32 billion parent company, Kimberly-Clark, reach out to them. As a result, ASC was able to begin an environmental dialogue with a company 160 times its size.[1] As another example, JetBlue Airlines ran a "One Thing That's Green" sweepstakes challenging consumers to commit to one of five simple actions: changing a lightbulb, reducing shower time, combining car trips, washing clothes in cold water, or adjusting their thermostats. The online campaign went viral and was a marketing success on many fronts, but it also succeeded by educating tens of thousands of people about five simple greening activities they could easily embrace.

A Primer on Green Certifications and Eco-Labels

As you embark on the green planning process, you'll inevitably come upon two tools that have become part of the sustainability market-place—green certifications and eco-labels. Depending on your industry, you may want to explore these options in the early stages of the planning process. Proceed with care. It's not always easy to distinguish the good from the not-so-good. Here are a few insights to guide you through the process.

Third-Party Green Certification

In order to establish credibility and gain access to valuable resources, you may want to consider obtaining a third-party certification. Organizations such as B Corporation offer company-wide green certification and programs, such as 1% For The Planet, which certify businesses as being financially committed to environmental issues. Groups such as the GreenPlumbers and the Green Restaurant Association offer industry-specific education, technical assistance, and credentials. In a competitive marketplace these kinds of third-party endorsements can serve as valuable tools for improving your qualifications, expanding your offerings, and differentiating yourself from the competition. Third-party certifiers provide all or some of the following benefits:

CASE STUDY

SCOTT HAGUE: AN ADVOCATE FOR SMALL BUSINESS

Scott Hague, founder and president of Small Business California and first vice chair of the National Small Business Association (NSBA), has made a second career out of doggedly promoting the interests of small businesses and, most recently, of energy policies and programs that help small business and the environment. He learned the ropes through the San Francisco Small Business Network and the Chamber of Commerce there. It took him eighteen years to create a Small Business Commission, but it was ultimately created through a ballot measure. He then succeeded in getting a $10 million grant from the California Public Utilities Commission (CPUC) that enabled the creation of a program called Power Savers, which involved working with small businesses to reduce their energy use around lighting.

In 2005, he created Small Business California, which, he says, "takes on what I call the global issues that affect small business." Not long afterward, he and Hank Ryan, who had run the Power Savers program, received an EPA grant to assist small businesses and promote on-bill financing. Through on-bill financing, a utility provides 0% financing loans to a business for

- Green credentials
- Green marketing support
- Green education and training programs
- Knowledge of green best practices
- Green tools and practices
- Access to information about how to green your business
- Networking opportunities
- Green growth opportunities
- Green vendor and supplier information

investments in energy efficiency improvements. "You're basi-cally paying the [loan] back with your energy savings," says Hague. (See "On-Bill Financing," page 122). Hague promoted on-bill financing throughout the country and testified before the Senate in 2007. As a result, on-bill financing was incorpo-rated into the Federal Energy Bill and signed into law by the president. "It's a pretty well-accepted statement that small businesses waste about 30% of their energy use. They waste 30% because they don't know what to do to resolve the prob-lem," says Hague. "But with encouragement from government and governmental policies, small business would, I believe with very little effort, reduce their energy use significantly."

According to Hague, there's still plenty of work to be done. Small Business California is strongly advocating for funding in-creases, and focused on energy-related legislation and policy-making where small business interests are often overlooked. He encourages small business owners to get more involved. "They're not going to be like me—spending twenty-five hours a week on this," he says. "But just spend a little bit of time to get out there and speak to the issues that affect us."

Caveat emptor: Not all trade-certifying organizations are created equal. Some provide fewer benefits than others. As a general rule, the more consolidated the industry, the less likely they are to have a green credentialing group of any worth—because the big boys generally don't need assistance, technical or otherwise. For example, the restaurant in-dustry (not particularly consolidated) has a stronger green credentialing group than the hospitality industry (consolidated). Other industry orga-nizations that promote green practices may be the offspring of manu-facturers or trade alliances seeking to promote green products and services rather than implement sustainable practices. Look at the membership list to see who is represented and feel free to call a few random members to ask their opinion of the group. That being said, whether you're a plumber, a restaurateur, a builder, or someone who services them, there's probably a green trade association out there for you.

Here are a few examples of green certification programs:

- The B Corporation, through its B Rating System, certifies companies as having implemented social and environmental standards at www.bcorporation.net.
- Green America's Business Seal of Approval program certifies that companies have successfully completed a screening process and have been approved to be listed as green businesses in a National Green Pages directory at www.coopamerica.org/greenbusiness/sealofapproval.cfm.
- 1% For The Planet certifies that companies donate 1% of sales to environmental nonprofits at www.onepercentfortheplanet.org.
- The Green Restaurant Association provides credentials, endorsements, and technical assistance not only to restaurants, but also to manufacturers, vendors, organizations, and media that serve them at www.dinegreen.com.
- The National Association of Home Builders' Certified Green Professional designation certifies builders, remodelers, manufacturers, vendors, and service providers, and other industry professionals at http://nahb.org.
- Green Advantage certifies contractors, subcontractors, tradespeople, educators, consultants, manufacturers, and vendors at http://greenadvantage.org.
- GreenPlumbers offers a training and accreditation program focusing on energy efficiency and water-saving technologies at http://greenplumbersusa.com.
- The Association of Energy and Environmental Real Estate

Professionals (AEEREP) awards the EcoBroker certification to commercial and residential real estate brokers at www. ecobroker.com.

■ There are programs led by the U.S. Green Building Council (USGBC) such as the LEED Accredited Professionals (AP) program for individuals and USGBC membership for organizations at http://gbci.org.

ABOUT LEED

 The U.S. Green Building Council's Leadership in Energy and Environmental Design (LEED) Green Building Rating System is a nationally accepted set of benchmarks and a certification program for the design, construction, and operation of buildings. The standards encourage the adoption of sustainable green building and development practices by requiring the use of products and adoption of practices that have a lesser or reduced impact on the environment and human health.

A word about LEED standards: LEED is a certification process that provides benchmarks rather than a set of standards. Developers and building owners pick and choose from a laundry list of greening strategies to reach a green building design that aggregates green standards. As a result, LEED certification can actually be achieved even in the complete absence of, for example, important energy efficiencies. This loophole remains a major criticism of the LEED program. Additionally, LEED ratings exist for new construction, existing buildings, commercial interiors, core and shell, schools, retail health care, and homes, so the benchmarks vary depending on your building use and whether you are building from scratch or renovating an existing space. For small projects, it may not be feasible to seek LEED certification. It may make more sense to follow individual

LEED criteria to achieve the *intent of greening* without the certification itself. As long as your approach is holistic—and not just eye candy—your greening strategy is still legitimate. In general, this thinking can be applied to other burdensome criteria—as long as avoiding the criteria does not lead you to make use of unsustainable practices or exaggerate environmental achievements (aka greenwashing).

Eco-Labels

The sheer number of [eco-labels] can be enough to make your shopping trolley spin. Marine Stewardship Council certified fish. ENERGY STAR electronics. LEED certified buildings. Standards. Criteria. Verification. Assurance. We found ourselves asking who's deciding what's green, and what do these labels actually mean?

—**Ecolabelling.org** home page

Eco-labels—third-party seals and logos indicating that a product has met certain environmental or social standards—are popping up everywhere. Eco-labels are the topic of some debate. On the one hand, government regulation of eco-labels has been lax, which has led to skepticism among consumers as to the value of them. On the other hand, eco-labels are viewed as a valuable way of disclosing environmental information to consumers. Many eco-labels adhere to strict standards, such as ISO 14000, and hold products to meaningful degrees of quality. Meaningful standards put pressure on businesses to maintain levels of excellence. In other words, if your competitors live up to a certain environmental standard, you will have to as well in order to stay competitive.

 The International Organization for Standardization (ISO), the world's largest developer of international standards on a variety of subjects, publishes the ISO 14000, a set of standards for environ-mental management in business. [link] For the essential features of the ISO 14000 standards, go to www.iso.org/iso/iso_14000_essentials.

Do eco-labels really affect consumer behavior? It depends. Eco-labels can influence consumers by establishing green criteria at the point of purchase and providing a point of comparison based on green standards. However, research suggests that not all eco-labels are created equal. In fact, consumers indicate that they are more likely to make green purchase decisions based on widely recognized eco-labels such as the recycling Mobius loop and the ENERGY STAR logo.[2]

Whether you are a manufacturer (and have to decide whether to qualify for an eco-label) or a reseller (and have to choose products to sell that have eco-labels), it makes sense to know about the labels in your industry. Do your research and be informed as to why—or why not—you have chosen certain labels.

If used responsibly, eco-labeling can play a significant role in your marketing efforts. The key is this: Know what's what, and use only eco-labels that are issued by independent third parties and recognized as legitimate.

[link] The Consumer Reports Greener Choices Eco-Labels Center provides everything you need to know about eco-labels. The site features search by label, certifiers, and product functions; a glossary; and excellent information about what makes a good eco-label at www.greenerchoices.org/eco-labels/eco-home.cfm.

[link] Another independent guide to hundreds of eco-labels can be found at http://ecolabelling.org.

Setting Priorities

Before drafting your strategic plan outlined in Chapter 5, you'll want to review Part Two of this book. The chapters in Part Two present a wide variety of green practices that involve varying investments of time and money. Not every area covered in these chapters will be relevant to your business. For example, most of the water conservation practices presented in Chapter 9 won't be relevant to retailers. And sole proprietors can breeze right past Chapter 11, which covers green human resources practices. But before proceeding to the planning stage, you'll want to review Part Two to determine which areas of your business are likely candidates for greening and to get a better understanding of the range of possibilities. No need to dig too deep into the details yet. At this point, use the information in Part Two to explore your options, begin to set priorities, and focus your planning efforts.

Part Two breaks down into the following overarching areas:

- Reducing Waste and Recycling
- Energy Management (including green information technology strategies)
- Water Conservation
- Green Office Supplies
- Green Human Resources
- Green Transportation and Shipping
- Green Marketing and Communications
- Green Business Travel
- Green Purchasing

As you review these chapters, you'll begin to identify practices that make sense for your business. You'll begin thinking about how to best use your time and capital. When you do, recognize that economic sustainability is essential to any green business model. So don't try to take on too much, too fast. Gradual, incremental progress is a worthy goal. For most small business owners it makes sense initially to focus on making changes that are cost-effective and don't have a significant impact on productivity. Remember, you can always launch more aggressive green initiatives once you are sure you can sustain them.

Turning Dilemmas into Opportunities

Approach the options outlined in Part Two with an open mind. If a particular practice appeals to you—from an environmental and business perspective—but seems too expensive or time-intensive, don't dismiss it out-of-hand. Refer back to your SWOT. Look for hidden costs that may be associated with *not* making the change—such as rising prices or changes in the regulatory or competitive environment. Explore ways to offset costs—such as tax credits or rebates, or finding partners. And look for hidden opportunities. For example, when Ikea started charging 5 cents for each plastic bag, they uncovered a hidden opportunity. Not only did plastic bag consumption in Ikea stores drop by 92%, but they ended up selling millions of dollars in 59-cent reusable bags. So, let's say your restaurant sells a lot of to-go food, but shifting to biodegradable packaging seems too expensive. Before ruling it out, consider charging a to-go fee, like a fuel surcharge. In general, if the cost of a material represents a small portion of a product's total cost, the greater the potential for markup. So if the biodegradable to-go container surcharge is a small enough percentage of the total cost of the food, you may even be able to turn the surcharge into a profit center.

Finally, before proceeding, recognize that going green inevitably involves trade-offs. As you begin to learn more about sustainable practices, you may start asking yourself questions that have never occurred to you before: Is it better to use organic or locally produced products? Should green materials be shipped from overseas? Are the CO_2 savings from compact fluorescent lightbulbs worth the extra mercury they contain? Is an employee subsidy for purchasing a fuel-efficient car better than promoting carpooling? Should linoleum floors be ripped up and replaced with bamboo? Is it better to keep an older computer or buy a new energy-efficient model? Don't lose sight of the forest for the trees. Think about tactics that are cost-effective for your business and good for your customers—and that you can afford to do. Then, to quote Nike, just do it.

Fast, Cheap, and Good—Pick Two

There's an old marketing adage: Fast, cheap, and good—pick two. Fast refers to the time required to complete a project, cheap refers to the total cost of the project, and good is the quality of the final project. In most cases you can only hope to achieve two out of the three. While many of the "Fifty Easy Ways to Make Your Workplace Greener" can actually be achieved quickly, inexpensively, and properly, it is unrealistic to plan for your green program to be fast, cheap, and good. My vote—at least at first—is for cheap and good. If your green program is planned deliberately, then you should be able to do so properly and economically.

Ultimately, going green is a way to reduce costs and improve efficiencies. In fact, in Part Two, you'll find a variety of strategies for streamlining operations, implementing best practices, and improving operating efficiencies—all of which are inherently green. And in Chapter 5, you'll find tools to help you weigh the costs and benefits of investing in specific sustainable practices. By setting clear priorities and following through on them, you'll be able to create a green program that is both consistent and sincere.

5 DEVELOPING YOUR PLAN

A goal without a plan is just a wish.

—Antoine de Saint-Exupéry, writer and aviator

This is where you begin to craft a strategic plan that will take your business into the future. You originally embarked on creating a green program because you wanted to achieve specific goals—related to reducing waste, costs, and the use of energy and other resources. By developing a coherent plan, you'll determine how to take advantage of opportunities to green your business and become more competitive.

Before you proceed, be sure to take the following steps:

1. Review the chapters in Part Two. Use your mission statement and SWOT as your guide, and focus on the areas of your business where you believe you can have the greatest impact. Familiarize yourself with the options. If you're a water-intensive business, you may want to review Chapter 9 most carefully. If fuel efficiency is a major concern, focus on Chapter 8. But be sure to look at all the relevant chapters in Part Two; you may identify green opportunities you never imagined.

2. Next, read through this chapter before beginning the planning

process in earnest or committing a plan to paper. This will help you understand the process and avoid false starts.

3. Once you've completed Steps 1 and 2, you're ready to craft your plan in earnest by working through this chapter, step by step. You'll be using the insights you've gained about your business from the preceding chapters and the ideas you've gathered from Part Two to develop, fine-tune, finalize, and implement your plan. To guide you through the process, this chapter breaks down into four sections:

    *   Measuring Your Use
    *   Setting Priorities
    *   Green Brainstorming
    *   Implementation

Measuring Your Use

I come from the metering industry where there's an old saying: If you can't measure it, you can't manage it.

—**Chuck Sathrum,** program manager, North Carolina State Energy Office

“” ECO CHAT

Sustainability is a journey, not a destination, so don't worry about whether you're "green enough" (you're not . . . but if you commit to the journey you'll make progress, and that's what matters). First, do the green improvements that are good for your bottom line. While the marketing benefit of being able to say you're green is nice, it's probably not going to be the fundamental driver of success. The more you do to green your business in ways that help to build your financial success, the easier it is (and more fun) to continue down the green path, and to take on opportunities where the economic benefits are harder to measure.

—**Randy Paynter,** founder and president, Care2

Why measure what you use. Measuring your activities allows you to generate data about how you spend your money and under what circumstances. This will give you a greater insight into your business practices and allow you to manage the financial side of your business more efficiently. The more efficiently you manage, the more you'll be able to reduce waste and the more productive you'll become. It all starts with measuring where you are today. For example, by measuring how much you spend on office supplies and what activities use the most office supplies, you can use the information to make decisions about whether or not to alter your office supply purchases and how to develop policies for reducing office supplies waste.

You can use measurements to:

■ Determine which activities and customer requirements are most important.
■ Develop baselines against which you can assess progress.
■ Establish targets against which the results can be evaluated.

How to measure what you use. Assessing how much energy, water, and other resources you use doesn't have to be complex, but it will probably take some time. In general, assessing your use requires an annual estimate of the amount of energy and resources consumed, and the dollar costs of operating various aspects of your business. You can take a four-step approach:

■ **Step One:** Using the chapters in Part Two as a guide, assess one material, resource, or process at a time—for example, energy use, water consumption, or paper. Otherwise, you will be unfocused and overwhelmed.
■ **Step Two:** Walk around your office, store, or plant, and take inventory of assets and materials that you use. This step will vary depending on what material or resources you're focusing on at the moment. As an example, if you are focusing on energy

use, take an inventory of everything that uses energy—lights, PCs, cash registers, appliances, machinery. If you're focusing on paper use, take inventory of all the ways you use paper—copying and faxing, producing brochures or direct mail pieces, correspondence and business stationery, receipts. If you're a manufacturer focusing on waste, you'll want to take an inventory of every step in the manufacturing process that generates waste.

■ **Step Three:** Review historical bills and accounting records to establish both the quantities and the dollar amounts expended on line item goods and services.

■ **Step Four:** Make a list of all your business expenses by dollar amounts in descending order. Once you've compiled information on what you spend historically, it will be much easier to set priorities, identify opportunities, and establish goals.

■ The Next Step: Setting Priorities

To green something that doesn't make sense to the consumer or make sense for the economics of the business, is not necessarily a net positive.

—**Leah Edwards,** marketing and strategy consultant

Focus on your largest expense areas. Consider targeting all expense areas over a certain threshold amount. You can measure this in dollars or as a percentage of overall expenses, such as any expense on which you spend over $500 a month, or that represent 10% or more of total expenses. If health insurance is your most significant expense, look at ways to green your human resources practices by hiring HR consultants to examine efficiencies in paper processes (such as electronic delivery of benefits documents), and negotiate contracts with carriers who will pass that reduction in costs on to you. If business energy is a top expense, look at ways to reduce energy use. Use your list of business expenses to guide your planning process and start with the areas of your business that will have the greatest financial impact. But keep in mind that you may not be able to change things as dramatically as you'd like, especially at first. Look for actions that are achievable and cost-effective to implement. Take energy use as an example. If you've noticed that your customers and staff leave lights on in unoccupied rooms (bathrooms, conference rooms), you may want to make turning off the lights in unused areas a priority. If you lease space, that step may be as simple as posting signs on light switches. If, on the other hand, you own your facility and the lights are generating significant added costs, you may want to install motion sensors or bilevel light switches.

Consider your customer requirements. Think about your business. What practices are essential to your competitive advantage? Fast delivery? Then make sure you look at the ways in which greening your shipping and transportation will positively—or negatively—impact delivery times before making changes. Will hiring local subcontractors reduce transportation time to job sites and reduce your fuel costs? Is customer service a key competitive advantage? Before making changes, be sure you look at the ways in which greening your human resources policies and call center activities will positively—or negatively—impact customer service measurements. By equipping your employees with mobile technology, can you reduce transportation expenses and improve customer service? Then that's another possibility you'll want to explore.

A good way to confirm your customer requirements is to solicit customer input. Listening to your customers is essential for setting your priorities. Studies have found that up to 85% of new B2B ideas come from customers, and that customer-generated ideas are more original and more valuable to users than those generated from within the business.[1]

Talk to your customers. Consider conducting a quick online survey in which you ask customers what green offers or innovations your business could provide that they might find desirable. Talk to your sales reps and customer service people. The people who deal with your customers and prospects every day are an excellent source of information about customer preferences—about what they do and don't like about your business. Understanding and anticipating undeveloped customer needs can provide you with a real competitive advantage.

 Risk management is a discipline for managing external threats that may face your business now and in the future.

Manage your risk. In the SWOT analysis conducted in Chapter 3, you considered the external threats that face your business now and in the future. Planning for those threats is risk management. Now that you have identified exposures, you can try to mitigate the negative outcomes with a plan. If you are in a business that emits significant amounts of greenhouse gases or uses a significant amount of energy, these issues will be of immediate concern. If not, reducing waste, especially of limited and natural resources, still makes sense. By reducing your dependence on scarce resources, you will be managing the risk that there will be insufficient supplies in the future. And of course, there is great opportunity to be had for those who supply solutions that mitigate those risks.

The risks associated with climate change affect every business, large and small. Increasingly, companies will be forced to address those risks—as we see more legislation and regulation. Smart companies will be the ones that stay ahead of the curve, anticipate those risks, and take steps to mitigate them.

Keep in mind that environmental requirements and regulations are going to get stricter. We will see a greater reliance on market-based controls, such as cap-and-trade systems. It only makes sense to plan ahead for the days when regulation and scarcity of resources will change the way you do business.

Take the case of Mokugift.com. The firm's product, a unique give-aplanted-tree-as-a-gift service, is all about sustainability and was originally targeted directly to consumers. When other companies began approaching the company about reselling the firm's branded service, Mokugift.com launched a new service just for a new target market: Mokugift Rewards for Business. The new target market became the firm's largest growth area. Or take the example of Grossman Marketing Group in Somerville, Massachusetts, a fourth-generation marketing services provider. In 2007, the firm began offsetting 100% of its energy use with Green-e certified wind power and became the only firm in its industry to offer envelopes produced exclusively using clean energy. Recognizing the marketing benefits of being green in a brown industry, Grossman Marketing Group absorbs the 5% premium on their energy costs as a capital expenditure instead of passing the cost on to customers. The result? Since the program began, the firm has produced almost a quarter-billion pieces of direct mail through its wind initiative for clients such as Google, Green Mountain Roasters, and the National Park

Foundation. This program helped boost Grossman's envelope sales by 20%—quite an achievement for a 100-year-old business operating in a competitive and mature marketplace.

Green Brainstorming

Get your staff and customers involved. Tell your employees, your people, or even your family members what you're doing, why you're doing it, and open it up like a competition. Say: We want to cut our paper waste by 100% in 18 months. Any ideas? Someone might say, we can start doing everything by PDF instead of printing out three copies of everything."

—**Jason Holstine,** founder and president, Amicus Green Building Center

Once you've reviewed your SWOT and set your priorities, it's time to get specific. Gather your green team and work together to generate ideas about how you can go green within the framework of your SWOT and priorities. Ask the group: How can we expand our products or services to meet the needs of new consumers or businesses that care about sustainability? How can we reduce energy (or cut transportation costs or improve advertising efficiency)? How can we affect supplier behavior to be greener? How can we influence the decisions of customers so they can be greener? How can we use our green program to sell more? How can we use our green program to improve market share? How can we communicate our green efforts and achievements?

Brainstorm ways to mitigate your weaknesses and eliminate threats. How can going green help you compete with a new business in town? If you need to upgrade systems, can you do it in a green way? Can you justify paying or charging higher prices for green products? Will greening your supply chain make it more secure? Can you anticipate impending environmental legislation in a cost-effective way? What will *not* going green mean for your business?

During the brainstorming session, don't forget to make the most of things you're already doing that are green to turn them into opportunities. Remind the team to consider leveraging your current activities into formal greening strategies. For example, if you already supply reusable mugs in the break room, consider implementing a nondisposables break room policy. Also, remember to consider making small-scale green choices, when large-scale ones are not feasible. Say, after a careful analysis, you decide that moving to 100% PCW recycled content copy paper company-wide is too costly; you might consider increasing the recycled content of copy paper to 30% PCW and using 100% PCW content paper for products that you use less of—such as stationery, business cards, or Post-it Notes.

The key to a good brainstorming session is to encourage the free flow of ideas. You can moderate to keep things on track, but resist the temptation to instantly reject or accept any one idea. Write every idea down on a white board or have someone take notes. Compare solutions. At the end of the meeting, vote on the best ideas or combinations of ideas. (Give yourself veto power if necessary—you are the boss after all.) Then select the best ideas to move forward to the next stage.

Calculating Return on Investment (ROI) and Payback

The beauty of going green is that it can sometimes save you money. Nonetheless, before making any significant investment in greening your business, you'll want to make sure it's financially viable by calculating the potential cost savings and potential returns. As the ENERGY STAR website states: "Behind every energy strategy is a measurable rate of return."

Determining the return on your investment will enable you to build a business case for or against green upgrades and purchases. To help you with this process, there are plenty of free financial calculators available online from both third parties and suppliers. Use them to calculate the returns for specific purchases you may be considering, such as for buying high-efficiency lightbulbs or web-conferencing services. A good list of calculators appears in the resources section at the end of the book. However, if what you're looking for is not listed, ask potential suppliers if they have ROI calculators. Many vendors make these tools available, because they know helping you make a business case for their products will help them make a sale. In any case, keep in mind that some investments also provide what are called soft returns on investment, such as improving customer satisfaction and brand building.

ENERGY STAR makes two powerful, free calculators available online: the Financial Value Calculator and the Cash Flow Opportunity Calculator.

- The Financial Value Calculator measures the impact of energy investments on a company's finances. To use the calculator, you'll need an estimate of your utility bills and commercial building floor space as well as the initial costs of the investment you're considering and the projected annual cost savings with respect to energy use. Go to www.energystar.gov/ia/business/financial_value_calculator.xls.

- Based on the assumption that the potential annual savings of an investment in energy efficiency equipment equals a defined cash flow opportunity, the Cash Flow Opportunity Calculator provides a simple payback calculator for evaluating energy efficiency investments. In other words, it helps you determine: (1) how much new energy efficiency equipment can be purchased based on the anticipated energy savings generated from the equipment; (2) whether the equipment should be financed now or would it be better to wait and use cash from a future budget; and (3) if money is being lost by waiting for a lower interest rate. Go to www.energystar.gov/ia/business/cfo_calculator.xls.

How to Green Your Landlord

If, like the majority of small businesses, you lease your facilities, you'll find that some recommendations in this book require the cooperation of your landlord. You may also find that your landlord does not yet see the financial benefits to making efficiency-related capital improvements because, in a typical commercial lease, the landlord pays for improvements but the tenants, who pay the utility bills, reap the benefits of the savings. Despite this, don't give up hope. The inclusion of environmental criteria into relevant lease clauses, such as requiring ENERGY STAR appliances or providing recycling services, are becoming more commonplace.[2] So, the best time to talk to your landlord about greening is when you are signing or renegotiating your lease. If it is not time to sign a new lease, however, you can steer your landlord to Building Owners and Managers Association (BOMA) International and their "Guide to Writing a Commercial Real Estate Lease, Including Green Lease Language" (aka "The BOMA Green Lease Guide"). It provides landlords with ideas on how to incentivize tenants to reduce the consumption of energy, water, and materials; reduce waste; improve recycling; and choose energy-efficient and environmentally friendly products, furnishings, and office equipment. Remember, your landlord may want the right to pass through capital costs that result in lower operating costs for you. That may not be such a bad way to green your business: In the end, you'll be greener and you won't have to bear the up-front costs. For more about BOMA's Green Lease Guide, go to http://boma.org.

Implementation

Plans are only good intentions unless they immediately degenerate into hard work.

—**Peter Drucker,** writer, professor, management consultant

Now the hard work begins. There are four general steps to implementing your green program: (1) formally develop green policies and procedures; (2) document your objectives by creating a formal policy statement; (3) create an action plan and deadlines; and (4) communicate your plan.

The first step to implementation is to formally develop green policies and procedures. To do this, you will need to define and write down realistic green objectives and targets for each aspect of your business that you want to green. They should be based on the identified goals such as resource reduction, reuse, recycling, pollution prevention, legal or other requirements. Establish measurable green targets that can be accomplished within a reasonable time frame. For example, if one of your objectives is to improve green purchasing practices, then set some targets that can realistically make that happen. You might decide to provide green purchasing training to staff; formally identify opportunities to purchase green products and services; or require the use of green criteria in all future contracts. If an objective is to increase participation in recycling programs, you might decide to provide recycling training to staff; post reminder signs above all bins; and purchase additional recycling bins to place in individual offices and near copiers, printers, fax machines, and in break rooms.

Then, document your objectives by creating a formal policy statement. Remember to include targets, and to review and update them on an established schedule, such as quarterly or annually. Targets should measure positive environmental impacts as well as progress toward meeting your green purchasing and practice objectives. For example, measure increases in the amount of PCW recycled content in your office supply purchases: "We will increase our purchases of 100% PCW copier paper by 20%." Or measure reductions in energy and water use associated with products implemented to increase efficiency: "We will reduce our electricity usage in kilowatt hours by 20% and expenses by 10% compared to the month of August last year."

Next, create an action plan and set deadlines. Assign team members specific duties. Who is going to count the recycling bins? Who is going to do the research to determine the costs of Xeriscaping? Who is going to run the financial analyses? Once you determine who is going to be responsible for what, set deadlines and schedule interim update meetings to make sure progress is being made and goals can be met.

Finally, as described in Chapter 6, you need to communicate your company's green mission and the progress you're making toward achieving it.

6 COMMUNICATE. COMMUNICATE. COMMUNICATE.

When all other means of communication fail, try words.
—*Anonymous*

Communicating your company's green mission and strategy may be the most important thing you can do to ensure you achieve the business outcomes you desire. You embarked on creating a green program because you wanted to achieve specific goals. Now is your chance to communicate those goals and the progress you're making toward them. How effectively you communicate your commitment, objectives, and successes to customers, employees, and other stakeholders will help determine how much value you will get out of your green program.

Once you've established your green guidelines, it's important to communicate your green initiatives and goals internally through newsletter articles, emails, and signs in key areas, such as in break rooms and near copiers. Use every tool at your disposal—including newsletters, meetings, and e-communications—to promote specific programs and practices, and publicize your environmental successes. Externally, share your green mission and your results with stakeholders whenever you communicate with them, as well as with the community and your industry—through local news outlets, trade publications, and other media. Your key messages: We're committed to this process. These are the steps we're taking. These are the results we plan to achieve. And going forward, this is a part of how we do business.

Marketing Your Greenness
Creating Green Value

 Positioning is the representation of what a product or service does in comparison to the competition. Positioning strategies typically focus on the effect on the consumer (i.e., is healthier, saves money) or how it differs from (read: is superior to) that of the competition (uses less water, gets better gas mileage).

Marketing is all about positioning—how you define your product or service for your customer. What's the value you're creating for them? And how do your green initiatives relate to your overall marketing message? According to an article in *Environment* magazine: "Research indicates that many green products have failed because of green marketing myopia—marketers' narrow focus on their products' 'greenness' over the broader expectations of consumers or other market players (such as regulators or activists)."[1] The authors define five fundamental benefits that consumers associate with green products and services:

- Health and safety
- Convenience
- Efficiency and the associated cost savings
- Performance
- And (sometimes) status[2]

The key to successfully marketing your greenness involves leveraging these core benefits. That means focusing your green marketing efforts not solely on environmental attributes or customer satisfaction, but on both. All green products and services can gain from focusing on some or all of these five benefits. And if your products and services don't seem to embody any of them—say your product is produced in a way that uses less water but consumers can't see that—you can bundle your product features with one or more of the five benefits to create a compelling value proposition. For example, in addition to promoting the absence of the controversial ingredient, aluminum, Tom's of Maine deodorants are also positioned as safe, natural, long-lasting, and highly effective in fighting odor. So the company's marketing message extends beyond greenness to appeal to other attributes people expect from a good deodorant.

If you're marketing a green product or service, look for ways to position it that first and foremost meet all consumer needs for the product. Pentel's Handy-line S Highlighters have all the features consumers want in a highlighter: They are a compact, retractable, have a chisel tip, and come in assorted colors. But they are also successfully positioned as green products because—*in addition to the core product features*—they are made from 54% post-consumer recycled plastic, are refillable, and are branded as part of the Pentel Recycology program. Through marketing, Pentel lets consumers know that no compromise of product features comes with their green products.

Once you can say that your product meets the fundamental consumer needs, then consider how it might incorporate some or all of the five core benefits that consumers desire from green products and services. Is it healthier? Does it save time or money? Is it a high-performance product? Think back to Milgard Manufacturing. The company positioned its high-performance windows not only as energy efficient, but also as products that enhance comfort and protect furniture. It's important to reframe the way you think about marketing green in order to make the most of the attributes your products or services possess.

How to Avoid Greenwashing

If we are strong, our strength will speak for itself. If we are weak, words will be of no help.

—John Fitzgerald Kennedy

It's impossible to talk about marketing your greenness without talking about greenwash, a subject that's come up throughout this book. The definition of greenwash, which appears in an earlier chapter, bears repeating here: *Greenwash refers to efforts by companies to portray themselves as environmentally responsible in order to overstate environmental benefits or misrepresent, mislead, diminish, or divert attention from environmental wrongdoing.* 🔗 To learn more about what exactly constitutes greenwash, go to TerraChoice's Six Sins of Greenwashing at www.terrachoice .com/Home/Six_Sins_of_Greenwashing or the Greenpeace Greenwash Criteria at http://stopgreenwash.org/criteria.

In a 2008 *BusinessWeek* interview, Kim Jeffery, the CEO of Nestlé Water North America, makers of Poland Spring waters, suggested that his company has been unfairly judged by consumers and environmental advocates. According to Jeffery, the company has not been given the credit they deserve for their environmental efforts, in part, because Nestlé management considered such actions "business as usual." Yet Nestlé Water, and in fact all other bottled water companies, are still under fire for greenwashing. The argument is not with their green practices; the argument is with the practices they continue to implement that *aren't* green. As part of normal business operations, these companies do promote certain green practices, many of which save the company lots of money. *And they are doing many of the very things you are learning to do in this book.* Are those practices good for the environment? Of course. But that's not really what greenwashing is all about. Greenwashing is about consumer marketing and positioning, because this is where the real greenwashing occurs. Here's the fundamental problem: The bottled water companies exaggerate and misrepresent their environmental achievements in order to divert attention away from the environmental problems inherent to their industry.

There are many ways in which businesses greenwash, ranging from mild miscommunication to flagrant misrepresentation of facts. How do you know if you're crossing the line? It's all well and good for companies to tout their environmental practices, but unless those practices are affirmatively good for the environment, that should not be the focus of the messaging. In other words, don't position your products or services as being green unless they are affirmatively good for the environment. Here are two questions to ask yourself if you're ever in doubt:

- Is my industry inherently polluting or unsustainable?
- Do any of the trade groups I belong to lobby against pending or current environmental laws and regulations?

If the answer to either of these questions is yes, then it's unwise to position your business as green. The best you can do is to fully and honestly communicate your sustainability efforts and admit that you are trying to be green in a brown industry. The airline industry provides a good example. While some airlines have significant sustainability initiatives, given the current state of the industry, no airline is positioning itself or its products as green. Although you've never seen an advertisement touting the company's environmental achievements, Continental Airlines has invested $16 billion in more efficient aircraft, technology, and ground equipment, and it has thirteen full-time environmentalists on staff. Virgin Atlantic has new, more efficient fleets, innovative recycling programs, and leading-edge brother companies—Virgin Green Fund and Virgin Fuel—that invest in new products and technologies that will help reduce CO_2 emissions.

To decide whether you can position a particular product or service as green, ask yourself these questions about your marketing:

- Does it exaggerate an environmental achievement in order to divert attention away from an environmental problem?
- Does it focus on one environmental achievement but conceal other environmental impacts?
- Does it tout environmental achievements that are required or mandated by existing laws?
- Is it impossible to substantiate the environmental claims?
- If you use a third-party certification or eco-label to promote your business, does it have reasonable yet stringent criteria?
- Are the environmental claims vague or meaningless?

If the answer to any of these questions is yes, then you should not consider positioning the product or service as green. You can either fix the issue so the answer becomes no, or you can mention the environmental achievement, but not use it as a positioning strategy. Say you're a retailer that sells some green products. Instead of calling yourself a "green retailer," you can credibly advertise a section in the store devoted to green products. Take the office supply industry as an example. None of the major office supply retailers call themselves green—because they all offer products that are not eco-friendly. However, they all have significant green sections on their websites and in their catalogs.

Sometimes it may be hard to tell if you are stepping over the greenwash line. As you go through the greening process, many of the practices you'll be implementing—such as waste reduction strategies—will be eco-friendly initiatives, but that doesn't mean you can call yourself a "green business" or call your product "green." Let's say you reduce the weight of a product's packaging. Achievements in this area would rarely merit an ad campaign focused on how green the new packaging is. However, mentioning dematerialization efforts on packaging and in ads (as one of many waste reduction practices) is perfectly legitimate. Apple does not market the iPod by talking about the lightness and recyclability of the box it comes in, but it is fairly common knowledge that Apple is known to be constantly improving the sustainability of its packaging. It is all in how you communicate.

So, the lesson is: Position your products and services with honesty and accuracy, and sell the core consumer benefits first and foremost. At the same time, let your customers know about what you're doing to green your operations. It matters to them, but not if they think you're trying to divert them from the facts. As for the water companies, the charges of greenwash will not go away until they change their advertising and PR campaigns. As business owners, you'll want to resist this type of messaging—because greenwash erodes consumer confidence and diminishes the value of legitimate environmental successes.

If you are curious about what you can and cannot say legally, the Federal Trade Commission has guidelines for the use of environmental marketing claims at www.ftc.gov/bcp/grnrule/guides980427.htm.

Communicating with Stakeholders

How to Communicate Your Green Mission

In Chapter 3, you wrote a green mission statement. Once you've set your green strategy in motion, it's time to publicly share that mission statement. Remember, your green mission is the basis for your competitive advantage. You'll miss a valuable opportunity if you don't put it at the forefront of your communication and marketing efforts. So share it with customers, employees, vendors and suppliers, and the broader community:

- Post it on your website where people can find it. It deserves a tab on your main navigation bar.
- Post it in your offices or retail space.
- Include a link on emails, online newsletters, and all printed materials.

■ Include an abridged version on all company press releases and in the About Us section of your website.

Remember to communicate your achievements. Once your green program is up and running, it is essential to measure the results of your efforts. (See "Measuring Your Use" on page 62.) Sharing your results is as important to stakeholders as sharing your objectives, so you will want to report on your progress periodically. Once you've begun your green program, you'll also want to elicit feedback. That will help you ensure that you're achieving the results you expected, gauge customer and employee response, and uncover new opportunities.

Making a Business Case with Employees

For most small businesses, getting employees behind your green plan involves *talking* to them. Some employees will be enthusiastic; others, less so. Therefore, when you address the issue, the key is to make a strong business case—not just an environmental plea—for participation. Says Consultant Leah Edwards: "If the employees don't all have the same environmental values as the business owner, then the business owner has to give employees reason to care. You may have to be pragmatic—it could involve saying: 'The businesses in our industry are very competitive, and all of our competitors are putting out messages of being better global citizens.'" Christine Nevers is manager of the NYLO Hotel in Providence/Warwick, which has successfully launched a series of green initiatives. She, too, advises talking to employees from both an environmental and a business perspective: "It's a collective message . . . Obviously, this is something that is important to the environment. And we've made an effort to say: This is what we're going to do. This is what we're going to continue to do. Then it comes down to the bottom line: This is bringing more business into the hotel . . . This is the future. This is where the business is going." In others words, treat your green initiatives as you would treat any other business initiative. Tell your employees: This is a move that will make us more competitive, more cost-efficient, more profitable—*and* help the environment.

Communication, Marketing, and PR Tools

Signage

Signs are a valuable way to reinforce your commitment to your green practices, and for getting people to stick with the program. If there's a green aisle in your retail store, post a sign. If you're starting a carpooling program, post a sign—and a rideshare sign-up—on your office bulletin board. Whenever you're promoting a program internally, use signs as reminders. In fact, studies have shown that people significantly increase their recycling behavior when signs are present. So posting signs around your workplace reminding everyone to conserve and recycle is one of the most effective and inexpensive green practices you can implement. Here are the keys to posting effective reminders: Include a specific re-

Images courtesy of www.RecycleReminders.com

NORTH CAROLINA: BUILDING AWARENESS, GENERATING RESULTS

CASE STUDY

Back in the seventies, in the wake of the Arab oil embargo, North Carolina created a State Energy Office. But it wasn't until 2001, when energy prices really started going up, that the state upped the ante with a series of mandates to control energy use, ultimately creating the Utility Savings Initiative Program to control costs in state agencies and universities. In 2007, the state passed a law expanding the initiative to all existing and new state buildings as well as the state's 140-campus network of community colleges, the largest in the nation. Today, the award-winning program is managed by a staff of three, including Program Manager Chuck Sathrum, who has more than thirty years of experience in the energy industry's private sector. "We run this like a business," he says. "We treat it as a profit and loss center; we see profits in our mind when we decrease energy or water consumption." The results are impressive: From 2002 to 2008, the Utility Savings Initiative Program has enabled North Carolina to avoid expenditures of more than $150 million.

The program's goal is explicit: "The energy consumption per gross square foot for all State buildings in total shall be reduced by twenty percent (20%) by 2010 and thirty percent (30%) by 2015 based on energy consumption for the 2002–2003 fiscal year." So far, the state is on target, putting North Carolina on the leading edge. "We're on track to get to this

quest (i.e., turn off lights when leaving); place signs in close proximity to the area in which people are expected to respond; and request actions that are convenient for the end-user.[3] The examples of signs on page 83 come from www.RecycleReminders.com, where you can customize, download, and print free recycling and conservation signs.

20% level. Some people have cut their consumption—not just their intensity, but overall consumption—by a huge amount," says Sathrum. "One community college has cut its electricity consumption by 30% despite the rising student population."

Initially, the program met some resistance from overstaffed agencies. "People complained about having to collect their information, their data. It's like collecting the information for your income tax," he says. But once they started seeing the results, it cemented their commitment. "Once people get hooked by it," says Sathrum, "they'll like it." At several of the universities, the students have become involved—creating Conservation Action Teams and competitions. "The dorms have had contests to see who could conserve the most energy and water. They post signs around the dorms and get people excited. And it's fun," he says, adding, "It's all about awareness."

According to Sathrum, the program itself is pretty simple. But the commitment is the key. "Even for a small company, it has to be brought in at the top. It can't be poor old Crusty the janitor who has to do everything." Engage everyone in the process. "Everyone has to be aware," says Sathrum. "Then, when you have staff meetings, everyone can see how well they're doing. They can see their progress." That's where the results come in.

Newsletters and Intranets

Consistent communication is one of the most effective—and easiest—greening strategies. Remind your customers, your suppliers, and your staff about the importance of greening your operations with daily, weekly, or monthly communications via:

- Your website's home page
- Email
- Online newsletters
- Promotions
- Event invitations
- Press announcements
- Intranet posts
- Bulletin board posts
- Blog posts
- Twitter tweets
- Holiday greetings

Remember to include facts about your progress and other hard information about the impact of conservation. You will see your communication pay off.

New Media

 New media refers to nontraditional, usually digital, ways of delivering advertising or promotional messages, and includes everything from the Internet to mobile advertising.

Public relations is often the first green marketing step small businesses take. Typically, that involves issuing press releases so the mainstream media (television, radio, magazines, and newspapers) will publish or air a piece about their green strategy or activities. While it's a good place to start, there are ample opportunities to publicize your business through new media—nontraditional avenues such as the green-targeted social media, mobile marketing, and text messaging. Keep in mind that new media, by definition, are emerging daily. By the time you are reading this, there will surely be new media not mentioned here.

Remember to send press releases to green websites like Green

Options Media (http://greenoptions.com), Greener World Media (www
.greenerworldmedia.com), and TreeHugger.com. If it's in the budget,
consider signing up with an environmentally targeted press release service like Environmental News Network (ENN).

Social Media

 Social media refers to Internet sites and mobile-based applications that rely on user participation and user-generated content.

Social media is a powerful communication tool. At its best, social media
leverages the reach of the Internet, and the power of content-sharing
and direct engagement. Social networking sites such as Facebook,
MySpace, and LinkedIn allow people to both network and to connect
personally. Blogs and blogger networks provide forums for targeted content to be shared over the Internet. Twitter, a cross between instant
messaging and blogging, keeps time- and attention-pressured users in
the loop. Community forums exist for every topic imaginable and media
sharing sites like Flickr and YouTube media for sharing photos and vid-
eos are becoming mainstream. The social media arena is exploding. Online communities — such as Care2.com and Change.org or green groups
on LinkedIn.com — provide an effective and green way to communicate
with large numbers of eco-minded people.

Start to blog. A blog, short for weblog, is a diary on the web. As a
communication tool, blogging can help you network, make sales, and
activate your stakeholders at a fraction of the cost of traditional media.
There are two basic ways to blog about your business. You can start your
own blog and build a reputation as an industry expert. A good example
of this is the blog "Inside Sustainable Packaging" (http://blog.sala
zarpackaging.com), written by Dennis Salazar of Salazar Packaging.
Known as a reputable and unbiased source of information, Salazar's blog
is effective because it is more than a repository for press releases. It

contains valuable information about industry trends as well as product information.

The other way to blog is to become a contributor to an existing blog. This can give you a platform from which to communicate your expertise and often requires less time than writing your own blog. Find a blog that reaches your market and ask if they are looking for contributors. Many blogs actively seek writers. Either option provides an excellent way to communicate your green positioning in a public forum.

The good news about blogging: You can reach a wide and diverse audience. The downside: It takes time and a genuine interest in engaging the community. It is essential to become an active member of your green online community. In other words, don't use your blog exclusively to promote yourself. Spend time reading posts, comment when you have something to offer, and promote your fellow bloggers. Also, if you want your blog posts to be read, make them personal and insightful. Everyone loves the insider scoop.

Finally, submit your blog posts to popular social bookmarking sites like Stumble.com, Digg.com, Reddit.com, and Tipd.com as well as to green-themed sites like Care2.com.

Open a Twitter account. Twitter.com, a cross between instant messaging and blogging, is a free website where users post text containing up to 140 characters. People receive updates or "tweets" from people whom they have chosen to follow. You can tweet to announce promotions, specials, coupons, and events; make new blog posts; provide customer service; and convey any other information that can be stated in a few words. There is an active green community on Twitter (as well as on most social networking sites). Get involved and let social media help spread the word about your initiatives.

Post events. If you sponsor and hold events, post them on social event calendars as a way to attract new attendees. Most social networking sites (including Facebook, LinkedIn, etc.) have event listing applications. Greenbiz.com and SustainableIndustries.com offer free, targeted event calendars as well.

TWO

ASSESSING
YOUR
GREEN OPTIONS

INTRODUCTION

How to Use Part Two

This part of the book features hundreds of green practices from which you can pick and choose to develop your own program. Designed as a reference tool and resource guide, Part Two is organized by subject area—energy management, water conservation, business travel, and so forth. It's your guide to the full range of green practices and possibilities—and it's designed to be used in conjunction with Part One. Part One offered insights on how to take a step-by-step approach to greening your business, advising you to start with small steps and to approach greening as an ongoing process. Part Two presents hundreds of actions you can take—from the simple to the complex. Some of these will be more relevant to your business than others. Some may not be appropriate for some time to come. It's up to you to choose which ones you want to implement—and when. You'll base those decisions, in part, on what you learned by working through the earlier chapters of this book.

A word of friendly caution: If you haven't read Part One carefully, you may have missed out on important information about how to maximize the benefits of your green program and minimize the challenges. To develop an effective green program, you'll want to refer back and forth between the two parts of this book—over weeks, months, and even years.

Use the chapters that follow to:

■ Explore your options. By reviewing Part Two before you start the planning process outlined in Chapter 5, you can begin to explore your green options and opportunities.

■ Set priorities. When you begin to craft your plan, the information in Part Two will help you set priorities and focus your planning efforts.

■ Find resources. Once you have a plan in place, use Part Two to find the resources you need to implement your plan and put your new green initiatives in place.

■ Expand your green program. Finally, use Part Two again and again as you expand your green strategy in the future.

How to Use the Icons

Again, some of the practices outlined in the chapters that follow will make sense for your business. Others won't. Not every green practice will fit everyone's needs or budget. To guide you through Part Two, each green practice is marked with an icon that indicates the level of time and/or money involved in implementing the practice, as follows:

Ø—No meaningful time or money.

†—A short amount of time or a modest one-time commitment of time.

††—A medium amount of time.

†††—A significant amount of time or an ongoing time commitment.

$—A cost of $10 or less.

$$—A cost of $11 to $100 or less.

$$$—A cost of $100 or more.

7 REDUCING WASTE AND RECYCLING

Make good use of bad rubbish.
—*Elizabeth Beresford*

In some respects, waste is immeasurable—it touches every aspect of your business, from the scrap paper that fills your waste bins to the fuel you use for avoidable business travel. As such, specific strategies for addressing various types of waste appear throughout Part Two of this book. Addressing waste issues requires that you think carefully about every aspect of your business to uncover sources of waste. This chapter provides an overview of sustainable practices related to solid waste—including approaches that involve reducing waste, reusing materials, and recycling. How you apply these strategies will depend on your business. And however difficult it may be to measure waste, one thing is clear: The success of waste reduction programs can often be measured in dollars saved, improved profitability, and higher revenues.

Virtually every conservation program starts with efforts to reduce, reuse, and recycle—a process that involves raw materials, consumables, products, by-products, and just about every form of waste. For small businesses, the benefits of these practices go beyond conservation. The first step to reducing waste is to minimize—as opposed to eliminate—the use of resources. As a result, whatever your industry, you can achieve real impact and savings through some simple, inexpensive waste reduction and recycling efforts. Given that there's a strong business case to be made for implementing these practices, addressing waste-related issues is a good place to start your green program.

Defining the Problem

The era of mass-produced products brought with it an unanticipated increase in the amount of solid waste. Goods were designed and manufactured with by-products that held no apparent use or market value. And as the U.S. economy grew and expanded, our level of waste production grew exponentially. As of 2006, the average American produced 4.6 pounds of nonindustrial waste every day and that amount is projected to increase by .5% every year. In 2010, that will add up to more than 266 million tons of trash. If current rates of recycling hold, 67.5% or 179.8 tons of that trash will be discarded or incinerated. More than half of it will go into the nation's landfills with waste from schools and commercial locations accounting for 35% to 45% of the total. That's no less than 62.9 million tons of trash that will come from U.S. businesses every year.[1] In the United States, landfills are the largest human-related source of methane, accounting for 34% of all methane emissions.[2]

Waste-intensive businesses. Every business generates solid waste. If you're a restaurant, you may be tossing out Styrofoam take-out containers or wasting food that could be composted or donated to a local food bank. Even the way you design, produce, and dispose of your menus may be a source of waste. If you're a manufacturer, you may be wasting materials through inefficient production processes, generating waste through by-products of the manufacturing process, or wasting paper through inefficient packaging design. And you might be generating significant waste in your break room—with soda cans and paper cups. Just about every business generates paper waste, a subject that's addressed further in Chapter 10. For any small business, reducing, reusing, and

ECO CHAT

A landfill shortage crisis is looming within the next 10 years, unless the tonnages of wastes currently disposed to landfill are successfully and very rapidly reduced . . . There is no truly popular waste disposal method, other than minimizing and recycling waste so that it does not become a waste. There are just some waste disposal methods which are less unpopular than others.

—**"Landfills: Environmental Problems"** at Landfill-Site.com[3]

recycling are powerful ways to promote sustainability, manage costs, and increase efficiency.

To put it in perspective. Consider packaging as an example. Paper and paperboard account for 35% of the total materials discarded in the United States. When you reduce the size of a shipping package, you not only reduce the amount of paper you use—and the cost of materials—

ECO CHAT

AIM FOR ZERO WASTE

Preventing waste and expanding reuse, recycling, and composting programs—that is, aiming for zero waste—is one of the fastest, cheapest, and most effective strategies available for combating climate change . . . Wasting directly impacts climate change because it is directly linked to global resource extraction, transportation, processing, and manufacturing . . . The good news is that readily available cost-competitive and effective strategies to reduce, reuse, and recover discarded materials can be implemented on a wide scale within a relatively short time period.

—*Stop Trashing the Climate,* June 2008, GAIA, the Institute for Local Self-Reliance and Eco-Cycle

but you reduce the amount of space and energy required to manufacture and ship it. As an example, Wal-Mart discovered they could save $2.4 million in shipping, 3,800 trees, and 1 million barrels of oil by eliminating excessive packaging from a single private-label line of toys, Kid Connection. Or think about your break room. What happens to all those empty soda cans at the end of the day? If every small business in the United Sates recycled one aluminum can a week, it would save enough energy to run 165 million televisions for 24 hours.[4]

Best practices. The EPA's WasteWi$e program is a good place to start your overall waste reduction efforts. The EPA enlists partner companies to increase the overall recycled content in the products they purchase—by either buying more recycled products (and fewer virgin products) or increasing the level of recycled content in the products they already buy. WasteWi$e also encourages manufacturers to focus on producing greener products by incorporating a higher percentage of post-consumer waste (PCW). If you become a WasteWi$e partner, your business will enjoy benefits such as access to free technical assistance, seminars, networking opportunities, and free outreach and educational materials.

Here are a few examples of the kinds of goals WasteWi$e partners have set for themselves:

- Purchase recycled content products and supplies for the kitchen/break room and office areas as well as for maintenance and janitorial operations.
- Revise purchasing policies to allow greater purchase of recycled content materials and purchase at least one new product with recycled content each year.
- Increase the post-consumer recycled content in all product lines by 5% each year.
- Review bid lists to identify products with recycled content and institute a preferred purchase policy for products with recycled content.

Find out more about WasteWi$e and strategies for improving efficiency and cutting costs through a waste reduction program at www.epa.gov/epawaste/partnerships/wastewise/wrr/cost.htm.

Taking action. When addressing waste issues, it's best to first focus on reducing what you use. This applies to every aspect of your business. Reduce the amount of energy you use, the products you consume, and the miles you travel. Use high-efficiency, environmentally preferable products *and* use less of them. Sometimes eliminating waste simply involves using less. But since no one expects you to reduce consumption down to zero, the next best thing is to reuse what you have. And the third preference is to recycle. This approach to setting priorities, called the Waste Hierarchy, is illustrated here, in order of desirability:

The rationale for the hierarchy is this: Ideally, you want to extract full use or value from every product and, as a result, generate the minimum amount of waste. Consider bottled water as an example. From a sustainability perspective, the greenest approach is to reduce the amount of bottled water you use—that is, by drinking tap water (which you can filter) instead of bottled water. In so doing, you eliminate the need to produce, ship, and discard a bottle—which not only uses valuable resources, but also generates added waste. Reuse is the next best option. When you reuse a water bottle, you not only keep it out of the waste stream, but eliminate the need to produce another one. Recycling, while lowest in the hierarchy, is still an important green strategy—because when you recycle materials, although resources are expended to collect, process, and produce recycled products, it takes far fewer resources than it would to produce brand-new ones. For example, recycling a single pound of clear plastic PET bottles saves about 12,000 BTUs of heat energy—which is equal to the amount of electricity twelve households consume in a year.[5,6]

Green Waste Reduction and Recycling Strategies

Based on priorities articulated in the Waste Hierarchy, the green practices outlined in this chapter fall under three main headings: Reduction, Reuse, and Recycling.

In this chapter, you'll find general insights into waste-related practices. More specific practices—for everything from fuel to paper to water—appear in the chapters that follow. *One note: The costs and time involved in implementing these generic practices will vary from business to business, so some of the icons used in other chapters to indicate the time/dollar investment required do not appear here.*

Reduction Practices
Simple First Steps

Ø **Use less.** The most straightforward reduction strategy involves simply using less of a product or material. This will typically save you money on the purchasing side. Virtually everything you use in your business can be assessed to determine if you can use less. For example, using two-sided printing reduces paper use—and lowers paper costs. Reusable mugs save on the cost of restocking paper cups.

Once you take simple steps such as these, you may want to implement more sophisticated reduction strategies that are relevant to your business. As an example, green hotels and restaurants are beginning to filter and carbonate tap water, and bottle it themselves in reusable carafes and specialty bottles. In so doing, they buy less bottled water and recycle fewer water bottles—which lessens everything from the energy used for shipping bottled water to the number of bottles that go in the recycling bin. It's possible for an eco-friendly restaurant to pay hundreds, even thousands, of dollars a year in recycling costs associated with glass and plastic bottles.

Ø **Reuse instead of purchasing new.** You can easily reduce consumption by eliminating the need to buy new things. For example, reuse shipping materials such as packing material and containers. If you worry about what your customers will think, let them know you are making a deliberate choice by placing a sticker or label on the outside of the package.

Ø **Reduce incoming and outgoing mail.** Eliminate multiple subscriptions, remove yourself from mailing lists, and change the way you communicate with your customers (See also "Paper Reduction Strategies" in Chapter 10.) If necessary, appoint a staff member to manage incoming mail on an ongoing basis, or make it a rotating responsibility. See the resources section at the end of the book for links on how to reduce the amount of junk mail your business receives. To remove your business from catalog mailing lists, go to www.catalogchoice.org.

Supply Chain Acquisition Strategies

There are a number of strategies that can reduce the physical distance between where materials are sourced and where they are used. These strategies not only help reduce travel-related emissions, but also often result in shorter times to market and lower inventory holding costs. If any of the strategies could work for you, check with vendors about the availability of local resources.

The supply chain consists of all the steps involving vendors, suppliers, transportation, and processing that relate to getting raw materials (for manufacturing) or finished products (for retail sale) to the end-user.

- Buying local is an excellent greening strategy, in part because of evidence that there are significant social, environmental, and economic benefits to creating local economies. At this writing, some thirty-six cities and towns—from Albuquerque to Tampa—have adopted programs to label and promote locally owned businesses. It is always worthwhile to check with your vendors about the availability of local products and materials. Buying local also provides business owners with more control over their materials and end products. As an example, Evan Smith of Cherry Capital Foods, a wholesale distributor of locally grown food products in Traverse City, Michigan, says the ability to customize purchasing is a key benefit of buying locally. He tells the story of being able to deliver poultry products that are cut to customer specifications quickly and on a regular basis, something that would be impossible if he were using larger, more distant vendors. The Business Alliance for Local Living Economies (BALLE) is a good resource for finding a local business network in your area at www.livingeconomies.org.
- Near-sourcing refers to the practice of obtaining goods from lower-cost locales that are relatively nearby. In the United States, this typically means sourcing internationally from Mexico or Latin America, as opposed to Asia. But it also refers to warehousing in ways that reduce transportation. For example, in a reversal of a trend toward large distribution centers, some retailers have moved back to smaller, regional

warehouses to reduce transportation costs and maintain better access to goods.

■ Ship to point-of-use strategies are employed in the manufacturing sector when raw materials or components are shipped directly to the point of assembly or manufacturing location, thus reducing transportation costs and the need for protective packaging. As an example, beverage companies can receive plastic bottles as unblown "test tubes" and mold them into shape on-site. The unblown bottles require far less space on a truck than blown ones and thereby can reduce the number of truckloads required to deliver bottles by as much as 90%.

Next-Generation Reduction Strategies

 Source reduction, waste prevention, resource optimization, de-materialization, and waste elimination all refer generally to the alteration of the design, manufacture, or use of products and materials for the purpose of reducing the amount used, and/or toxicity of the product itself and the associated waste.

Many of the following reduction strategies can save you money. How you apply them—as well as the time and cost involved—depends on the nature of your business.

■ Change the way you design, manufacture, or use products and materials to reduce product toxicity, waste, and the materials it takes to get a product to market. By optimizing the use of raw materials, you'll not only minimize waste, but you may also be able to reduce materials, labor, and transportation usage and costs. For example, in order to comply with new environmental regulations, the John Roberts Commercial Printing Company in Minneapolis, Minnesota, switched to a less toxic solvent to clean their printing press wipers. In the process, the company reduced its solvent costs by 72%. They also purchased new equipment to extract and recover solvent from used wipers before sending them off to the cleaners. This new equipment allowed them to recover more than 5,000 gallons of solvent a year—keeping those chemicals out of the waste stream. The changes involved an initial investment of $15,000 and saved $50,000 in the first year—a payback of less than four months.[7]

■ Explore waste exchange, also called materials exchange programs. These programs provide a marketplace for the exchange of by-products or surplus goods that have a market value. Often the industrial waste of one company can become raw materials for—or be reused by—another business. For example, a Massachusetts food manufacturer sells 1,000 used plastic buckets every month to a business that converts them into biohazard waste containers. Find out if there's a waste exchange in your region, or ask your waste management company about finding markets for your surplus or scrap materials. Recycler's World is an online waste exchange network at www.recycle.net.

■ Look for material donation programs that serve your industry. By donating surplus goods and materials, you not only reduce the need to produce more and help other businesses save money, you also keep those materials out of landfills. As an example, each year the nonprofit organization First Book distributes millions of books donated by publishers with overstocks that are too costly to warehouse but that had, in the past, been destroyed and sent to landfills. Of course, if you are in need of the kinds of materials such programs provide, material donation programs can also serve as a valuable resource for your business. The Redo.org Donation Program matches donors with recipients of available goods at www.redo.org/Material%20donation/redo's_material_donation_program.htm.

■ Find ways to pool your resources. Pooling enables companies to maximize the use of resources, increase efficiency, and save money. For example, when a Seattle accounting firm and the nonprofit organization with adjacent offices joined together to replace their garbage containers with one large shared recycling cart and a large garbage bin, they saved $30 a month and enabled a waste management solution that would otherwise have been too expensive. Car- and vanpooling, and buying groups, are other examples of pooled resources.

Reuse Practices

In its simplest form, reuse involves keeping materials out the waste stream by passing them on to others or finding ways to reuse them in your own business. The idea of reuse is often associated with products that are passed on with little or no reconditioning, repair, or reprocessing. However, increasingly, reuse involves adding value back into used products and materials by taking steps such as cleaning, replacing worn elements, or refilling consumable components. Markets for reused products have spawned a variety of remanufacturing and refurbishing businesses. From an environmental perspective, reuse is a way to keep used products out of the solid waste stream. But by collecting, processing, and adding value to products, components, and materials—and then marketing them to people who want them, reuse strategies can have economic benefits. It can be simple to implement policies that reuse resources.

Reuse products and materials that are:

■ Refillable
■ Refurbished
■ Remanufactured
■ Repaired
■ Reusable
■ Used

IDEAL JACOBS: THE CASE FOR WASTE REDUCTION

CASE STUDY

Andrew Jacobs, president of Ideal Jacobs Corporation, a commercial printing company, has always been an environmentalist. And when a big customer asked him to get EPA certified nearly ten years ago, he didn't hesitate to pursue it. Since then, the company has been recognized by both the EPA and the Occupational Safety and Health Administration (OSHA) for environmental and social responsibility. One of the few, small independent manufacturers in the EPA's Performance Track program—a program for companies with the best environmental management systems in the country—Jacobs is an ardent believer that quality, environmental, health, and safety standards are all intertwined, and that setting and meeting the highest standards is the surest route to profitability and competitiveness. Says Jacobs: "You can't get the best profits, you can't even compete worldwide unless you are the ultimate in making as little garbage as possible, having the least amount of it around so your people won't get sick, and being one of the safest you can be. So by being the best employer, you're also being the most profitable."

Jacobs chose to focus on two high-impact areas of his business: solid waste and hazardous waste. "After working through the EPA application [twice], I realized the correlation between

Ø **Promote reuse.** According to the Reuse Development Organization, there are more than 6,000 reuse centers around the country, ranging from specialized programs for building materials or unneeded school supplies to local programs such as Goodwill and the Salvation Army to online marketplaces such as Freecycle.org.

Find out more about reuse practices and locate reuse centers at www.redo.org, a nonprofit organization that promotes reuse and in-reducing solid waste and higher profit margins. It suddenly dawned on me: Of course, create less pollution and [you'll] have more end product." Jacobs took his commitment to the next level. "We invited in OSHA, which was unheard of at the time," says Jacobs. "Then, I realized that the healthier and safer our place was, the more money I was making. Every click we made in terms of quality, environmentalism, and safety, every time we notched up, we made more money."

Ideal Jacobs is proof that good sustainability practices are good for business. Since 2002, the company has reduced its solid waste per dollar of sales by more than 50%. By substituting less toxic materials in its sheet-fed printing operations, the company achieved an 18% reduction in pounds of solid waste per $1 in sales and a 23% reduction in pounds of hazardous materials used per $1 in sales. How? "To achieve these goals, Ideal Jacobs broke down every process, identified inadequacies in the system, and implemented a system to improve overall efficiency," according to an EPA report. Jacobs describes his management system as rigid, extremely structured, and comprehensive—it's a single, unified system for quality, environmental, health, and safety standards.

cludes a database of reuse centers (http://redo.org/SearchRedo.aspx) and web resources (http://redo.org/Links/body_links.html).

 Remanufactured products have been disassembled, inspected, cleaned, repaired, given replacement parts, reassembled, and refinished to "like new" condition and returned to the market for sale.

Refurbished (also called reconditioned) products are "touched up" or cosmetically improved and then returned to the market for sale.

Reused (also called used or as-is) products are returned to the market for sale without repair or improvement to their appearance.

Check out Freecycle.org, which is made up of thousands of groups with millions of members who exchange stuff for free.

Recycling Practices

Recycling, which involves collecting used materials and converting them into new products, is a key part of the Sustainability Hierarchy because it is an essential and fundamentally sustainable practice. Recycling conserves resources, reduces the need for landfills and incinerators, saves energy, and prevents pollution.

Recycling basics. The recycling process consists of:

COLLECTING RECYCLABLE MATERIALS

MANUFACTURING NEW PRODUCTS FROM RECYCLED CONTENT MATERIALS

BUYING AND SELLING PRODUCTS MADE OF RECYCLED MATERIALS

The State of Connecticut has put together an excellent primer called "Setting Up a Recycling Program at Your Small Business." Find it at www.ct.gov/dep/cwp/view.asp?a=2714&q=324900&depNav_GID =1645.

Collecting Recyclable Materials

The first step to implementing or beefing up a recycling program for your business is to determine what type of recycling you need and what services are available in your area. Here are some important first steps:

- Check with the local government or public works department that is responsible for recycling. It goes without saying that, at a minimum, every business should recycle whatever the local municipality legally mandates. While many cities and counties provide residential recycling programs, they don't always extend those services to business. So while business recycling is common, it's not yet required everywhere.
- Check with your landlord. If you lease space, check with building management to see if they have a recycling program on-site. Some office buildings provide in-office pickup; others offer a central location where businesses can drop off their recyclables and the building management takes care of the rest.
- Explore private recycling providers. If you don't have access to a public recycling service, you should be able to find a private recycling company to pick up and recycle your collected items. Check with your local waste management service or public works department to find out what private services are available in your area. Be sure to ask about rates.
- Explore drop-off options. If pickup recycling is not an option in your area, many cities have recycling centers where you can drop off what you've collected to be recycled. Because this means you'll be hauling it yourself, you might want to enlist

some help. Many centers pay by the pound for your collected material, so you might entice employees to assist in the effort by using the money earned from recycling to purchase a gift card or other token of appreciation for the employees who help out the most.

🔗 To find recycling services in your area, go to http://earth911.org and use their recycling search tool to locate collectors and drop-off sites.

What Can Be Recycled?

Once you've determined what you *can* recycle, the next step is to determine what you *choose* to recycle. The most commonly recycled office items include newspapers, boxes, paper, plastic, and glass. Electronics such as computers and cell phones can be recycled, but you'll want to check with your recycler to see whether they can be dropped off at the same location or require a different procedure. (See "E-Waste" on page 110.)

Items Commonly Collected for Recycling

- **Paper:** Boxes, catalogs, envelopes, magazines, newspaper, high-grade office paper (white paper and stationery); mixed office paper (white, colored, folders, manila envelopes, paperbacks); paper bags.
- **Corrugated Cardboard.**
- **Plastic:** Soft drink and water bottles, milk jugs, food containers, grocery bags.
- **Glass:** Some localities require that glass be sorted by color (clear, brown, and green) although many accept mixed.
- **Metal:** Aluminum cans, aluminum foil, tin/steel cans.

- ■ **Office Equipment:** Computers, fax machines, CRT monitors, printers, small electronics, toner cartridges.
- ■ **TerraCycle:** Cookie wrappers, corks, drink pouches, energy bar wrappers, yogurt containers.

These simple-to-implement strategies are an excellent place to start a recycling program:

Ø **Recycle paper.** More than 75% of office waste in the United States is composed of paper, most of which can be reused or recycled. Separating paper for recycling can reduce waste disposal costs and prevent it from going to landfills or incinerators. Shredding companies often recycle as part of the service so if you use a third-party shredder, consider using one that picks up and recycles.

HOW TO DECIPHER
RECYCLING SYMBOLS

You're probably familiar with the recycling symbol, called the Mobius loop, that appears on recyclable plastics. When used on packaging, these symbols commonly have a number in the center—a plastic resin code that helps recyclers sort plastics by type. Different jurisdictions and recycling vendors accept different plastics, so check with your recycling vendor or local recycling program for guidelines. For details and images of all seven plastic recycling symbols, download a PDF at www.americanchemistry.com/s_plastics/bin.asp?CID=1102&DID=4645&DOC=FILE.pdf.

 ✓ **PET or PETE (polyethylene terephthalate)**—commonly used for water and soda bottles.

 ✓ **HDPE (high-density polyethylene)**—commonly used

for milk jugs, laundry/dish detergent, fabric softeners, bleach, shampoo, and conditioner.

 ✓ **PVC (polyvinyl chloride)**—typically used in construction products such as pipes, fittings, siding, carpet backing, and windows.

 ✓ **LDPE (low-density polyethylene)**—commonly used in dry cleaning, bread and frozen food bags, and squeezable bottles (i.e., honey, mustard).

 ✓ **PP (polypropylene)**—used for ketchup bottles, yogurt containers, margarine tubs, and medicine bottles.

 ✓ **PS (polystyrene)**—a rigid plastic used for CD jackets, grocery store meat trays, egg cartons, aspirin bottles, cups, plates, and cutlery.

 ✓ **Other**—this code denotes that the package is made with a resin other than the six listed above, or is made of more than one resin listed above and used in a multilayer combination.

Images courtesy of www.PackagingGraphics.net

E-Waste

 E-waste consists of discarded electronic equipment—such as computers, radios, fax machines, and cell phones, and the components that go into them—and includes a broad range of electronic devices.

Ø **E-cycle your e-waste.** In other words, reuse and recycle electronics instead of sending them to a landfill. More than 3 million tons of TVs, computers, printers, scanners, faxes, mice, keyboards, and cell phones are discarded in a year. Although the EPA is working on voluntary guidelines, there are no federal laws on the books regarding e-waste disposal. The only e-waste disposal laws come from the states themselves. As a result, if there is no law in your state, there may not be an easily accessible electronics recycling program. However, public pressure is mounting and many manufacturers and retailers now have take-back programs or sponsor recycling events. Also, if you are lucky enough to live in a state that has implemented e-waste disposal laws, you will probably be able to find an e-cycling program nearby. 🔗 For an interactive map of state e-waste legislation, go to www.electronicstakeback.com/legislation/state_legislation.htm.

Look for end-of-life programs that take back and/or properly dispose of products once they have reached the end of their useful life. You may even get rebates or credits based on the value of the materials. Or you may be offered services such as compliance documentation and secure data removal. 🔗 For a list of manufacturer and retail take-back programs, go to www.earth911.com/electronics/proper-disposal-and-recycling-of-e-waste.

As mentioned, many states have passed legislation to require end-of-life programs and there is growing pressure for more to do so in the future.

How to Find an E-Waste Recycler

There is no heaven for cell phones. Wherever they go, it seems that something, somewhere, to some extent always ends up being damaged or depleted.

—**Jon Mooallem,** "The Afterlife of Cellphones," *New York Times,* January 13, 2008

When it comes to e-cycling, not all recycling is created equal. The proper recycling and disposal of electronics is complicated by two facts: (1) E-waste generally contains substances that are toxic if not handled properly, and (2) certain components (such as copper and gold components) of e-waste are valuable. Many e-cyclers are not concerned about being green, but rather sell and send e-waste overseas to be dumped or disposed of improperly. So when looking for an e-waste recycler, reseller, or asset management firm, make sure they are environmentally responsible. Look for:

- E-cyclers that participate in the Basel Action Network's (BAN) Electronics Recycler's Pledge of True Stewardship.
- E-cyclers that adhere to the EPA's R2 Responsible Recycling standards, which are in development and environmentally responsible, although far less stringent than BAN's.
- Corporate take-back programs operated by reputable companies such as Dell, HP, Staples, OfficeMax, and Office Depot. Although not typically participants in either of the above programs, corporate take-back programs are believed to be reputable given the high cost associated with greenwash claims should they prove to be improperly managed.

Recycle

† **Encourage employee participation.** Once you know what you'll recycle, and how it will get to a recycling center, let your employees know the details.

† **Communicate.** Use signs throughout the office to increase awareness of your recycling policies. Include information about your procedures and recycling container locations in memos and newsletters. Don't forget to track progress and communicate results. (See page 83 for information on signs.)

† **Join TerraCycle**, a company that provides turnkey recycling programs for typically unrecyclable materials such as cookie wrappers, drink pouches, energy bar wrappers, yogurt cups, and wine corks. If you run a retail children's products, health and fitness, or liquor business, TerraCycle programs can help bring new customers to you when they come to use your drop-off facilities.

$ † Make Recycling Easy

■ Provide clearly marked containers throughout the workplace; if you don't already have recycling bins in your office, purchase them.

■ Locate bins in places where people need them, such as in copy, printing, and kitchen areas.

■ Place paper recycling bins in individual offices when possible.

† Explore opportunities to turn your recycling efforts into a profit center. If your business generates scraps, toner and ink cartridges, or e-waste (computers, laptops), there may be a market out there. The most valuable recyclable items include ink and toner cartridges, cell phones and laptops, and certain industrial by-products. For example, Ideal Jacobs Corporation, a New Jersey–based manufacturer of custom-designed, screen-printed labels, often prints on polycarbonate plastic sheets. Instead of disposing of the waste, Ideal Jacobs resells it so it can be reground into new materials. So not only are they recycling, but they're getting paid for it. (See "Ideal Jacobs: The Case for Waste Reduction," page 104.) Also, see the discussion of waste exchanges on page 102.

 The EPA provides information about common wastes and materials with good market opportunities at www.epa.gov/osw/conserve/materials/index.htm.

Items You May Be Able to Resell

• Camcorders
• Cartridges — ink and toner
• Cell phones

- Computers
- Digital cameras
- Gaming consoles
- GPS devices
- Laptops
- LCD monitors
- LCD TVs
- Networking gear
- MP3 players
- Pagers
- PDAs
- Portable hard drives
- Satellite radios

See the resource list at the end of the book for help locating responsible e-waste buyers.

$ † Recycle as many of your office supplies as possible. (See Chapter 10.)

$ † If your municipality doesn't provide recycling pickup for small businesses, appoint a recycling team to handle routine drops at a nearby facility.

8 ENERGY MANAGEMENT

Considering the many productive uses of petroleum, burning it for fuel is like burning a Picasso for heat.

—An anonymous Big Oil executive[1]

Whatever your industry, managing costs is good for your business, and increasing energy efficiency and reducing energy costs does just that. And although energy is the number one expense for almost one-third of small businesses, many don't have a well-defined energy management strategy. When you begin to address the issue of energy efficiency, a planned approach can produce twice the savings of an unplanned one, providing opportunities to cut energy consumption without adversely impacting operations. Furthermore, research suggests that companies with a clear energy management strategy have a competitive advantage. According to studies by Innovest Strategic Value Advisors, leaders in energy management achieved superior stock and financial performance over "laggards," with leaders achieving significant financial premiums over competitors.[2] Given rising energy prices and a growing awareness of the importance of energy conservation, a carefully conceived energy management strategy may well be one of the most important steps you can take to sustain and grow your business.

“” ECO CHAT

As the cost of energy rises . . . and carbon emissions are increasingly priced (in the U.S. it's just a matter of time), companies that sell products that consume less energy and emit less carbon either in their manufacture or use (ideally both) will profit. Soon it may not be necessary or relevant to appeal to consumers' environmental consciousness; whether you're selling a lightbulb or jet engine, the products that are the most efficiently manufactured, and most efficient to use, will win because, ultimately (and simply), they'll cost less.

—**Gardiner Morse,** senior editor, *Harvard Business Review*, in a blog comment on March 14, 2008.[3]

An energy management plan is a strategy that enables a business to identify, monitor, manage, and reduce the environmental impacts of energy use.

In this chapter, you'll find guidance and resources to help you develop an energy management plan as part of your overall green program. Even the most basic energy management plan can produce significant energy savings; however, your best approach to conserving energy involves developing a long-term plan. There are plenty of straightforward, low-cost practices outlined in this chapter that will allow you to create a simple energy plan, improve energy efficiency, and reduce energy costs right away. In fact, you may be amazed at how much energy you can save by taking a few simple steps.

This chapter also covers energy-efficient equipment. Given the cost involved in upgrading equipment, energy efficiency alone is not likely to justify such investments. But as part of your overall green program, you may want to make a commitment to such upgrades when you're leasing equipment, remodeling, retrofitting, or replacing current assets. In addition, the chapter includes information on green information technology (IT) practices, a moving target in today's environment, but a major source of energy consumption for any small business that has even a single computer. And finally, the chapter reviews renewable energy options to consider as part of your green strategy.

Defining the problem. Consider these facts:

- A typical office building's energy usage represents 30% of its operating costs.
- Global demand for all energy sources is forecast to grow by 57% over the next 25 years.
- U.S. demand for all types of energy is expected to increase by 31% within 25 years.
- Electricity demand in the United States will grow by at least 40% by 2032.
- New power generation equal to nearly 300 power plants will be needed to meet electricity demand by 2030.

The reality is that regardless of what business you are in and whether you currently pay directly for your energy use, rising energy demand, global climate change, and inadequate energy supplies are likely to impact the relationship between your energy use and profitability—now and in the future. Managing the energy you use (and waste) is an easy and highly effective way to control costs and minimize your risk in the future.[5]

ECO CHAT

Whether your business is manufacturing, real estate, retail, health care, education or government, controlling and cutting costs is important for success. Reducing energy use and increasing energy efficiency is a proven strategy for cutting and controlling costs with good returns.[4]

—"Good Energy Management Is Good Business," ENERGY STAR website

Energy-intensive sectors. The larger your facility, the greater your energy use. Obviously, a 100,000-square-foot facility uses more energy than a 100-square-foot home office. But technology-intensive activities require more energy per square foot; in other words, the more computers you use, the greater the energy use. So it is possible for a 1,000-square-foot IT facility to use as much energy as a 10,000-square-foot warehouse. That being said, all businesses use energy. Since reducing energy use and increasing energy efficiency is a proven strategy for cutting and controlling costs, energy efficiency is an issue every business should address.

To put it in perspective. If every small business in the United States replaced one 75-watt incandescent bulb with a 23-watt CFL, it would save up to $1.16 billion in electricity costs and would eliminate CO_2 emissions by more than 7.7 million tons.[6] If every small business in the United States installed ENERGY STAR–qualified exit signs, it would save up to $246 million in electricity costs and prevent up to 6.15 tons of greenhouse gas from being emitted annually.[7]

Best energy management practices. ENERGY STAR for Small Businesses breaks best energy practices down into two categories: Sure Energy Savers and Larger Opportunities. The Sure Energy Savers practices include actions that you can implement quickly with limited time and money:

- Lighting strategies
- Office and kitchen equipment maintenance
- Water conservation
- Heating and air-conditioning maintenance
- Food service equipment

Larger Opportunities, involving greater time or cost, include:

- Building shell improvements
- Lighting upgrades

- Commercial food service equipment
- Heating, cooling, and ventilating upgrades
- Office equipment and appliance purchases
- Refrigeration equipment

🔗 The ENERGY STAR for Small Business site is the portal to extensive resources at www.energystar.gov/index.cfm?c=small_business.sb_index.

🔗 Specifications for more than fifty categories of ENERGY STAR–rated products can be found at www.energystar.gov/index.cfm?fuseaction=find_a_product.

🔗 The Industrial Technologies Program (ITP) of the DOE's Office of Energy Efficiency and Renewable Energy has developed a set of best practices for corporate energy management that provides valuable guidelines for establishing an energy management program. While created specifically for the corporate industrial sector, the ITP's Best Practices provide insight into the key elements of a successful energy management plan. For a PDF of "Best Practices: Corporate Energy Management," go to www1.eere.energy.gov/industry/bestpractices/corporate_energy.html#Management_Strategies.

🗨️ ECO CHAT

When I look at the world of small business, I see opportunities to save energy in every nook and cranny . . . Here's the icing on the cake. Small business energy efficiency doesn't require years of expensive R&D. All the technology needed is available now. And a fast turnaround is possible because energy efficiency upgrades for small businesses involve doing the same simple thing over and over again in lots and lots of places . . . In the small business world, little things mean a lot.

—**Byron Kennard,** founder and executive director, Center for Small Business and the Environment (CSBE)[8]

Taking action: creating an energy management plan. When it comes to energy, make conservation your priority. While purchasing renewable energy credits or installing solar panels may sound sexy, the most important steps you can take to save money and conserve energy relate to reducing consumption and waste. Generally speaking, greening your energy consumption boils down to reducing wasted energy use and improving efficiencies. This process involves four key steps.

- Begin monitoring and collecting usage data. This can often be done at the equipment level via internal monitors or plug-in power meters that measure power use from the electrical outlet. You can also refer to a year's worth of energy or utility bills.
- Review the practices outlined in this chapter to determine which low-cost and no-cost energy-saving practices you can implement immediately to reduce costs and improve efficiency.
- Establish a set of policies to decrease energy consumption and eliminate energy waste. This step will lead you to a basic energy management plan with a clear set of measurable goals and objectives.
- Lastly, when possible and appropriate, upgrade equipment, systems, and fixtures to improve energy efficiency—typically when making new purchases, leasing, remodeling, retrofitting, or replacing assets.

Green Energy Practices

Many of the energy-saving practices outlined here can be implemented with little investment of time or money. Others involve up-front effort, but yield significant efficiencies with relatively short payback periods. Go to www.DSIRE.org for a comprehensive database of state, local, utility, and federal incentives and policies that promote and help finance renewable energy and energy efficiency.

The EPA offers strategies for energy management through a range of tools and resources. Based on the successful practices of ENERGY STAR partners, the Getting Started section of the ENERGY STAR website has lots of good advice on:

✓ Identifying projects
✓ Finding funds
✓ Selecting contractors
✓ Prioritizing projects
✓ Managing projects

Find it at www.energystar.gov/index.cfm?c=sb_guidebook .sb_guidebook.

General Energy-Saving Practices

Although there are many energy-saving solutions specific to the type and use of a facility and detailed in sections below, there are a few general energy-saving practices that any business can employ.

† **Get an energy audit.** Ask your utility company if they offer free or inexpensive energy audits.

Energy Crossroads has a comprehensive state-by-state listing of utility-sponsored energy efficiency programs available for small businesses at http://eetd.lbl.gov/EnergyCrossroads/2ueeprogram.html.

Small manufacturers interested in facility audits can check out three sites:

■ DOE Industrial Assessment Centers (IAC) provide eligible small- and medium-size manufacturers with no-cost energy assessments at www1.eere.energy.gov/industry/bestpractices/ iacs.html.
■ DOE's Save Energy Now initiative conducts free energy assessments to help manufacturing facilities identify immediate opportunities to save energy and money at www1.eere.energy .gov/industry/saveenergynow/assessments.html.

A NEW WAY TO FINANCE ENERGY EFFICIENCY IMPROVEMENTS

On-Bill Financing (OBF) is an emerging option for financing energy efficiency improvements. Through an OBF program, a utility company allows qualified commercial customers to pay for energy-efficient business improvements through an interest-free loan on their monthly bill. The energy savings are used to offset the loan, so the monthly expenses are lower than taking a conventional loan and may be completely offset by energy savings. When the loan is paid off, the utility bill stays lower permanently. Although at this writing, OBF is only available in parts of California, Connecticut, Rhode Island, and Massachusetts—and programs are under serious consideration in New York, Pennsylvania, Nevada, Wisconsin, and Oregon—small business organizations are lobbying aggressively to make it available throughout the country. So check with your utility company.

■ Department of Commerce's National Institute of Standards and Technology's (NIST) Manufacturing Extension Partnership (MEP) provides technical assistance to manufacturers at http://blue.nist.gov.

$ **Use rechargeable batteries** to reduce the environmental impact of battery disposal. One rechargeable battery can replace as many as 1,000 alkaline batteries.

Reduce Standby or Vampire Power

 Standby power, also called vampire power, refers to the electricity used by inactive electronics.

Standby power is yet another excellent example of how the law of large numbers affects the environment. Each individual piece of equipment may only draw a watt or two of electricity while idle, but every business in America contains five or ten such devices and the numbers really add up. Look around your office. How many devices have remote controls, permanently illuminated digital displays, or LEDs? All these components of common office electronics draw standby power; and all electronic products with external power supplies or adapters, such as laptop computers and cordless telephones, do as well. Standby power—which has little utility beyond the convenience of "instant on"—is responsible for a huge amount of environmental waste—approximately 1% of global carbon dioxide emissions.[9]

- Ø When shopping, search for low standby products. Many commercially available, off-the-shelf products use low power wattage while in their standby power consuming mode. All ENERGY STAR products have lower standby thresholds.
- Ø † Unplug infrequently used devices (toasters, coffeemakers, conference room televisions, etc.).
- $$ Install Smart Strip Power Strips, Wattstopper Plug Load Controls, and PlugMisers, which sense activity and turn on electricity accordingly.
- $$ For retail coolers, and vending and snack machines, you can achieve an average energy savings of 46% by installing EnergyMiser plugs that power the machines down when not in use, while still maintaining readiness to dispense products and keeping products cool.
- Ø Look for new technology-enabled electronics that automatically reduce standby power when making purchases in the future. New technologies are emerging that reduce standby power by as much as 90% while maintaining core consumer benefits.

Lighting

Although many of the lighting solutions suggested here involve little cost, consult with a lighting professional to determine what makes sense for your facility.

Ø **Turn off lights (and other equipment) when not in use.** Turn lights and signage off at night.

Ø † **Keep bulbs clean.** Dirty bulbs can reduce light by as much as 50%.

$ † **Replace worn-out incandescent bulbs with higher-efficiency bulbs.** Existing incandescent lightbulbs can be replaced with energy-efficient CFL or LED bulbs. Get the most bang for your buck by replacing 60–100 W bulbs that are on several hours per day. Also, consider upgrading to T8 (1" diameter) fluorescent lamp tubes that are more efficient than older T12 (1.5" diameter) tubes.

Maximize Lighting Efficiency

■ Ø Use daylight to reduce artificial lighting needs during cold months; use solar screens or shades during hot months.

■ $ Buy light-colored or translucent lampshades and consider $$ painting your walls light colors to improve brightness, all of which reduce the need for lighting.

■ $$$ Reduce consumption with lighting retrofits or technology upgrades. Retrofitting involves refurbishment of components of the lighting system with counterparts that make it use energy more efficiently. Technology upgrades involve replacing all or part of the lighting system with new, more efficient technology. Also, consider eliminating some of the lighting fixtures in your facility. You may still have acceptable light levels, especially if it's done in conjunction with a lighting retrofit.

Reduce the Amount of Light Used in Your Facility

■ $ Use timers to turn lights on and off automatically.

■ $$ Use bilevel switching to control groups of fixtures or lamps;

for example, bilevel switches could be set to allow users to turn half the lights in a room off at one time.

- ■ **$$** Install switch plate occupancy/motion sensors in proper locations to automatically turn off lighting when no one is present and back on when people return. Be careful not to install sensors behind doors or furniture such as coatracks or bookcases.
- ■ **$$** Install ENERGY STAR–qualified exit signs, which use far less electricity than conventional exit signs.

Weatherization

Decrease the heating or cooling needed in your facility by reducing unnecessary heat and air-conditioning loss. Often, the two most beneficial energy savings measures are air sealing and adding more insulation. These two measures combined often lead to a majority of the savings to be had.

$$ Use weather stripping and caulking to block leaks around doors and windows. If you have fireplaces, install chimney plugs.

$$–$$$ Upgrade or install insulation in ceilings, walls, attics, floors, and windows.

$$ Install heavy curtains at windows and doors to keep drafts out.

$$ Hot water tank blankets are inexpensive and effective ways to insulate your hot water heater.

$$$ When replacing **windows**, make sure they are double or triple glazed.

Heating and Air Conditioning

$ Install a programmable thermostat that can automatically turn your HVAC system on at specified times. Set the thermostat to turn on just before arrival instead of heating or cooling unoccupied spaces. Set goals to shift temperatures +/– 3 degrees. Use an ENERGY STAR–qualified thermostat for best results.

$ Change (or clean if reusable) HVAC filters monthly during peak cooling or heating season. New filters usually only cost a few dollars. Dirty filters cost more to use, overwork the equipment, and result in lower indoor air quality.

$$ Use fans to delay or reduce the need for air conditioning—a temperature setting of up to 5 degrees higher can feel as comfortable with fans. When the temperature outside is more comfortable than inside, use fans to push air out and pull outside air in.

$$ Take care of your heating, ventilating, and air-conditioning (HVAC) system with an annual maintenance contract. All HVAC systems will perform best when regularly maintained. You will save energy and money, and your system will likely last years longer.

Food Service and Cleaning Equipment

Ø **Use cold(er) water.** Use unheated—or the least heated—water whenever possible. Lower the hot water temperature controller on dishwashers and washing machines. Whether you are washing clothes, floors, or dishes, heating water uses lots of energy so heat water as little as possible.

Ø † **Clean refrigerator coils twice a year, and replace door gaskets** if a dollar bill easily slips out when closed between the door's seals.

$$ Have refrigeration systems serviced at least annually to maintain optimal performance. Again, you save energy and money, and reduce dangerous chemical leaks, and your system will likely last years longer.

$$$ Consider **retrofitting existing refrigerators and display cases** with antisweat door heater controls, variable speed evaporator fan motors and controls, and replacement refrigerant chemicals. Consult a professional for advice and estimates.

$$$ Install ENERGY STAR–qualified commercial food service equipment. Commercial equipment uses a lot of energy so going energy efficient can have a big impact. For example, qualified refrigerators and freezers can save over 45% of the energy used by conventional models, which equals as much as $140 annually for refrigerators and $100 for freezers. Buy GreenChill-certified refrigerators and display cases, in new construction and store remodels.

GreenChill is a free, voluntary, nonregulatory alliance between the federal government, the supermarket industry, and manufacturers to promote practices that reduce ozone-depleting refrigerant leaks. A list of participating supermarkets and information on industry best practices can be found at http://epa.gov/ozone/partnerships/greenchill/index.html.

Office and break room equipment. For more information about conservation practices in your office and break room, see Chapter 10.

Green Information Technology

The system of nature, of which man is a part, tends to be self-balancing, self-adjusting, self-cleansing. Not so with technology.

—E. F. Schumacher, *Small Is Beautiful,* 1973

For a small business, IT may not seem like a likely candidate for greening, but given the scale of computer use among small businesses, it is. Obviously, the environmental impact of your IT operations will vary greatly depending on how much computer hardware you need to run your business. But incrementally, you can reduce your energy consumption and your energy bills even if you only have a single computer on-site.

There is no area of business more subject to the law of large numbers than information technology. Consider these facts: Having a single computer on-site can increase the amount of electricity a business uses per square foot by an average of 60%, and the percentage generally goes up as you add more computers.[11] The Energy Information Administration

" " ECO CHAT

When it comes to energy use, the web is both a crusader and a culprit.

—Richard Martin, "Can the Internet Save the Planet?"[10]

forecasts that electricity consumption for computers and office equipment will grow more than twice as fast as electricity use as a whole, and notes that the energy consumed in commercial buildings by PCs and other types of office equipment consumes about as much as is needed to air-condition those same buildings.[12] It is also estimated that CO_2 emissions related to the operation of PCs, computer servers, and telecommunications networks contribute more than 2% of the world's annual greenhouse gas emissions. That's generally the same amount of greenhouse gasses being produced by all the world's airplanes.[13]

At the same time, technology is one of the greatest assets in the greening movement. Nothing is more effective for reducing use and waste of resources than technology. Internet technology is expected to contribute significantly to reductions in energy consumption in the future.[14] E-commerce replaces energy-intensive bricks-and-mortar stores. Electronic content management systems replace paper processes. Digital advertising replaces paper-based advertising. GPS systems reduce idling. The list goes on and on. *The ultimate goal is to design operations so that you employ the most energy-efficient technology available to implement the most resource-reducing practices possible.*

And finally, industry is being forced to change the way it thinks about the life cycle of the technology it produces. Everything about the electronics life cycle is in flux—from the way materials are sourced to the way goods are constructed to the way end-users manage power to managing global regulations that put limits on toxic chemicals and emissions to the development of adequate end-of-life recycling programs. Environmental groups are working to educate consumers about the environmental impacts of manufacturing processes and about the critical need to embrace responsible e-waste recycling. Because the awareness surrounding the environmental impact of technology is changing, there are few universally agreed-upon rules and best practices. As a result, advice to small business owners varies widely. It can be more confusing than ever to green your IT operations. 🔗 *Green IT for Dummies* (John Wiley & Sons) is an excellent introductory resource. If you just want a primer, HP sponsored a free, condensed, limited edition "Green IT for Dummies" guide for download at www.hp.com/hpinfo/globalcitizenship/environment/productdesign/greenit4dummies.html.

Power Management

 Power management is a feature of electrical appliances that turns off the power or switches the system to a low-power state after periods of inactivity.

In the world of IT, one of the most common recommendations, and most hotly debated topics, is power management for small businesses.

💬 ECO CHAT

In business-to-consumer e-commerce, for instance, a warehouse holds far more product per square foot than a retail store, and uses far less energy per square foot. We calculated the ratio of building energy per book sold in traditional bookstores versus on-line retailer Amazon.com to be 16-to-1. Internet shopping uses less energy to get a package to your house: Shipping 10 pounds of packages by overnight air—the most energy-intensive delivery mode—still uses 40% less fuel than driving roundtrip to the mall. Ground shipping by truck uses just one-tenth the energy of driving yourself.

—Joseph Romm, executive director, Center for Energy and Climate Solutions[15]

In its simplest terms, turning off electronics when they are inactive is beneficial because it simply lowers power consumption. Power management strategies can dim or switch off a screen, reduce processor speed, shut down the hard drive, or put an entire computer into "sleep" mode after periods of inactivity. Lowering energy consumption has the added benefit of lowering heat generation, a major by-product of technology. Less heat requires less cooling and increases system stability. All these factors also require less energy, which saves money and reduces the impact on the environment.

Power management tools come preloaded with virtually all computers these days. And despite the fact that enabling power management settings can yield annual energy savings of $25 to $30 per desktop computer, there is still some resistance among IT professionals. Some experts feel that power management tools adversely affect productivity (owing to power-up lag times and update interference) and can lead to file corruption. I believe in power management strategies, with the caveat that if you want to use power management, remember to institute policies and systems to close files and applications when computers are left inactive. This simple practice will enhance system performance, reduce power, assure data integrity, and maintain the system security.

Ø The most basic power management strategy is to **turn off computers, monitors, and peripherals every night**. Just shut them down! The majority of the energy consumption happens while the equipment is in the *on* mode, not in various low-power modes like *sleep* or *off*.[16]

Ø In addition, **basic power management strategies** can be enabled by activating preloaded settings that come standard in most desktop and laptop computers. Review the owner's manual or call tech support to enable the settings. Whether to turn on, plug in, turn off, or unplug can be confusing. And while there is some debate on the details, it is generally agreed that best practices include:

■ Set computers to enter sleep mode when they are inactive; try ten minutes and adjust if you need a longer active period.

■ Set display monitors to enter sleep mode when the computer is inactive; try five minutes and adjust if you need a longer active period.

■ Set computers to put hard drives to sleep when possible.

■ Turn computers off when not in use. When a computer is off, unplug it to eliminate standby power use (see page 122 for standby power reduction strategies). Despite rumors to the contrary, turning a computer back on uses far less energy than leaving it on for an extended period of time.[17]

■ Keep computers plugged in when in use. About 20% more electricity is required to operate a computer in battery mode and then recharge it, compared to simply leaving it plugged in. There is some debate about how running computers while plugged in affects the life of the battery. Every manufacturer issues its own recommendations; check with the manufacturer for advice for your specific equipment.[18]

■ Change your energy settings on your laptop so that they are the same whether or not your laptop is plugged in. Most laptops are set up to use less energy when they aren't plugged in, since battery life is at a premium. As soon as they start receiving electric power, however, they're often set to start running at higher speeds—and thus use more energy. If you have not reset your laptop's power settings before, chances are it uses more energy when it's plugged into the wall.

$ Install eco-buttons. Eco-buttons hook up to and sit on the table/desktop next to a computer. With a simple tap, the computer automatically enters a power management mode. Available at www.eco-button.com.

$$ If you run a network, consider using **software that allows the settings on computers to be controlled centrally**. This software is available from companies like LocalCooling.com, which is free, or Faronics.com and Scriplogic.com, which costs approximately $20 per computer. These companies have worked out the power management productivity and security kinks. Check with your utility company to see if they give rebates to companies that use these services.

 Cloud computing refers to a range of computing activities that are consumed outside of a company's own servers. It includes everything from using virtual servers available over the Internet to any third-party software that is housed on another company's hardware (i.e., YouTube). Cloud computing also encompasses Software-as-a-Service (SaaS); on demand (as opposed to licensed and housed in-house); and subscription-based or pay-per-use services where an application is hosted as a service provided to customers across the Internet.

Ø **Use cloud computing.** Cloud computing and especially SaaS are excellent ways to increase your IT capacity or add capabilities without investing in new computer hardware, training new personnel, or paying for new software. Cloud computing is inherently green because not only is buying less IT equipment more cost-effective and efficient than owning your own data center, but data centers that house the software and store the data running in the cloud are inevitably more energy efficient than your IT operations; they are operated out of consolidated, virtualized data centers and—more important—their bottom line depends on it.

Hardware

Ø **When purchasing new computers and peripherals**, buy only ENERGY STAR or EPEAT registered products—including peripherals, as they become available. You can also request that vendors provide the EPEAT rating along with price quotes.

EPEAT Purchaser Resources has easy-to-use tools and resources for how to incorporate EPEAT into the purchasing process at www.epeat.net/Procurement.aspx#.

The Electronic Product Environmental Assessment Tool (EPEAT) is a system to help buyers evaluate, compare, and select desktop computers, notebooks, and monitors based on their environmental attributes. EPEAT evaluates electronic products according to three tiers of environmental performance—Bronze, Silver, and Gold.

$$ Buy laptops. Laptop or notebook computers use as much as 80% less energy than desktops. Laptops are designed to be more energy efficient than comparable desktops because preventing overheating and maximizing battery life are key to operations. As a result, laptops use the most energy-efficient components available (displays [LCD], adapters, hard disks, and CPUs). In addition, they don't use power-hungry monitors. As a final added bonus, laptops require less packaging and energy to manufacture.[19]

$$ When purchasing monitors, choose flat-screen LCD monitors rather than cathode ray tube (CRT) models—the energy consumption of an average LCD display can be one-half to two-thirds of what an average CRT uses.[20]

Hosting

Ø Switch to a green web-hosting provider when your current contract is up. There are many hosting providers that are powered by alternative energy such as wind or solar either directly from solar panels and wind turbines or by buying renewable energy certificates (RECs). At Greenhance, we use AISO.net, a provider that boasts a 100% solar-powered data center. Go to www.hostreview.com for a decent list of green web host providers.

Other Green IT Strategies

If your business uses only a few servers and a part-time IT staffer, then the power management and SaaS strategies will probably be sufficient for making your computer technology more energy efficient. However, if you are updating or building a data center, or experiencing rising IT costs, other green IT strategies may make sense. In that case, consult with your IT staff and ask them to consider the following strategies:

- Virtualization for servers and storage
- Data center design—in particular improving hardware and HVAC efficiency, and consolidating servers
- Other green IT equipment that has come to market

Using Technology to Become More Efficient

There's a sweet spot where good ethics meet good business. And IT can—and should—be sitting at the nexus.

—Elana Varon, executive editor, CIO.com[21]

As mentioned earlier, nothing reduces the use and waste of resources more efficiently than the effective use of technology. Within each chapter in Part Two, specific technologies are recommended that will allow you to implement the most resource-reducing practices possible. As examples, reducing paper with an electronic content management system and buying high-efficiency printers and copiers are ways to use technology to reduce waste. In the area of transportation and shipping, GPS systems are a technology that promotes fuel efficiency, and spend management systems are a technology-based approach that promotes efficiency in the purchasing practices. When determining which technology solutions to implement, be sure to include IT or other staff members responsible for technology in the decision-making process.

Consider technology-enabled energy management solutions. New technologies, such as those employed by companies like EnerNOC and Prenova, are transforming the way businesses use energy. These companies use technology to manage demand response (reducing energy demand during peak-use times in exchange for payments) and monitor energy use, which allows businesses to use energy more efficiently, minimize energy expenses, and generate revenue by modifying *when* energy is used.

Renewable Energy

New Energy is the term that we apply to new sources of energy that are currently not recognized as feasible by the "scientific establishment," but for which overwhelming and compelling evidence exists.

—**Dr. Eugene Mallove,** science writer and author

 Renewable energy, also called clean energy, green energy, green power, clean power, and new energy, is power that is produced by renewable sources that are naturally regenerated.

If you're located in Texas or Iowa, your business may be surrounded by commercial wind farms that provide a natural, renewable source of energy. If you operate in an appropriately windy location, you may be in a position to install a wind turbine to generate energy for your business, or you may be able to purchase local renewable energy from your local power company at an affordable rate. If you are located in the sunny Southwest, solar energy may provide your business with similar options.

So, when it comes to renewable energy, there are two basic options to consider—and a complex array of choices. The first option: buying your electricity from renewable sources—through your local power company, or a variety of local and national suppliers. At present, you'll be paying more for electricity—how much will depend on any number of factors—but paying a premium may offer some value to your business in the form of supporting renewable energy or appealing to your customers. The second option: installing a renewable micropower source at your facility—such as a small solar, wind, or geothermal system. Micropower energy from renewable sources can be harnessed on-site to power your business or heat your water supply. For now, you may be limited by your geographic location, front-end costs, or the fact that you lease your facility. But in truth, the renewable options are growing every day. And as new technology and innovations emerge—for everything from renewable sources to managing the power grid, the energy options for small businesses will continue to increase.

 Micropower refers to small, modular solar, wind, and hydropower technologies that generate electric power on a relatively small scale and that are typically designed to produce power for use on-site.

Buying Clean Energy

Most energy from renewable sources—such as solar and wind—are fed directly into power grids the same way as energy from nonrenewable energy sources such as coal, nuclear, oil, and gas. In today's energy market, you generally have three options when it comes to buying electricity from renewable sources:

- Pay a premium to buy clean energy directly from your existing utility company (called green pricing).
- Choose an alternative electricity supplier from among competitive suppliers.
- Buy financial instruments—such as renewable energy certificates (RECs) and carbon offset programs—to compensate for your energy use.

$$ Opt in to clean energy sources from your existing utility company. More than 750 utilities in more than thirty states offer green pricing programs whereby you can pay a premium for electricity generated by clean energy sources directly from your existing electricity supplier. Check to see if your utility company provides green pricing.

$$ Purchase green power from an alternative electricity supplier. If retail electricity competition is allowed in your state, you may be able to choose from among several suppliers, some of which may offer green energy products. Many states have implemented electricity competition.

To find out what green power options are available in your state, go to the DOE's interactive green power map, where you can click on your state to view available green power products at http://apps3.eere .energy.gov/greenpower/buying/buying_power.shtml.[22]

Offsetting Emissions

Carbon offset programs typically refer to financial programs aimed at directly or indirectly counteracting or offsetting the impact of greenhouse gas emissions. This is typically done by funding projects that reduce the equivalent amount of emissions. Carbon offset programs typically fund activities such as tree planting or developing clean energy, and are an increasingly common method for calculating and compensating for a company's carbon footprint.

Renewable energy certificates (RECs) are tradable commodities that represent the environmental attributes of a specific amount of electricity generation. For every certificate purchased, 1 megawatt hour (MWh) of renewable energy is produced and delivered onto the power grid. These certificates are sold and traded, and the buyer of the REC can claim to have purchased renewable energy. A green energy provider (such as a wind farm) is credited with 1 REC for every 1 MWh of electricity it produces. A certifying agency gives each REC a unique identification number to make sure it doesn't get double-counted. The green energy is then fed into the electrical grid and the accompanying REC can then be sold on the open market. RECs are sometimes treated as carbon offsets, although they are not actually offsets. In theory, carbon offsets directly counteract greenhouse gas emissions by mitigating them, while an REC represents a quantity of energy produced from renewable sources. In that regard, an REC is more accurately defined as an *indirect* offset since it does not mitigate emissions; instead, it reduces the need for an equal amount of nonrenewable energy. Nonetheless, for the purposes of this book, RECs are treated as a mechanism for offsetting emissions since a business using either instrument is attempting to achieve the same benefit: offsetting emissions—as opposed to actually reducing them.

A word about offset programs: However noble the concept may be, they don't always help the environment as much as advocates suggest. It can be difficult to determine the true value of these programs. In theory, the more RECs and carbon offsets that are sold, the more environmentally friendly power projects and carbon-mitigating projects will be created. However, there are a number of problems with the premise. For one thing, the concept is a bit misleading. Take the example of using tree-planting activities as a carbon offset strategy. To absorb all the CO_2 generated by human activities in the year 2008, we would have to plant more than 3 million trees *and* it would take seventy years for those 3 million trees to absorb all that CO_2. We simply cannot plant trees fast enough to offset carbon output. In the case of RECs, it is commonly agreed that investments often do not lead to new renewable energy projects, but simply make existing programs more profitable.[23] Finally, and possibly of greatest concern, is the fact that buyers are purchasing offsets instead of actually taking essential steps to reduce the amount of greenhouse gases they emit.

That said, if you're genuinely committed to greening your business, offset programs can be a reasonable practice as long you're not using offsets to replace activities that would actually reduce your emissions. In other words, use offsets only after you've taken all possible measures to reduce your emissions and only for cases in which they are the best or only option available. If you do buy RECs or carbon offsets, be sure to use a reputable provider, one that verifiably sends its money where it says it does.

$$$ Buy renewable energy certificates to offset your energy use.

While it may not be feasible for every business to install a wind or solar energy system, any company can buy RECs. RECs are a viable mechanism to use renewable energy without switching from your existing energy supplier. Also, keep in mind that finding local, cost-efficient renewable energy sources may not be possible. Often, the least expensive RECs will come from somewhere far away.

Generating Your Own Clean Energy with Micropower

If you're interested in generating your own energy from a renewable source—such as a wind turbine or solar installation—research your options carefully. Local regulations governing such installations vary significantly, and as importantly, renewable options vary significantly in terms of efficiency, appropriate applications, and payback period. Your location will determine what codes and regulations you will need to follow in order to add a micropower system to your home or small business. Check with your state energy office or a local renewable energy supplier to determine the requirements that apply in your locale.

For information on micropower local codes and requirements, go to http://apps1.eere.energy.gov/consumer/your_home/electricity/index.cfm/mytopic=10690.

The National Renewable Energy Lab's Learning About Renewable Energy site covers all aspects of renewable energy including extensive information on biofuels, geothermal heat pumps, passive solar heating, solar electric systems, solar hot water systems, and wind energy at www.nrel.gov/learning/small_business.html.

Solar Power

I'd put my money on the sun and solar energy. What a source of power! I hope we don't have to wait until oil and coal run out before we tackle that.

—**Thomas Edison,** 1931

NYLO: BUYING RECS IN RHODE ISLAND

When the NYLO Providence/Warwick Hotel in Rhode Island was under development, the owners knew they wanted to have a renewable energy component. "Green is associated with the brand," explains the property's general manager, Christine Nevers. The challenge was figuring out how exactly to go about it. "We looked at all the different facets," says Nevers. "Whether we could have hydro connected to us, whether we could actually generate energy with a wind turbine. [We asked] what are the available sources right here in our community?" Ultimately, buying renewable energy certificates (RECs) was the only viable option—but Nevers had to decide whom to work with, where to buy them, and whether to commit to 50% renewable energy or 100%.

After extensive research, she decided to work with People's Power & Light (PP&L) in Rhode Island. "We specifically chose a nonprofit. And above and beyond that, it was a nonprofit that was local," says Nevers. The key: NYLO wanted to communicate its commitment to *local* renewable energy sources. "And,"

When you think about solar power, the vision of large reflective panels may come to mind. However, as of today, solar energy technology commonly comes in two forms: solar thermal collectors, and solar electric or photovoltaic (PV) technology. Solar thermal collectors gather the sun's heat and redistribute it; they are used almost exclusively, and quite effectively, for heating water stored in tanks. Solar electric or PV technology, which is costlier than solar thermal technology, directly converts the sun's energy into electricity. PV solar technology makes use of the panels that we generally associate with solar power. A variety of factors determine whether a solar energy system makes sense for your business, including your geographic location, architecture, energy use patterns, and payback period.

she adds, "I felt very strongly that, if we're going to do it, I wanted to be able to do it 100%." Nevers used PP&L as a re-source, to understand the options and make informed deci-sions. She advises: "If you find that right source, you'll really learn a lot about what's available in your area and what is going to work best for your individual business."

In the end, the NYLO Providence/Warwick ended up paying a 5-7% premium for clean energy generated by local sources including wind, solar, and low-impact hydro—versus buying conventional energy off the grid or buying renewables from a national source, which can be significantly less expensive. The result: As the first hotel in the state to open completely powered by renewable energy from local resources, the NYLO Providence/Warwick was able to make a high-impact statement about environmental leadership. Says Nevers, "We saw an opportunity to help the environment and help the business."

$$$ If your business uses a lot of hot water, **consider installing solar thermal water heaters**. There are many systems to consider and the appropriateness of each will have to do with factors such as how much hot water you use, whether the temperature drops below freezing in your area, and the desired payback period. Keep in mind, the less hot water you use due to practices that reduce your demand for hot water—both the total amount of water and the amount of *heated* water—the smaller and less expensive the solar thermal system needs to be.

$$$ If you want to power your facility with solar power, **consider installing a solar electric system**. In the end, it may be difficult to make a purely financial argument in favor of solar electric power since the payback periods are still quite long. However, demand for affordable solar electric products is bringing prices down. Check with a qualified solar energy provider, who will be aware of available tax incentives or rebates and able to provide estimates and advice.

Southface, a nonprofit organization that promotes sustainability through education, research, advocacy, and technical assistance, provides information about the mechanics and financing of solar thermal and electric systems at www.southface.org/solar/solar-roadmap/commercial%20solar/commercial_intro.htm.

Wind

It is now possible for any size business in a suitable location to use small wind turbines to convert wind energy into electricity. Wind turns the turbine blades, which spin a shaft, which connects to a generator and makes electricity.[24] Owing to the increased availability and affordability of small wind turbines—thanks in large part to the 30% federal Investment Tax Credit—the market is projected to grow 300% within as little as five years,[25] and this will make small wind turbines even more affordable in the near future. Keep in mind, wind power isn't an option in geographies where there's not enough wind, or in locations where noise pollution would be a problem. The American Wind Energy Association provides information about installing a wind power system, promoting wind power in your community, and the Small Wind Investment Tax Credit at www.awea.org/smallwind.

$$$ Consider installing a small wind turbine to generate electricity. Smaller turbines are now on the market, including rooftop models, which can make wind power a viable option for smaller facilities.

Geothermal

$$$ For new construction, **consider installing a geothermal heat pump**. Geothermal heat pumps draw heat from the ground to heat and cool buildings. They are only suitable for new construction. All areas of the United States are suitable for geothermal heat pumps.[26]

9 WATER CONSERVATION

When you drink the water, remember the spring.
—*An old Chinese proverb*

Water misuse tends to be invisible, because most people give little thought to where water comes from—and where it goes after they use it. Most businesses waste water without even realizing it. And while many industries have been working toward reducing the impact of industrial chemicals that are spread through the water system, it has taken a longer time for the importance of water conservation to reach the industrial mainstream.

Defining the problem. It may seem as if our fresh water supply is endless, but population growth and a host of other natural and human factors are putting stress on our fresh water supplies. Today, the average American uses 100 gallons of water every day—the equivalent of more than 1,500 cans of Red Bull. In California, the average is more than twice that number. Increased consumption, along with contamination from pollutants, floods, drought, waterborne diseases, and shifting rain patterns, have put significant stress on fresh water supplies across the country and the globe.

Scientists agree that water shortage, following only global warming, is the second most worrisome problem for the new millennium. A recent government survey showed at least thirty-six states will face catastrophic water shortages within five years owing to the combined impact of drought, rising temperatures, urban sprawl, and population growth. As a result, water has become a national priority. However, if we all start using water more efficiently, we can help preserve water supplies and save money at the same time.

> ## ❝❞ ECO CHAT
>
> I think we're really in the infancy of the water conservation movement. All around the country, water is the sleeper problem. For example, in Atlanta, you hear that they were praying for rain. It's something that's going to be of major consequence if we don't address it right now.
>
> —**John Roeber,** Roeber's Inc., one of the nation's first green-certified plumbing companies

Water-intensive businesses. Even if you're not in a water-intensive business, you may use a significant amount of water for activities unrelated to your primary business. In fact, it's estimated that nonprimary water use represents 35% to 50% of a business' water use. Whatever your industry, if you're responsible for all or part of the water bills for a toilet, sink, shower, washer, dryer, or irrigation system, you can achieve real savings through some simple, inexpensive conservation efforts. You stand to save considerably from water conservation practices if your business operates in one of these water-intensive sectors:

- Cleaning or janitorial/sanitation (jan/san) services
- Educational institutions
- Food service
- Gym/fitness facilities
- Health care facilities

- Hotels and motels
- Laundromats
- Multifamily housing properties
- Nursery and landscape

To put it in perspective. If every small business in the United States took steps to save a single gallon of water a day, we would save 26.4 million gallons every day. That's enough water to supply the entire state of Arizona for almost four days.[1] This does not even take into consideration the fact that a five-minute shower uses more water than the average person living in a poor area of a developing country uses in a whole day.[2]

 Potable water is water suitable for drinking. Greywater (also spelled graywater) is nondrinkable wastewater that can be reused for irrigation, flushing toilets, and other uses.

Best practices. There is a popular saying among water conservationists: The key to water efficiency is reducing waste, not restricting use. And that's where you'll want to focus your efforts. Given advancements in water-efficient products, consider installing new, high-efficiency fixtures and devices, if at all possible. Minimum water efficiency standards were established in the Energy Policy Act of 1992 (EPAct 1992); WaterSense and ENERGY STAR also have published water efficiency standards.

For a comprehensive list of national efficiency standards and specifications for residential and commercial water-using fixtures and appliances, go to http://epa.gov/watersense/docs/matrix508.pdf.

There are three basic approaches to water conservation:

1. Reduce water waste by installing low-water-use, high-efficiency appliances and fixtures. Optimally, they should exceed EPA minimum standards by at least 20%. EPA and WaterSense

efficiency standards and specifications for water-using fixtures and appliances can be found at http://epa.gov/watersense/docs/matrix508.pdf.

2. Limit the use of potable water for landscape irrigation.
3. Reduce the amount of water used in cleaning.

Taking action. In truth, because there is so much needless waste, water conservation is one of the simplest green practices to implement. Whether or not your business uses a lot of water, there are a surprising number of ways to improve your water efficiency that take very little time and effort, cost very little, and yield great benefits by helping you lower your short-term operating costs, and extend the life of your fixtures and appliances. This chapter is full of simple steps—such as installing aerators on your faucets and fixing leaky fixtures—that every business can take, as well as straightforward options for water-intensive businesses.

Find out more about tax credits and rebates. You may be eligible for a variety of tax credits for improving water efficiency. Check out www.epa.gov/watersense/pp/find_rebate.htm for convenient links.

Green Water Practices
Discover and Repair Leaks

$ † Fix leaky toilets, faucets, and showerheads. Leaks can lead to a significant—and completely unnecessary—waste of water. Depending on the severity of the problem, a leaky faucet will waste anywhere from 3 to 100 gallons of water a day. And leaky toilets are the most common source of wasted water. Replacing inexpensive parts available at any home supply store (such as gaskets and flapper valves) can easily repair toilet and faucet leaks.

To find a host of simple, no-to-low-cost remedies for fixing leaky toilets, consult www.toiletology101.com.

gpf = gallons per flush

gpm = gallons per minute

psi = pounds per square inch

Toilets

$ † Insert water displacement devices in toilets. If your bathrooms are *not* equipped with 1.6-gallon low-flow toilets (standard since 1992), reduce the amount of water used per flush by inserting a tank dam or homemade device (such as a soda bottle filled with pebbles and water) in your toilet tank. For homemade displacement devices, make sure to place it in the tank where it will not interfere with the flushing mechanisms. Tank dams, available at most home supply stores, can reduce water use by up to 40% on a 3.5-gallon flush toilet.

$$ †† Replace older, water-wasting toilets and urinals with newer models. Any toilet that uses 1.6 gpf or less is considered high efficiency. Reasonably priced models are widely available. The EPA lists more than 200 toilets that meet WaterSense standards. Newer 1.28 and 0.9 gpf toilets are coming soon. Waterless urinals can save an estimated 40,000 gallons of water per urinal per year.

WaterSense is a U.S. Environmental Protection Agency program that certifies water-efficient products such as bathroom sink faucets, showerheads, high-efficiency toilets, urinals, and landscape irrigation services and control technologies.

Bathroom and Kitchen Sinks

$ † Install aerators on faucets. Easily installed in about a minute and available at any home supply store, screw-on, low-flow aerators can save from a half gallon to four gallons of water per faucet per day.

$ † Install sensor-operated and self-closing faucets to help to reduce water use in areas where people may run water unnecessarily for too long or inadvertently leave faucets on. These reduce water usage by up to 20% without any compromise to functionality.

Showerheads

$ † Use shower timers. Inexpensive devices such as the Shorter Shower and Shower Coach affix to the shower wall with a suction cup. The user simply rotates the small hourglass-style device to start the timer, which empties in five minutes and sends a signal to stop showering.

$ † Install low-flow showerheads. These reduce water usage by up to 50% without diminishing the quality of the shower experience. Look for showerheads that use less than 2.5 gpm of water.

$$ Install showerhead adaptors. These are for showers located a great distance from the hot water heater—a significant water waster. They are easily installed, affordable, and available online. For facilities with multiple showers, you may want to look into a recirculating pump that can heat the water in your pipes before it's turned on.

Water Efficiency Technology

$$ Install water-efficient appliances when making new purchases, leasing, or remodeling. This will substantially reduce your hot water use.

$$$ Greywater systems enable you to reuse the water from your lavatory sink or shower by filtering it to your toilet tank. Stand-alone systems, available that fit under your sink or lavatory, can save 30% to 40% in water use. Systems are also available for rainier climates to collect rainwater and circulate it to the toilet tank *Note: These must be installed by a licensed plumber to eliminate the possibility of cross-contamination, and greywater reuse is not permitted in every locale so check with local officials to learn your local codes.*

Cleaning Methods

Ø **Do not overdilute cleaning chemicals.** How much water you use to dilute cleaning supplies determines how effectively the job is done. Using too much water not only is wasteful, but can also lead to inadequate cleaning. *But be sure to follow the manufacturer's directions—too high a proportion of chemicals can do damage.*

Ø **Revisit your maintenance schedules.** You may be paying to clean all or parts of your facility too often. Review your maintenance schedules. Clean high-traffic areas—restrooms, carpets, and floors—more frequently than low-traffic ones.

$ † **Use entrance mats** to capture and concentrate dirt before it reaches your floors, and reduce the need for floor cleaning. Floor cleaning is one of the biggest users of water in non-water-intensive businesses. The Worldwide Cleaning Industry Association estimates it costs $600 to find and remove one pound of soil after it has entered a building.[3] Look for slip-resistant mats and clean them regularly to limit the spread of dirt.

$ †† **Change to water-free or water-efficient cleaning methods.** Ask your cleaners about new technologies the can reduce water use or look into it yourself. Practice dry cleanup—by using brooms, brushes, and vacuums to remove dirt before using wet cleaning methods, you can save a significant amount of water. Replace mops and hoses with brooms, microfiber flat mops, squeegees, steam/vapor cleaners, or vacuum cleaners; you can save up to 80 gallons of water per activity and thousands of gallons of water every year. If you must use wet cleaning practices, consider ways to reduce the water you use with water-saving hose nozzles. For example, as part of a larger water conservation program implemented to avoid water access fees, Sparta Foods in St. Paul, Minnesota, switched from garden hoses to high-pressure washers that use half the water for cleaning flour-processing equipment. By making the switch in this one area, the company reduced its water use by nearly 217,000 gallons a year—saving almost $1,050 annually. At a cost of $200

> ## ❝❞ ECO CHAT
>
> Green buildings and green cleaning continue to accelerate in the market-place . . . Interestingly, when the green movement began, the issue simply revolved around recycling and the use of recycled products. The movement evolved to pollution prevention and the use of less toxic products such as cleaning chemicals, paints, adhesives and other building materials. The new issue focuses on energy efficiency and alternative energy sources due to concerns relating to global climate change and the use of foreign oil. And the next step along this journey is predicted to be water efficiency and conservation. Savvy and sustainable building service contractors will find it in their best interest to be ahead of the curve.
>
> —**Stephen Ashkin,** president, The Ashkin Group[4]

for each high-pressure washer, the payback period was less than three months.[5]

Irrigation and Landscape

Ø **Water lawns and flower beds at night.** Water outdoor landscaping between 9 p.m. and 9 a.m., when water pressure is highest, and wind and evaporation rates are lowest. It may be most convenient to water in the early morning, before the start of business.

Ø If you don't take your vehicles to a commercial car wash, **park cars and trucks in the grass when you wash them**. The lawn will soak up the soapy, dirty water, in effect watering your lawn *and* diverting pollutants from storm drains and roadside ditches that lead directly to lakes and streams. Although the soil will filter out pollutants, it's best to use as little soap as possible (which will save you money) and find nonphosphorus cleaners.

$ † **Use mulch.** Applying mulch to the surface of the soil will reduce evaporation, keep soil temperatures from becoming too hot or too cold, and inhibit weeds that compete with plants for water. When possible, use fine-textured mulches, which are less likely to be scattered by the wind, do a better job of preserving moisture, and settle better than coarse-textured mulches. Mulching can reduce outdoor water use by as much as 50%.

$ † **Harvest rainwater.** There are several ways to capture rainwater and reuse it for irrigation. A network of gutters and downspouts that direct rainwater to planting areas, sloped terrain, channels, ditches, and swales can be used to distribute water to a planting area.

Another option: Collecting rainwater in barrels. According to the EPA, a rain barrel can save as much as 1,300 gallons of water during the peak summer months.

$ † **Install a drip irrigation system.** Drip irrigation is the slow application of water directly to a plant's roots, where the water is most needed. The beauty of these systems is that installation is relatively simple and inexpensive. A variety of kits are available online.

$ † When selecting new plants and grass to plant, choose drought-resistant varieties.

Find out more about smart planting strategies. The University of Georgia College of Agricultural & Environmental Sciences Cooperative Extension Service offers six simple steps for "water-wise" planting at www.p2ad.org/files_pdf/ProperPlanting3.pdf.

$ † To avoid overwatering outdoors, inexpensive **lawn and garden rain gauges** are available to determine the volume of watering or rainfall. Moisture in the soil at the root level is where it is most important and can be measured with easy-to-read moisture meters, which can also be used for watering indoor plants. Using simple soil moisture sensors/probes and rain sensors can reduce outdoor water use by up to 10%.

$ † An open garden hose or worn hose sprayer can flow more than 12 gallons of water per minute. A **water-saving hose nozzle** allows you to control the amount of water used by selecting the level of spray strength, typically from full force to a water-saving mist. Hint: Hose leaks can

IRRIGATION CONSULTANTS AND CONTROL INC.: SMART IRRIGATION

Remember the popular saying among water conservationists: The key to water efficiency is reducing waste, not restricting use. Nowhere is that more relevant than in the field of irrigation, where states and municipalities are beginning to impose rigid restrictions on when exactly people can operate their irrigation systems. For example, a municipal law might mandate watering on Tuesday only—legislation that runs counter to irrigation best practices. "The reality is that properly designed and properly managed irrigation systems need to have an open water window to accomplish their task, because with today's technology—including something known as a smart irrigation—controllers adjust themselves daily," says Tim Malooly, president of Irrigation Consultants and Control Inc. (ICC). "This irrigation system will operate based on changing weather and only deliver water when water's necessary. But in order to do that, it needs to have an open watering window during the

waste gallons of water per minute, so make sure your hoses are leak free.

$ † A hose timer can help avoid overwatering. The timer automatically shuts off the hose when it has completed the watering cycle.

$$ † Install a smart irrigation system. Smart irrigation systems—which automatically control water efficiency—are a good solution for any business with irrigation needs. Look for EPA WaterSense-rated systems and a certified landscape auditor, irrigation designer, or irrigation contractor for installation.

$$ †† Reduce water pressure. Reducing water pressure is an excellent long-term water conservation method. Check with your building

week." Malooly should know, as one of four EPA WaterSense
Partners of the Year in 2008, recognized for his irrigation practice. Malooly has a maxim of his own: Irrigation systems don't
waste water; people waste water.

According to Malooly, a well-designed irrigation system—
compared to one that's not well designed—can save at least
50% in water use. These smart irrigation systems are available
for as little as $600. The problem: Many contractors and land-
scapers don't know how to install and operate them properly.
"The irrigation consulting industry is literally in its infancy," says
Malooly. For golf courses, streetscapes, nurseries, or any business with landscaping needs, smart systems make economic as
well as environmental sense. "The savings generated over time
from using an efficient irrigation system far outweighs the cost
of the service in the first place. The payback is usually in three
years or less, depending on the size of the site," he says.

engineers to see if your facility can accommodate pressure-reducing
valves or, if they already have them, whether they can be used more
effectively.

**$$$ †† Implement an outdoor landscape water conservation
strategy.** Xeriscaping (pronounced "zera-scaping") is a comprehensive,
seven-step process that can reduce outdoor water use by as much as
50%. A popular method in drought-ridden states, Xeriscaping effec-
tively combines planting and design, soil analysis and improvements,
plant selection, turfgrass management, irrigation, mulches, and mainte-
nance to create a low-water-requiring landscape. Xeriscaping is not only
a sound gardening practice that promotes water efficiency, it's also an
environmentally sound, low-maintenance landscape strategy since it re-

quires less fertilizer and fewer chemicals to maintain your property—all of which saves time, effort, and money.

    🔗 Find out more about Xeriscaping. A University of Georgia Cooperative Extension guide describes seven steps for making your landscape more water efficient at http://pubs.caes.uga.edu/caespubs/pubcd/B1073.htm.

Appliances and Equipment

$$$ Replace appliances and equipment with high-efficiency models. Although the up-front replacement costs may be higher, virtually all high-efficiency appliances and equipment will pay for themselves in energy and water cost savings. Look for ENERGY STAR–rated and WaterSense-rated commercial appliances. New product categories are being added daily, and in many product categories, ENERGY STAR ratings are provided for both energy and water efficiency.

10 GREEN OFFICE SUPPLIES

Sometimes the situation is only a problem because it is looked at in a certain way. Looked at in another way, the right course of action may be so obvious that the problem no longer exists.

— *Edward de Bono, motivational author and physician*

No matter what kind of business you operate, greening your office supply practices is one of the most straightforward areas of your business to address. For one thing, it's easy to see the inherent waste associated with office supplies—paper waste being one of the biggest culprits. For another, it's easier than ever to shop for green office products. Although they're not yet available in every product category, environmentally friendly office supplies have become mainstream, and energy-saving office equipment is now widely available. Just as importantly, there are an array of green office practices you can put in place that involve no cost and very little effort—many of them related to reducing paper waste.

Defining the problem. Let's start with paper. In the United States alone, we use enough office paper each year to build a 10-foot-high wall that's 6,815 miles long, or two and a half times the distance from New

York to Los Angeles. Try to imagine the volume of resources used to produce that much paper—and where it all goes when it's discarded. Paper production requires enormous resources. It takes about 24 trees, 22,313 gallons of water, and 33.1 million BTUs of energy to make a ton of paper; that's enough energy to power a U.S. home for two months.[1,2] In addition, the process of extracting and bleaching wood fiber generates pollution. Add to that the fact that our landfills are full of paper and you've got a big problem. *So, from an environmental perspective, the paper challenge is twofold: to reduce waste, and to promote recycling and recyclables, which, ultimately, involves purchasing recycled products.* Implementing policies that reduce paper waste and shifting demand toward recycled content paper will save trees, conserve water, reduce energy needs, encourage recycling, and prevent harmful materials from ending up in landfills and incinerators.

Office supply-intensive businesses. Although all businesses use office supplies, white-collar businesses use disproportionately more. And for many of them, paper storage is a major issue. As an example, according to WebCPA.com, a typical CPA firm could have more than 20% of its physical space devoted to storing paper files. The paper reduction strategies outlined in this chapter can not only lower your paper costs, but also significantly reduce your storage needs, lower your administrative costs, and improve your overall efficiency. If you operate in any of the following sectors—or in an industry that's subject to federal regulations regarding secure document storage—you stand to save considerably from the conservation practices outlined in this chapter:

- Professional services such as law and accounting
- Insurance
- Advertising and marketing
- Financial
- Real estate
- Collection agencies
- Education
- Health care

Best practices. A viable green office supply strategy involves both waste reduction and green purchasing strategies. Use the reduction strategies in this chapter to address waste issues first, then implement a green purchasing strategy. For best practices in the purchasing arena, the EPA has established standards for office products through its Environmentally Preferable Purchasing program (EPP), which requires federal government procurement officials to buy green. You'll find the EPP standards for paper products, nonpaper office supplies, and office furniture at www.epa.gov/epp/pubs/buying_green_online.pdf. You'll want to meet or exceed those standards when you set up your own purchasing policies, a subject that's addressed in more detail in Chapter 15.

To put it in perspective. The truth is, when it comes to office supplies, your actions can have an enormous impact on the environment. For example, if every small business in the United States took steps to save a single piece of nonrecycled copy paper each workday, it would save more than 842,000 trees a year.[3] To get a sense of how much waste you may be generating—and how much money you could be saving by implementing a few simple practices—consider these facts:

- The typical office worker uses about 10,000 sheets (20 reams) of paper per year.
- The average document gets copied 19 times.
- You can reduce paper waste by almost 50% by using duplex

(two-sided) copying, and 89% by sending and receiving faxes via computer.

Taking action. Setting a green office supply strategy in motion involves addressing two basic issues: waste reduction and green purchasing. In terms of priorities, it makes sense to focus first on reducing the volume of office supplies you consume and then on switching to green alternatives. The money saved by reducing waste can often offset the added costs of buying green products. The office supply practices that follow break down into the following five sections: Paper Reduction Strategies, Purchasing Strategies, Nonpaper Consumables, Office Equipment, and Office Furniture.

■ Green Office Supply Practices
Paper Reduction Strategies

When it comes to office supplies, reducing paper waste is one of the most important actions small businesses can do to have a big impact on the environment at a relatively low cost. And by reducing the amount of paper you use, you'll save money not only on paper, but also on energy, ink, toner, maintenance, and time. Once you've decided which of these practices make sense for your business:

- Write them down as formal policies.
- Post the policies above printers and copiers.
- Get your staff and/or IT person involved in the process.
- Host training sessions to familiarize employees with these paper-saving techniques.

Ø **Don't print unless it's essential.** Encourage people to think before they print. For example, if you need to print only a paragraph or two of a document, highlight it and use the Print Selection function.

Ø **Use scrap paper for notes instead of printing.** Encourage staff to write down small bits of information, such as phone numbers and URLs, on scrap paper instead of printing.

Ø **Replace Post-it Notes with scrap paper.** If you use Post-its, use the recycled ones.

Ø **Add a message to your email signature.** For example: *By not printing this email, you've helped save paper, ink, and trees,* or some version of that.

Ø † **Whenever possible, use electronic forms** for purchasing, employment applications, record keeping, etc. You can use freestanding form-building software or build forms as part of a larger document management system.

Ø † **Have your payroll service issue paystubs via email.** Almost every payroll service or system now offers a variety of paperless payroll options.

Ø **Order supplies by phone or email.**

Ø **Send holiday cards and invitations electronically.** Services such as Sendomatic.com and ConstantContact.com have easy-to-use systems.

Ø **Use online banking** to pay invoices, transfer money between accounts, and monitor your expenses. Save PDFs digitally for record keeping.

$ **Allow your customers to opt out of receipts.** Consider implementing online accounts for customers, or do as Apple has done and send e-receipts to customers via email. For a fee, TransactionTree.com allows retailers using standard point-of-sale (POS) retail systems to issue paperless receipts.

Change the Way You Print and Copy

Ø **Print paperless.** Print and store documents in portable document format (PDF) whenever possible. PDF files have numerous benefits: They're easy to send via email, easy to store, and easy to use. (See "Send and Store Documents Digitally," page 161.)

Ø **Dedicate a copier or printer for draft documents.** Then fill the tray with paper already printed on one side. If you only have one copier or printer, designate one print tray for draft documents and fill it with paper already printed on one side.

Ø **Switch to duplex printing and copying.** If possible, set printers and copiers so they default to double-sided printing. This is an easy way to reduce your paper use by as much as 50%.

Ø **Use multi-up printing when possible.** Some printers have printer drivers that can print multiple pages on a sheet. Multi-up printing reduces paper and toner use, and speeds up the printing process. Some software, such as Microsoft Office PowerPoint, has this functionality built in as a standard feature.

Ø **Use Draft Mode or Fast Print as the default setting.** For most documents, printing in less than the highest quality (which uses the most ink) is perfectly sufficient. Set your printer's default to Draft Mode or Fast Print. Then revert to high-quality printing when necessary. Again, check your printer manual for instructions.

Ø **Use Print Preview and Shrink to Fit functions.** In word processing, use the Print Preview feature before printing to eliminate stray or extra text that adds unnecessary pages. Either delete the unnecessary text or use the Shrink to Fit function to proportionally decrease the font size to condense the text.

$ **Use high-efficiency toner and ink.** Look into new products such as Xerox's Ultra Low-Melt EA toner that saves energy by lowering fusing temperature, a process that accounts for as much as 80% of the total power used in printers and multifunction devices.[4]

$ † **Install software that eliminates unnecessary printout pages.** When printing a web page, banners, legal disclaimers, and page addresses can add unnecessary pages. Inexpensive software, like GreenPrint, FinePrint, and HP Smart Web Printing, all for Windows, can be used to eliminate waste. Each program works a bit differently and provides slightly different additional benefits, but their purpose is the same: to minimize paper waste. Paper savings can be significant. GreenPrint estimates typical savings of 1,400 pages a year. FinePrint cites an average savings of 30–60%.

Send and Store Documents Digitally

There are plenty of good reasons to digitize your documents. Conventional filing systems take up valuable—and expensive—physical space. Digital files are also easier to work with. You can share them over a network, send them by email, and save them to removable USB flash drives in a fraction of the time it takes to physically access and distribute hard copies. Electronic distribution saves time and postage. Hard copies of drawings, invoices, handwritten notes, and other papers can tear, fade, and get damaged. Digitizing the information also allows you to maintain the quality of the original.

When you convert to a digital storage system by scanning all your files, you'll uncover stuff you haven't seen in years. It's kind of like cleaning out the front hall closet. As an example, Delaware-based EBC Carpet Services went through a similar process—without scanning anything. They simply started storing current files digitally, and cleaned out a storage unit, moving only the essential paper files to their offices, and shredding and recycling the rest. (Of course, they checked with their accountant first.) In the process, they eliminated the need for a remote storage unit, saving more than $2,000 a year in rental costs.

Digital storage has numerous advantages. The documents are more accessible, saving you retrieval and filing time. And time is money. Consider these statistics:

- Professionals reportedly spend 5–15% of their time reading information, but up to 50% looking for it.
- American businesses spend $15 billion a year transferring data from paper-based forms, such as loan applications and purchase orders, into computer systems.

Digitize Your Paperwork

Ø **Store files electronically instead of on paper.** In the same way that you can save documents as PDF files instead of printing them, you can store PDFs on hard drives and CDs instead of filing them. Newer computers come with the ability to convert files to PDF. If your computer does not have the ability to convert files to PDF, you can download software (some of which is free) or use a web-based SaaS provider like FastPDF.com and pay per document. Storing files electronically is the most simplistic form of document management.

$ † **Use a scanner to convert documents to a digital format** so that they can be stored, retrieved, and transmitted in the future. Then do away with the hard copies. Many copiers have the capacity to save to a PDF. There are also several inexpensive ENERGY STAR–qualified scanners and multifunction machines with scanning capabilities on the market. Or cost-effective scanning services can do the job for you, either on-site and off-site.

$ **Use online services to replace paper processes.** An excellent array of online services are available to help you replace paper processes throughout your organization. Online faxing is a good example. A cost-effective service that allows for paperless document transmission, retrieval, and even signing, paperless faxing can also eliminate the need for a dedicated phone line to accommodate a fax machine, further reducing costs. Other online services that can help you go paperless include document management systems (see below), electronic signature systems, and customer relationship management systems (CRM). Some of these services are listed in the Resources section at the end of the book. (See "Green Key: Going Paperless," page 164.)

 A document management system (DMS) (also called enterprise content management [ECM]) is technology that imports, stores, and manages electronic documents and/or images of paper documents.

$$$ ┼┼ Use a document management system (DMS) to manage your company's documents electronically. A good DMS will facilitate document storage, and improve efficiency and reduce redundancy, and can cut overall document-related costs by an estimated 40%. Costs of new systems vary, and with the document management and storage market evolving rapidly, new offerings and features are coming out all the time.

If you don't want to invest too much up front, look for a SaaS DMS system, such as Ricoh DocumentMall. There are also industry-specific data management systems, such as those for accountants and lawyers.

Purchasing Strategies

It's easier to buy green office products than ever before. The three largest office supply retailers, Staples, OfficeMax, and Office Depot, each carry thousands of products with recycled content and other environmental attributes; and there are a number of green office suppliers online. For example, TheGreenOffice.com offers 40,000 products, both conventional and eco-friendly, and allows you to compare prices and "greenness" through a unique rating system. Dubbed GreenScreen, this rating system not only enables one-stop shopping, but also, according to Alex Szabo, "makes it easy and cost-effective for consumers to essentially vote with their dollar for sustainability in product design."

The key to saving money and resources on office supplies is establishing clear purchasing guidelines that integrate green specifications into your procurement policy, a process that's discussed in great detail in Chapter 15, which also includes a list of product attributes to look for when making green purchases (see page 232).

Greenseal, a nonprofit that certifies everything from hand cleaners to food service packaging, has issued the excellent "Choose Green Report on Office Products," which provides an overview of greening opportunities. The report includes information on purchase criteria, product recommendations, sourcing, and case studies. Down-

GREEN KEY: GOING PAPERLESS

CASE STUDY

Real estate is traditionally a paper-intensive business, with all the signed contracts and legal documents and multiple copies. For Green Key Real Estate, a San Francisco–based firm with four offices and a growing franchise, paper reduction is just one element of a green strategy that touches virtually every aspect of the firm's operations. According to founder Chris Bartle, the firm "is about selling green homes, and promoting green building and green remodeling. We want to be a catalyst for the creation of green inventory."

They buy 100% PCW recycled paper, but Bartle's aim is to go paperless, relying on PDFs, CDs, electronic faxing, electronic document storage, and an online signature service. The firm uses an online electronic signature service that lets their clients sign documents online. "I upload a PDF to their system," explains Bartle. "Then I go in with their tools and indicate where on each page I need my client to sign. Once that's done, [the

load the PDF at www.greenseal.org/resources/reports/CGR_officesup plies.pdf.

Recycled Paper Products

A word about recycled content products: Although the cost of some recycled content products remains higher than comparable products, there is a case to be made for making the switch from virgin to recycled content paper. *An eco-friendly paper policy is considered a core tactic for conducting business in an environmentally sustainable way.* It is easily communicated and can give you an edge over the competition if they do not have similar policies. Finally, instituting an eco-friendly paper policy helps build market demand for recycled paper and in doing so keeps prices down.

Ø **Address size and weight issues when you buy paper.** Think about your paper practices. You may be wasting paper simply by using a

service] sends it to the client. They go in and go click, click, click everywhere they need to initial or sign. And they're done. It's much faster than flipping through all the paper." Another benefit: The agent can walk the client through the document over the phone, which saves on driving to in-person meetings. At the end of the transaction, instead of using paper files, everything's stored electronically. For a monthly fee, the service will package all the documents into a CD for storage purposes. It saves on energy costs and storage costs.

"Not everybody is up to date on technology," says Bartle. "So sometimes we need to fax something—like when you have a wet signature. But I haven't physically faxed in I don't know how long." For faxing, the firm uses an online electronic fax service. First, Green Key uses its scanner to convert the hard copy to a PDF, then uses email or the electronic fax service to send it on.

heavier stock than necessary for routine tasks—or larger sheets than you need. The heavier the paper, the bigger the sheet, the more paper you're wasting.

$ Buy recycled paper. This simple measure reduces the environmental impact of paper production and keeps paper out of landfills. Choose recycled content paper with the highest post-consumer waste (PCW) content you can afford. Also, ask about the bleaching process and avoid paper processed with chlorine. Depending on the volume and timing, you may be able to lock in deals with a paper company that makes the premium for PCW content paper negligible.

Nonpaper Consumables

Nonpaper consumables—toner, ink, kitchen supplies, and cleaners— probably represent a good chunk of your office supply expenses. Again, the good news is that there are several ways to both cut your consumables costs and adopt environmentally friendly policies.

PAPER BLEACHING

When chlorine is used to bleach paper, the process can also result in the formation of harmful chemicals, which are known to cause cancer in humans. The Natural Resources Defense Council's order of preference for bleaching processes, on the basis of environmental criteria, is as follows[5]:

✓ **Best: Processed chlorine-free (PCF).** Recycled content paper produced without the use of elemental chlorine or chlorine derivatives.

✓ **Better: Totally chlorine-free (TCF).** Virgin paper produced without chlorine or chlorine derivatives.

✓ **Good: Elemental chlorine-free (ECF).** Replaces elemental chlorine with chlorine dioxide in the bleaching process. Next-generation processes include Enhanced ECF with ozone or hydrogen peroxide and ECF with extended or oxygen delignification, both of which are considered improvements upon ECF.

Toner and Ink

$ † Buy and sell ink and toner cartridges. While we addressed the many benefits of recycling cartridges in Chapter 7, the act of selling ink and toner cartridges is one of the easiest ways to make money and be green at the same time. You can save significantly on the purchasing end by buying refurbished toner and ink cartridges. To ensure quality, look for cartridges that meet original equipment manufacturer's (OEM) standards and provide money-back guarantees. You can save a good bit of money since remanufactured cartridges typically cost 30–50% less than new ones.

And on the revenue side, cartridges are valuable (some are worth as much as $22). Either way, by buying and selling cartridges you won't be contributing to the more than 350 million (and growing) cartridges that are discarded in U.S. landfills every year.[6]

The International Imaging Technology Council (IITC) has a directory of reputable cartridge remanufacturers at their Find a Dealer tool on www.consumerchoice.info.

Once you've identified the dealers near you, check out each company's website to find its product offerings, or call or email a sales representative. You'll want to ask two things: what type of service guarantee they offer and whether the company is Standardized Test Methods Committee (STMC)–certified—which means that its products have been quality tested by an independent third party. The International Imaging Technology Council also warns buyers to beware of scams and fraud, especially from "toner-phoners" who call with incredible deals.

$ † Refill cartridges. Ink cartridge refilling systems are popping up across the country and can save you as much as 50% off the price of a new cartridge. You can find refillers at retailers like Cartridge World, OfficeMax, and Walgreen stores. *Note: Don't refill cartridges by hand—it's messy and produces low-quality print results.*

Kitchen/Break Room/Bathrooms

$ † Eliminate disposable products in the kitchen. Provide reusable mugs, cups, plates, and cutlery in your break room and kitchen. If it's not possible for you to eliminate these products altogether, try hiding the disposables in cabinets. You'll be astonished how much less people will use when something's out of sight. Also, remember to provide dish soap and sponges for cleanup to avoid paper towel waste. IKEA and dollar stores are good places to find durable, inexpensive dishware and other kitchen items. Consider using personalized mugs that can double as gifts.

$ † Use environmentally preferable products. It's easy to find recycled content goods such as paper towels, napkins, toilet and facial tissue, trashcan liners, and other environmentally preferable products such as high-efficiency lightbulbs. You'll find more information on purchasing these and other items in the purchasing section that appears in Chapter 15.

$ † Use environmentally preferable cleaning products. It is easy to find environmentally preferable hand and dish soap, as well as other cleaning supplies. Gone are the days when using green cleaners meant inferior quality. In a recent survey, nearly 90% of janitorial and sanitation distributors believe green cleaning products to be comparable to conventional cleaning products. Commercial strength jan/san products are easily found on the web.

Office Equipment

The best office equipment is not only energy efficient, but also designed to use green accessories and other complementary products. In addition to computers (a subject that's covered under "Green Information Technology" in Chapter 8), ENERGY STAR qualifies a wide range of products, including:

- Copier and fax machines
- Printer, scanners, and all-in-ones
- Digital duplicators
- External power adapters
- Mailing machines
- Monitors
- Water coolers
- Point-of-sale retail terminals

If you're buying or leasing new office equipment, environmentally preferable equipment will save you money in the long run by saving electricity, using fewer supplies, and producing less heat when powering down, thus lowering air-conditioning costs.

Copiers, Printers, Faxes, and Scanners

The copier is the refrigerator of the office. It is an energy-sucking appliance that is left on 24/7. Greening your copier (and the refrigerator in your break room!) is one of the most powerful actions you can take. If you already have a copier, you can also adopt some or all of the tactics listed above under "Paper Reduction Strategies."

According to the EPA's *Green Purchasing Guide for Copiers*, the following are basic considerations for purchasing environmentally preferable copiers. When possible, choose copiers that:

- Are ENERGY STAR rated.
- Go to "sleep" or power down when not in use.
- Have the capacity to default to double-sided printing.
- Use returnable, recyclable, or remanufactured toner cartridges.
- Use an organic photoreceptor (if not organic, avoid hazardous metals such as arsenic, cadmium, or selenium).
- Do not use wet process technology.
- Minimize emissions of dust, ozone, and VOCs such as styrene.
- Contain no polybrominated biphenyls (PBBs) or diphenyl ethers (PBDEs).
- Are designed for remanufacturing and reuse of parts.
- Contain materials made with recycled content.
- Use minimal packaging and/or arrange for packaging taken back for reuse.
- Can be taken back by the vendor at the end of its useful life for remanufacturing, refurbishing, or recycling of parts.

$ Know your copy volume. Before upgrading your copier, calculate your monthly copy needs. Your copier probably has a counter so you can easily determine how many reams of paper you use in a given month. Choose a machine that matches your copy volume because using a machine with excess capacity can as much as double your energy use.

$ † Install a multifunction device (also called an all-in-one machine), a piece of office equipment that performs two or more primary functions of copying, printing, scanning, or faxing. This is a no-brainer if your office is small with lower equipment usage. By combining copy, print, fax, and scanning functions into a single unit, you save on front-end costs; given their compact size and the multiple capabilities, a multifunction device can reduce energy consumption by about 40%. Even if all other things were equal, one idling machine uses less energy than four.

Update your cash registers. Instead of running continually at full power, some new point-of-sale retail terminals are ENERGY STAR rated, power down when not in use, and have new thermal printers that draw power only when actually printing.

Office Furniture

American companies throw away about one million desks, eight million chairs, two million tables, and five million file cabinets each year. Given those numbers, greening your office furniture decisions is no small matter.

$$ † Refurbish your existing furniture. If you simply want to update your office, consider refurbishing the furniture that you currently own. Many areas of the United States have local or regional furniture refurbishers who will pick up your existing furniture, adhere to applicable environmental waste disposal regulations, and return it appearing virtually new.[7]

$$ † Buy remanufactured, refurbished, or reused furniture. Today, furniture refurbishers are able to restore high-quality office furniture to like-new condition using an array of environmentally friendly finishes and fabrics. Recycled office furniture can look as good as new and is typically 30–50% less expensive than new furniture. *Note: Furniture remanufacturing and refurbishing is a growing and unregulated industry, so make sure to conduct a thorough business check before signing contracts.* See page 105 for definitions for the different types of office furniture: re-manufactured, refurbished, and reused.

$$$ † Buy environmentally preferable furniture. It is now easy to find environmentally preferable office furniture. In fact, office furniture manufacturers such as Knoll, Herman Miller, and Steelcase are at the leading edge of sustainability. For example, several Herman Miller products, including chairs, desks, and storage units, are cradle-to-cradle certified. The following are basic considerations for purchasing environmentally preferable office furniture. When possible, choose furniture that is made with:

- End-of-life recycling programs.
- Environmentally preferable fabrics.
- Nontoxic glues, paints, foams, and other materials.
- Recycled, biobased, and nonhazardous materials.
- Sustainably harvested woods and other sustainable materials.

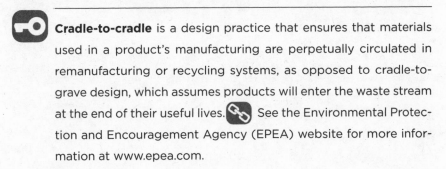

Cradle-to-cradle is a design practice that ensures that materials used in a product's manufacturing are perpetually circulated in remanufacturing or recycling systems, as opposed to cradle-to-grave design, which assumes products will enter the waste stream at the end of their useful lives. See the Environmental Protection and Encouragement Agency (EPEA) website for more information at www.epea.com.

Greenbiz.com features an excellent report from the Business Products Industry Association (BPIA) called "Recycled Office Furniture," which details the benefits of using recycled furniture, discusses the myths and misconceptions, and provides an office furniture buyer's checklist. Go to the BPIA report at www.greenerbuildings.com/files/document/O16F3340.pdf.

11 GREEN HUMAN RESOURCES

Human capital is a vital, yet often overlooked, means of establishing competitive advantage.
—The Conference Board, August 13, 2008

When it comes to sustainability practices, greening your human resources (HR) is about as innovative as you can get. When it comes to green employee benefits, even corporate America is still pretty much in the dark ages. From an HR perspective, there are three issues for small businesses to consider:

- The potential impact of your overall green strategies on morale, and on your ability to attract and retain good people.
- The possibility of adding green employee benefits — such as telecommuting, giving paid time off to volunteer for environmental causes, matching donations to environmental causes, and providing incentives for carpooling or other fuel-saving strategies.
- Strategies for greening your HR administrative practices, for example, by reducing paper and storage needs.

Some say the verdict is still out on the value of green HR benefits—that, while nice, they don't actually affect employment decisions or employee satisfaction. But there's ample evidence to support the notion that greening your business is a powerful way to attract employees and build loyalty. According to the 2008 Society for Human Resource Management Green Workplace report, companies that implement environmental responsibility programs report improved employee morale, a stronger public image, increased consumer confidence, a positive financial bottom line, and increased employee loyalty.

The good news is that green programs—such as recycling and using energy-efficient lights—are perceived as important to many employees, and that by simply implementing green practices, you are de facto providing green "benefits" to your employees. Green initiatives are particularly important to women and younger workers. In an April 2008 Adecco USA Workplace Insight survey, 69% of workers born after 1978 ("Gen Y") indicated that they want their company to be more environmentally friendly—and 63% of the working women in the study agreed, compared to only 54% of men and 52% of those born between 1946 and 1964 ("Baby Boomers").[1] In another study conducted by Experience Inc. later that year, 79% of Gen Y workers said that they would be more likely to accept a job offer at a green company than another company when evaluating two similar job offers.[2]

Although the value of green benefits may be hard to quantify, green employee initiatives can be an effective way to promote greenness, market your uniqueness, show empathy with employee values, and gain a competitive advantage in attracting talent. It's also important to remember that your employees are largely responsible for implementing your green practices. Green benefits may be a powerful tool for enlisting their support for your overall green program.

Defining the problem. Any successful green program involves reducing paper waste and decreasing energy emissions—two issues that can be addressed through green HR programs. According to the Federal Highway Administration, driving—even driving new-model

"" ECO CHAT

CSR - HR = PR

If employees are not engaged, corporate social responsibility (CSR) becomes an exercise in public relations. The credibility of an organization will become damaged when it becomes evident that a company is not "walking the talk."

—**Adine Mees,** president and CEO, and Jamie Bunham, senior researcher with Canadian Business for Social Responsibility[3]

cars—accounts for one-quarter of all air-polluting emissions, nationwide.[4] So, if your employees drive to work, any benefit aimed at reducing those emissions—from telecommuting programs to vanpooling—is a net gain for the environment. In addition, HR administration may well be your most paper-intensive function; the impact of paper waste on the environment is a problem discussed in more detail in Chapter 10.

HR-intensive businesses. The more employees you have, the more HR-intensive your business, the more you stand to gain from implementing some of the practices outlined in this chapter. Keep in mind: You depend on all your employees to implement your green strategy. And employees that routinely interface with customers have a special role in communicating your commitment to going green—a role that generally requires education and training. For more on engaging employees in your green program and building employee commitment, see Chapter 6.

Put it in perspective. If every small business in the United States allowed one employee to telecommute (and thus not drive to work) for one day, it would prevent more than 320,000 tons of car-emissions carbon dioxide from entering the atmosphere and save 9,720,000 hours of wasted travel time—73% of workers rarely or never get work done during their commute.[5]

Best practices. Green HR is such a new field that there's no ready resource for best practices. Use the practices outlined in this chapter as your guide.

Green HR Practices

[Green HR] programs need not be complex or expensive to implement. What is important is that they reinforce the message that the company is supportive in doing its part for the environment and encouraging its employees to do likewise.

—**The Total Rewards Role in "Going Green,"** *Workspan* magazine, March 2008

If yours is like most businesses, significant portions of your monthly expenses are devoted to paying and training your employees and maintaining their benefits. Whether you need to increase output and productivity without increasing head count in an increasingly competitive economy or you simply want to keep the folks you have, you should be getting the most out of your investment in your employees. To this end, everything you do to find good employees and keep them can be seen as a way to maximize your success in this area. It makes business sense to offer the best alternatives in compensation, safety, wellness, and benefits, some of which it might make sense to green. It also means that when providing direction for the people who work for you, it makes sense to be mindful of what motivates them and what are the most effective ways to educate, train, and communicate with them.

Ø † **Communicate to employees.** Getting your employees involved is crucial to the success of your green initiatives. After all, it's the employees who will be implementing these programs. Let them know what's going on. For example, one study found that when companies shared utility bills with staff, the employees began to adopt a more proactive attitude toward energy conservation.[6]

† **Provide all employees with access to the green team.** Depending on the structure and size of your business, you may want to invite all

employees to join the green team. If that's not feasible, provide a formal mechanism for suggestions, such as an email or blog system. Strategies for engaging employees in specific green initiatives such as recycling, paper reduction, and energy-saving programs are covered in their respective chapters in Part Two.

$$ † Don't discount the importance of atmosphere. Some green initiatives have an immeasurable positive impact on productivity, employee retention, and loyalty. For example, the offices of Green Key Real Estate have an open floor plan and all the furniture is made from recycled wheat straw. "As a recruiting and retention tool, when new agents walk into our offices, they see this really natural, comfortable environment and it's very different from a typical real estate office. There's no out-gassing of paints and carpeting like you smell in lots of offices," says CEO and President Chris Bartle. "Recently, we added a whole bunch of plants, just natural, living plants for the office, and that has really improved the mood of the place. Not only has it beautified it, but it's brought a livelier energy to the place—which is a very subjective observation."

◼ Benefits

Commuting Benefits

If your employees drive to work, consider the option of offering commuting benefits, which can have a big impact on reducing auto emissions. According to the Environmental Defense Fund, auto emissions are responsible for more than one-fifth of total U.S carbon dioxide emissions—and if all U.S. commuters worked from home just one day a week, it could save 5.85 billion gallons of oil and reduce carbon dioxide by 65 million metric tons a year. Commuter benefits also appeal to employees. A GfK Automotive National Survey on Attitudes and Behaviors found that 57% of commuters expressed interest in working for an employer that offers commuter benefits. That's not surprising given that such benefits save both you and your employees money. For example, when technology giant Sun Microsystems measured the impact of employees working from home or at a variety of company-sponsored, flexible-office locations, the findings were impressive. By working at home an average of 2.5 days per week, employees saved more than $1,700 per year in gasoline, and wear and tear on their vehicles as well as about two hours a week in commute time.

Find out more about commuter benefits at Best Workplaces for Commuters, which provides the resources you need to start offering commuter benefits. Employers that meet the National Standard of Excellence in commuter benefits—a standard created by the U.S. Environmental Protection Agency—can join the list of Best Workplaces for Commuters. For detailed information about implementation and available resources for dozens of commuter benefit programs, go to www .bestworkplaces.org/employ/benefits.htm.

The Carbon Tracker for the iPhone is a free application that allows users to easily calculate their carbon footprint from commuting, vacation, and business trips. A GPS feature automatically determines the length of each leg of the trip. Users can set monthly "maximum emission" goals as well as monitor their progress at www.clearstandards .com/carbontracker.html.

† **Promote public transportation.** Make it easy for employees to use public transportation. Make public transit resources available. Websites like GoogleTransit and HopStop can help staff find the quickest public route to and from work. **$$ † Consider subsidizing employees'**

public transit costs with rebates, bonuses, or prepurchase of transit vouchers (check with your local mass transit authority for options).

✝ **Promote walking and biking.** New Belgium Brewing in Fort Collins, Colorado, gives every employee a free bicycle after one year of employment and runs a program encouraging staff to bike to the office at least once a month. These practices have the added benefit of keeping your employees healthy and saving them money.

✝ **Support carpool/rideshare programs.** Encourage employees to drive with neighboring employees, post rideshare opportunities, and distribute information about how commuters can find rideshare partners through sites such as eRideShare.com or Carticipate, a social network rideshare application on the iPhone and Facebook. Keep up with the news, though, since new mobile, wireless rideshare tools are coming online every day. Many make use of GPS locators to match drivers with riders in real time, including Avego, a rideshare application on the iPhone. One application, Ecorio, tracks your travel miles and then lets you buy carbon offsets for your travels on the spot.

$$ If possible, **offer a shuttle or vanpool service**. A vanpool is a commuter vehicle that typically seats at least six riders plus a driver.

✝✝ **Offer telecommuting.** Telecommuting is often cited as one of the most valuable green benefits—to both employers and employees. Telecommuting has been credited with improving work-family balance, supervisor-staff relationships, job satisfaction, worker retention, productivity, and career prospects, as well as reducing stress, absenteeism, recruiting, office space, and parking costs. It may also be one of the most effective greening practices you can embrace: The American Consumer Institute projects that telecommuting alone will cut CO_2 emissions by more than a half-million tons over the next decade.[8]

Offering telecommuting will be particularly valuable if you hire young people. As far back as 2005, researchers found that 51% of Gen-Xers surveyed said they'd quit their current job if another employer offered them the chance to telecommute.[9] AT&T found that two-thirds of employees offered jobs by competitors decided not to leave the company and that telework was a major factor in their decision.[10] If you have employees who need to be on-site, consider allowing benefits that are akin to telework such as flex-time schedules where employee work four 10-hour days instead of five 8-hour days.

$ **Provide preferred parking** for hybrid and high-efficiency vehicles. Provide secure bike racks.

† Provide information about **car insurance companies that give discounts to noncar commuters**. For example, under its My Rate program, Progressive Insurance discounts car insurance rates for drivers who carpool, commute by mass transit, or use other "eco-friendly" options. The Allstate Green program provides electronic statements, up to a 5% premium discount, and a $10 contribution to a national, environmentally conscious organization. Other insurers are sure to follow.

▉ HR Administration

Greening your HR administrative practices involves using electronic processing to reduce paperwork—and paper waste. By replacing paper processing with online technologies, you can reduce costs in the long run and improve efficiency. In addition, there are a variety of reasonably priced software options or outsourcing firms that can help you manage all your HR functions electronically including payroll, benefits enrollments, performance reviews, compensation management, HR manuals, and employee handbooks.

Replace Paper Processes with Online Technologies

$ **Use an electronic signature service** that digitally stores and records documents including contracts, policies, procedures, and forms with legally binding e-signatures. Services like Docusign.com and EchoSign .com include several standard forms (W-9, W-4, I-9, etc.) that can be filled out online.

$ Offer direct deposit and eliminate printed paystubs and payroll reports. All payroll providers offer these services.

$ Convert company-specific paper-based documents to online templates. If you don't outsource your HR functions or choose not to go with a comprehensive web-based HR solution, you can still use online templates. Forms such as vacation requests and personal information changes can be completed by employees and then automatically integrated into your personnel files. Your company handbook, W-4 forms, I-9, and other internal documents can be uploaded for easy access. Use virtual files to communicate updated corporate policies, vacation schedules, new hires, birthdays, and more.

$$$ Web-based employee self-service programs allow employees to request forms, submit changes, and receive approvals online, and to electronically view and update information such as personal data and benefits changes. They also provide online access to W-2 forms, paystubs, company handbooks, benefit enrollment choices, professional licenses and certifications, and H1B visa expiration dates.

$$$ Outsource your HR functions. Given the rising cost of providing employee benefits and the complexity of the associated paperwork, more and more businesses are outsourcing HR functions. In the long run, it can save time, money, and paper. When exploring outsourced options, be sure to ask vendors to outline a program that will cut paper use as well as increase efficiency. Payroll processing and training are the two most commonly outsourced functions, and areas where a significant amount of the paperwork can be managed online, but many other paper-intensive processes can be automated and streamlined.

▮ Training and Recruiting

Ø When hiring, prescreen candidates online or on the phone. By prescreening, you save the paper, time, and cost of printing application forms.

ENGAGE PR: AN AWARD-WINNING COMMUTER PROGRAM

 CASE STUDY

Engage PR is a technology public relations firm located in Alameda, California, fifteen miles from San Francisco. About a third of the firm's eighteen-person staff lives in the city, and commutes to Alameda on a daily basis. "People don't actually want to come out to Alameda," says Bitz. "It's not the most sexy place. That means to retain employees, we have to find creative ways to compensate them." When gas prices began to spike in the summer of 2006, partners Jeanette Bitz and Molly Miller got serious about commuting strategies.

"It took us a while to get the program off the ground—to work out the numbers and to really get a grasp of what the options were for employees," says Bitz. "First, we asked: How do I compensate an employee that may live far from here? Then we asked: Why not encourage those employees and their neighbors to commute together?" They implemented a series of initiatives to address the problem: First, they offered a "Commuter Relief" program, which provides a $40 stipend to employees who average more than forty-five miles a day on the road. Then they added a stipend for anyone who carpools—for example, $20 for carpooling eight to eleven days a month as an incentive. Employees that carpool more than forty-five miles a day receive both stipends.

Ø **Accept résumés online.** For every résumé you accept online, that's one less piece of letterhead and envelope wasted.

Web 2.0 is an umbrella term describing the second generation of Internet interface with user-defined activities and collaboration such as the use of blogs, social networking sites, wikis, and other forms of user-generated online interaction.

In addition, as part of its "Something Healthy Plan," Engage provides $50 a month for public transportation through the Bay Area Rapid Transit (BART). And the firm provides a one-time bonus to employees who trade up to a more fuel-efficient car—$100 for a car that gets 25% or better gas mileage than the original car; $200 if the new car gets 50% better gas mileage.

Today, Bitz estimates that half their workforce routinely carpools; three people routinely take advantage of the mass transit stipend; and a handful of people have purchased more fuel-efficient cars. That's no small accomplishment in California's commuter-oriented culture. "I tell people, you can really think of it two ways: It's good for the environment and it's keeping people," says Bitz. Attrition rates for the firm are at about 15%, compared to 40–50% for the industry, and it received the "Best Workplaces for Commuters" designation in 2006 from the EPA and the U.S. Department of Transportation. For four of the past five years, Engage PR has been named one of the "Best Places to Work in the Bay Area"—and Bitz credits the commuter program, at least in part, for the firm's high profile.

†† **Use blogs, wikis, and social networking tools to recruit or to communicate with staff.** Engaging employees through education and training is one of the most effective ways to connect with potential employees, and facilitate employee socialization and intracompany learning—all of which will improve retention rates and promote recruitment, especially among younger employees. A 2008 Aberdeen Group study found that 52% of organizations that utilize these kinds of Web 2.0 tools achieve a significant improvement in employee engagement.[11]

Depending on the applicant pool, they can also support recruiting efforts. Take the example of Connected Ventures (CV), an online content producer and retailer in New York City with fifty-five employees. The company made a video of staffers lip-synching to Harvey Danger's 1998 hit "Flagpole Sitta," and posted it online. The postings at Vimeo.com, the company's video sharing social networking site, created a viral marketing event that boosted CV's brand and its recruiting efforts. Before the postings, CV attracted no more than fifty applicants for each open position, but after the video went viral, the company received as many as 500 résumés per open job.[12]

Ø **Include eco-initiatives in internal newsletters** along with information about programs and progress updates.

Ø **Encourage employees to conduct home energy audits.** Post phone numbers for local public utilities, most of which will conduct home energy audits for their customers free of charge.

Ø **Set up an actual or virtual bulletin board where employees can post eco-information.**

$ † **Hold training sessions on eco-issues.** By providing education to employees on environmental issues, you show support for their interests. Sessions can be as simple as lunchtime seminars/speakers or DVD screenings on eco-topics.

$$ **Provide online training courses** and eliminate lengthy training guides. Online classes also provide flexibility to allow employee to train at their own convenience. For information on online training options, check out *Training Magazine* at www.trainingmag.com.

12 GREEN TRANSPORTATION AND SHIPPING

If GM had kept up with technology like the computer industry has, we would all be driving $25 cars that got 1,000 mpg.

—*Bill Gates, chairman of Microsoft*

Every business transports goods, materials, or people. Whether you're a florist delivering bouquets, an online retailer shipping to consumers, a software developer shipping a booth to a trade show, or a real estate agent showing houses, you're transporting something. What kind of transportation you use and the number of miles your employees or goods travel per year will have a tremendous impact on your carbon footprint. By making greener transportation choices and cutting unnecessary miles, you can lower labor and fuel costs, and improve operational efficiencies.

Sustainable transport, also commonly referred to as sustainable transportation or sustainable mobility, refers to transportation that minimizes fuel consumption, CO_2 emissions, and pollutants. Sustainable transport includes transport options such as public transit, carpooling, walking, and cycling, as well as those incorporating fuel-efficient technologies such as electric and hybrid vehicles.

For starters, promoting sustainable shipping and transport practices means rethinking how you use transportation in your business—to ship goods, provide services, and move products and raw materials. Today, fuel efficiency and environmental imperatives are driving new approaches that conserve fuel, reduce emissions, and save money. Your goal is to find ways to reduce the environmental impact of the transport and shipping choices you make. When you begin to rethink those choices, use the Green Transportation Hierarchy as your guide. The hierarchy puts cyclists and pedestrians first—at zero environmental impact. Next comes public transit, followed by commercial vehicles and trucks, which have elevated status because they perform vital commercial functions. Here's how the hierarchy breaks down:

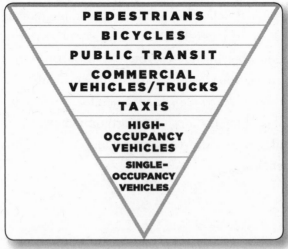

Image courtesy of Transportation Alternatives

From here on out, take your transport and shipping decisions off autopilot. Instead of automatically moving people by plane or car, consider a train or mass transit. When you're planning a meeting, choose a hotel or event venue within walking distance of the site. If you routinely make deliveries, try matching vehicles to specific routes. As an example, UPS makes deliveries by bicycle in congested urban areas. If you routinely make service or sales calls, plan your routes and schedules to minimize travel and maximize fuel efficiency. And if you're shipping packages, ask your suppliers what they're doing to conserve fuel and reduce emissions. Those are the kinds of green strategies you'll find in this chapter.

Defining the problem. All in all, the transportation sector produces more than 28% of total U.S. CO_2 emissions and is second in emissions only to the industrial sector. Air transport is the worst culprit. It yields higher fuel consumption and greenhouse gas emissions per ton-mile than any other form of transportation. And then there are cargo ships: Two-thirds of the goods from overseas are transported via cargo ship; each one emits more pollution than 2,000 diesel trucks. While trucking emissions are improving every day—and are actually projected to decline in the next ten years despite increases in trucking miles traveled—commercial trucks currently contribute 23% of U.S. highway carbon emissions, 40% of nitrous oxide emissions, and 60% of particu-

" ECO CHAT

A trip is a trip. Each trip allows us to reach a location at which we conduct personal or commercial or cultural business. [The Green Transportation Hierarchy] is called environmental but really has to do with efficiency: What are the benefits and costs associated with each trip? Whose costs, whose benefits? The trip with the lowest environmental and financial costs is the one that is "highest" on the scales.

—*Green Transportation Hierarchy: A Guide for Personal and Public Decision-Making*[1]

late matter emissions. The bottom line: Anything your business can do to reduce transport-related emissions is good for the environment.[2,3,4]

Transport-intensive sectors. The green practices outlined in this chapter break down into two parts: green transport practices and green shipping practices. If you have your own fleet of vehicles, or your employees routinely use their vehicles for conducting business—a florist or a real estate agency, as examples—you'll want to explore the green transport practices; if you rely on third parties to transport your goods and services—like an online retailer or a trade show exhibitor—you'll want to explore the green shipping practices. Either way, your goal will be the same: to reduce your carbon footprint by employing some of the fuel-saving practices outlined here. The more miles your vehicles—or goods—travel, the more attention you'll want to pay to this chapter.

To put it in perspective. If every small business in the United States reduced a delivery truck's idling time by five minutes a month, it would save 26.4 million gallons of fuel a year and prevent more than 270 tons of CO_2 from being emitted into the atmosphere.[5]

Transport best practices. The EPA has joined forces with the freight sector to create the SmartWay Transport program that provides business tools for improving energy efficiency and reducing greenhouse gas and air pollutant emissions, and offers financial incentives and low-cost loans for purchasing SmartWay vehicles. According to Smart-Way, the most effective steps a driver can take to improve fuel efficiency are:

❝❞ ECO CHAT

The real problem is that we use too much oil. It's that simple and that difficult. If we truly want to reduce our vulnerability to high prices, the best way to do so is to reduce consumption.

—**Richard Heinberg,** author of *Peak Everything*, May 14, 2008[6]

- Reduce idling.
- Lower speeds.
- Improve aerodynamics.
- Maintain/replace tires.
- Conduct driver training.
- Use low-friction lubricants.

🔗 Find out more about the SmartWay Transport program at www.epa.gov/smartway/transport/index.htm.

Shipping best practices. SmartWay and other sources provide best practice information for shipping customers, some of which improve fuel efficiency, some of which are simply good for the environment:

- Avoid expediting/air freight whenever possible.
- Consolidate shipments.
- Implement a no-idle policy for carriers when loading.
- Buy local whenever possible to reduce the need for shipping altogether.
- Use more environmentally friendly rail/intermodal shipments— that is, when appropriate, make use of more than one transportation mode such as train-to-truck.
- Increase shipping with carriers that have measurable green programs.
- Incorporate a carrier's environmental practices into the contract bidding process and give preferences/points to carriers with measurable green programs.
- Develop employee awareness focused on green strategies, such as those listed here.

🔗 For information on how to choose a SmartWay shipper, go to the SmartWay partner list at www.epa.gov/smartway/transport/partner -list/index.htm.

Taking action. There are two guiding principles for greening your transportation and shipping: minimize miles traveled and eliminate fuel waste. The first involves using transportation strategies that enable you to move the same amount of goods or people with fewer and shorter trips—a process that's simplified by a variety of low-cost technology solutions. The second involves employing fuel-efficient driving practices and vehicles. For shippers, a core strategy involves using environmentally preferable vendors to reduce your carbon footprint.

Green Transportation and Shipping Practices

Green Transport Practices

If you have your own or lease a fleet of vehicles, or your employees routinely use their own vehicles for conducting business, many of these green practices will be relevant to your business.

Reduction Strategies

The quickest way to green your transport practices is by minimizing the amount of transportation required to do business—an approach that's also going to save you the most money. This involves reducing the number and distance of trips through practices such as buying local, consolidating shipments, and optimizing routes.

 Third-party logistics providers (3PLs) are companies that provide outsourced transportation and logistic services. 3PLs often specialize in integrated warehousing and transportation services, and may have other specializations such as trade show logistics or reverse logistics.

$$$ Adopt technology to help manage the transportation process. Technologies such as transportation optimization and transportation management systems are software solutions for logistics management. Companies with larger fleets or greater transportation demands will want to consider implementing such a system, or even hiring a third-party logistics provider. Regardless of the size of your fleet, a technology solution reduces the need for manual and time-consuming logistics.

† Balance daily deliveries so that you service clients in the same area on certain days. This will decrease inefficient routing and empty miles, and save fuel.

$ or † Employ route optimization, which makes use of software to optimize routes and schedules, and often includes nifty help such as turn-by-turn directions. These programs reduce the time vehicles are on the road and therefore reduce fuel costs. Look for **$ web-based systems** like Netrouter or Routesmith or software like MapPoint Fleet Edition. If you don't want to invest in the technology, use **† maps** or **† Internet sites** to determine the quickest and most direct routes. If you outsource the driving, **† use multiple shippers** to secure the most direct routing.

†† Plan ahead to reduce the number of empty or underutilized miles traveled, a process that may involve analyzing your transportation needs. This means sending full trucks or vans out whenever possible—a practice that's better for the environment than using multiple, partial shipments. If you charge a flat fee for delivery and a buyer's shipment requires less than a full truck, use the opportunity to help them figure out what else they can order to fill up a truck and pitch it to them as a cost-savings measure. Software is also available to help optimize or improve trucking utilization.

$$$ Use wireless technology to make your mobile workforce more fuel efficient. Mobile workers are people who spend a significant amount of time—say, 25% or more—working away from their primary place of work or home. They might work on-site and move around the facility, travel regularly on business, work primarily off-site at client locations, or work on the go. Adopt wireless technology such as mobile phones, wireless laptops, electronic messaging, and remote access to an internal corporate network. By equipping your employees with mobile technology, you can reduce transportation expenses by eliminating unnecessary trips to offices and warehouses to process invoices, obtain

EBC CARPET: DOWNSIZING THE FLEET

"We're big on measurements here. We measure a lot of things to make sure we're doing things right," says Chip Rankin, president of EBC Carpet Services. A Millicare franchise with eighty full-time associates and offices across the Mid-Atlantic region, EBC leases a fleet of vehicles to transport its cleaning crews and equipment in their respective markets. In 2007, Rankin began implementing a variety of green practices and, as part of that process, decided to examine the efficiency of his fleet.

He took an eight-week period, and had the scheduling people measure—for the first time—how big each crew was that went out every night. "We realized," he says, "over an eight-week period, half of our cleaning was being done by a two-person crew or even a one-person crew. But we were running pretty big minivans or even commercial-type vans for every cleaning." Since then, EBC has begun moving to a much smaller fleet, gradually replacing some of its minivans and full-size trucks with smaller Chevrolet crossovers. The smaller vehicles accommodate the cleaning equipment and two people; the

parts, and so forth. It also reduces expenses by moving your workplace toward paperless processes.

✝✝✝ **Transport 24/7—or as much as possible.** Trucks are most valuable when they're transporting goods. So keep them moving, and you'll reduce the amount of equipment you have to buy or lease. It may be as simple as owning fewer vehicles and just using them more often. For example, if possible, use one vehicle twenty-four hours a day rather than three vehicles eight hours a day.[7]

Improve Fuel Efficiency

Ø **Establish no-idling policies.** Depending on the vehicle, idling (which gets you zero miles to the gallon) wastes one-half to one full gal-

vans carry four or five people. At this writing, EBC has four crossovers in operation and four more on their way. While Rankin still has twenty large vehicles in operation, he says: "The plan is, until we get our fleet to half and half—50% small vehicles, 50% large—we won't be reordering any of the larger vehicles." The transition process is expected to take several years.

The results: "We've already increased fuel efficiency by as much as 50%," says Rankin. In addition, the cost of leasing the smaller vehicles—without any change in terms or time—is $125 less per vehicle per month. So Rankin is saving money all around. But he doesn't just measure the program's value in terms of dollars—it's the potential impact on the environment. "I do consider it just one of the many little things that we can do to lower our footprint," he explains. "And I believe, if every business, no matter how small, just did one or two of these little things—that's where we could have an impact."

lon of fuel per hour. There are three good rules of thumb when it comes to idling:

- ■ If you stop for more than 20 seconds (although not at red lights), turn off the vehicle.
- ■ Turn off vehicles immediately upon reaching a destination.
- ■ Do not turn the vehicle back on until all people and cargo are fully loaded and ready to depart.

$$ **Use anti-idling technologies**, if appropriate. If your drivers idle in vehicles for heat or air conditioning, consider adding anti-idling technologies such as Alternative Power Units (APUs), particularly in sleeper

units. Companies report as much as an 80% reduction in engine idle time after installing APUs.

Ø Establish anti-idling rules for receiving as well as deliveries. Post signs in loading areas requiring drivers to turn off engines when making deliveries.

SmartWay Transport has extensive information about the benefits, technologies, and strategies for idling reduction at www.epa.gov/otaq/smartway/transport/what-smartway/idling-reduction.htm.

Ø Avoid left turns. UPS found that, when trucks idle while waiting to turn across traffic, it wastes time and gas and holds up idling traffic behind them, further compounding the waste. Therefore, the company redesigned its routes to avoid left-hand turns. As a result, UPS eliminated 28.5 million miles from its delivery routes, saving 3 million gallons of fuel and cutting CO_2 emissions by about 34 million tons.

Ø Lower speed. Reducing highway speed by 5 mph can cut fuel use and greenhouse gas emissions by more than 7%.

Ø Avoid rush hour. If you can travel at off-peak times, you'll spend less time in traffic and consequently consume less fuel.

Ø Travel light. The heavier the vehicle is, the worse the fuel efficiency. Eliminate anything unnecessary before heading out.

$ † Driver training ensures that drivers are aware of and understand all the driving rules. A few simple changes in driving techniques — such as cruise control and progressive shift — can produce fuel savings of more than 5%. Include rules for staff that use rental cars.[8]

†† Make 100% on-time delivery your standard. Living up to this standard forces you to put more efficient systems in place to manage routes and fleet scheduling, and eliminate waste.[9]

$ Use low-friction lubricants. Synthetic engine and drive train lubricants can improve fuel economy by about 3% in diesel trucks.[10]

$$ Mind your tires. Specifying single wide-base tires on trucks can result in fuel savings of 2% or more. Automatic tire inflation systems can improve fuel economy by almost 1% and extend tire life by more than 8%.[11]

$$ Improve aerodynamics. Aerodynamic drag (wind resistance) accounts for most truck energy losses at highway speeds. Reducing drag improves fuel efficiency. By enhancing the aerodynamics of tractor-trailers with add-on drag reduction devices (fairings) on the roof, in the gap between the trailer and the cab, underneath the truck, and/or rear-mounted on the back, trucks can be made significantly more fuel efficient.

$$$ Make your own fuel. Buy a self-contained micro-refinery, like E-Fuel100 MicroFueler, to make environmentally friendly ethanol at about $1 a gallon. Both a pump station and an ethanol distiller, it uses sugar to produce up to thirty-five gallons of ethanol per week. Eligible for federal tax credits.

$$$ Drive environmentally friendly company cars and trucks (and forklifts). Consider reducing or eliminating gas-driven cars and trucks with hybrid or alternative-fuel fleets when upgrading. For example, replace diesel trucks with compressed natural gas vehicles. If your fleet consists of big minivans or commercial vans, consider switching all or some to smaller vehicles that get better gas mileage. If you use forklifts, move to electric power (for energy efficiency) or refurbished ones (often a greener option).

The National Renewable Energy Lab's Learning About Renewable Energy site has a primer on "Biofuels for Small Business Owners" at www.nrel.gov/learning/sb_biofuels.html.

Green Shipping Practices

If you ship a lot of goods, either directly to consumers or to commercial customers, you can have a big impact on your environmental footprint—and often your bottom line—by reviewing your shipping practices. That includes how you ship and which shippers you use.

Ø Buy—and hire—local whenever possible. Purchasing materials and goods from local suppliers, and hiring local subcontractors, will reduce transportation miles and therefore fuel use.

Ø For long-distance shipping, **make ground transport your first preference**. Avoid air freight and cargo ships, if at all possible.

Ø **Reuse packaging materials.** Reusing boxes and shipping envelopes will keep them out of landfills. Use crumbled newspaper, used plastic bags, or egg cartons instead of packing peanuts or bubble wrap. If you are worried that customers won't understand, include a note inside or message on the outside telling them that you are deliberately and proudly reusing your boxes and materials. (See Chapter 7, and "Packaging" on page 210.)

Reused Packaging!
Paper and paperboard accounts for 35 percent of the total materials discarded in the U.S.
Americans throw away 10 times their own weight in garbage every year. Please reuse this packaging again.
©Greenhance.com Helping small businesses grow greener

Image courtesy of Greenhance

† **Use transportation contracts.** Contracts will make carriers more competitive and force them to improve fuel efficiency. Look first at SmartWay for certified carriers who will likely be able to offer better prices as a result of better operating costs.[12]

† **Use backhauling**—that is, use an empty truck's return route to

SPECIALTY 3PLS

If your company exhibits at trade shows, it may make sense for you to hire a 3PL that specializes in trade show logistics. These firms know how to move exhibits and booth materials to meet show deadlines and interface with the on-site logistics staff. To reduce transportation back and forth, some 3PLs can warehouse your things at a central location.

If you're a retailer or manufacturer, 3PLs that specialize in reverse logistics can help you streamline the collection, handling, and processing of returned, damaged, and obsolete items.

carry cargo—as a shipping strategy for deliveries that are not extremely time sensitive. Approximately 28% of trucker miles are driven empty without cargo on return trips.[13] Ask your shipper about backhaul rates, because they may be looking to fill empty trucks. For example, Maxus Technology, an e-waste recycler with a facility in Morgan Hill, California, always checks for backhaul rates first since transportation represents such a large portion of its total costs and backhauls are the most cost-effective.[14]

†† **Avoid air freight whenever possible.** Air freight has a low fuel-per-mile ratio, making it one of the most expensive commonly used shipping methods.

†† **Avoid expedited shipping and delivery whenever possible.** Expediting usually involves inefficient local messenger services or overnight air freight (see above). Generally, if you're caught in a bind where you're forced to use overnight air delivery or a local messenger, it's probably because you're not managing your schedules, the supply chain, or the production process effectively. If you're a retailer, provide alternatives to overnight shipping. If you're a web-based business, consider implementing self-service options or drop shipping for customers and suppliers to eliminate one step in the ordering process. If you must use local messenger services, opt for those that use bicycles or mass transit.

†† **Consolidate shipments.** By consolidating—for example, sending out one large shipment once a week instead of smaller shipments four times a week—you can reduce fuel use, facilitate more efficient packing and packaging, and lower overall shipping costs.

† **Review and correct address labels** to avoid unnecessary transport as well as costly address change surcharges[15] for packages that must be forwarded and returned to sender.

† **Give preference to carriers and shippers that employ measurable environmental practices.** For example, if your vendor uses Smart-Way trucks, their vehicles are up to 25% more efficient than an average truck. Check out what your shipper is doing to become more sustain-

able before you sign a contract. SmartWay lists hundreds of partners, including UPS and FedEx, on its website. It is possible to find green logistics providers that buy carbon offsets, use alternative fuel vehicles, warehouse strategically, and adopt other eco-friendly practices in their businesses.

13 GREEN MARKETING AND COMMUNICATIONS

> The philosophy behind much advertising is based on the old observation that every man is really two men—the man he is and the man he wants to be.
>
> —William Feather, publisher and author

When a business sends out a message via product advertising, a company brochure, a public relations program, or even by putting its name on a cap or T-shirt, it's engaged in marketing. Although marketing itself is intangible, it involves the use of paper, promotional items, and a great deal of other resources that generate—literally—tons of wasted resources.

Defining the problem. Oftentimes, marketing materials are, quite literally, waste—waste in the form of unwanted messages. Yet, given rising global competition and the dramatic expansion of the variety of marketing channels, the barrage continues—via television, radio, print and outdoor advertising, phone and mail, and now the Internet and mobile applications. The crowded marketing arena is also creating a surge in customized, personalized, and niche marketing, all of which require new materials and messaging to deliver tailored messages. In the end, however, successful marketing boils down to customer acquisition. And since customer acquisition is a numbers game—only 4% of people respond to a catalog, only 3% of people respond to a direct mail piece, only 0.5% of people respond to a newspaper ad, and so forth—marketers significantly overproduce materials in order to reach the right number of consumers. That leads to unwanted messages and materials—also known as waste.[1]

Take direct mail, or what is commonly known as junk mail. Each year 100 billion pieces of direct mail—equaling 4.5 million tons of materials—are printed and mailed in the United States. This represents 100 million trees and does not even take into account the resources necessary to produce, print, and ship. The real tragedy is that 44% of that mail goes directly to landfills without ever being opened, representing 2 million tons of solid waste and 44 million trees—all for nothing.

Marketing-intensive sectors. All businesses market themselves, but direct mail and printed materials create the most direct waste of resources and energy. If you use direct mail or printed materials to market your business, this chapter will be of significant benefit to you.

To put it in perspective. If every small business in the United States cleaned its mailing list and thereby sent *one* less piece of unwanted mail, it would save about 200 tons of solid waste, more than 10 million trees, and 13 thousand tons of CO_2—the annual equivalent of heating more than 3,000 homes.[2]

❝❞ ECO CHAT

We're not a manufacturer, or an airline, but we do use energy. Printing and publishing newspapers, producing films, broadcasting television signals, operating 24-hour newsrooms. It all adds carbon to the atmosphere.[3]

—**Rupert Murdoch,** chairman and managing director, News Corporation

Best practices. The world of marketing involves not only advertising and public relations agencies, but also advertisers, publishers, media outlets, production companies, printers, and paper companies. The broadly defined goals of the nonprofit Sustainable Advertising Partnership mandate that all players in the advertising process become more sustainable by adopting eco-friendly practices such as using renewable or recycled materials, employing clean production technologies, eliminating waste, and building in recycling and end-of-life programs. Find out more about the Sustainable Advertising Partnership, a nonprofit organization that provides tools for promoting sustainability in the advertising industry, at www.sustainableadvertisingpartnership.org.

Best practices for direct mail advertising, the most environmentally resource-intensive marketing channel, however, are more specific and can be found in the Direct Marketing Association's (DMA) Environmental Resolution, the Green 15, instituted in May 2007. The Green 15 calls on marketers to implement fifteen eco-friendly business practices. These practices can be used as a baseline for greening all printed marketing materials with a focus on five areas:

■ Paper procurement and use.
■ List hygiene and data management.
■ Mail design and production.
■ Packaging.
■ Pollution reduction.

To find out more about the Green 15, go to the Direct Marketing Association's Environmental Resource Center at www.dmaresponsibility.org/Environment.

Taking action. When it comes to marketing and communications, a good place to start is by looking at your printed materials—direct mail, collateral materials, and packaging. Since printed materials require lots of trees as well as processing on both ends, the greenest marketing and communications practice you can employ is to reduce the amount of direct mail, collateral materials, and packaging you use. Taking these three simple first steps can have an enormous impact:

- For direct mail: Eliminate duplicate, irrelevant, and unwanted mail.
- For collateral materials: Produce materials electronically.
- For packaging: Use smaller, lighter-weight, and environmentally preferable materials and processes.

If these strategies are not fully achievable, strive to design all printed materials with the smallest possible dimensions and as lightweight paper stock as possible.

Green Marketing Practices

Reducing the amount of paper-based materials and packaging you use is the best strategy for greening marketing efforts. The good news is that the Internet has created significant opportunities for paperless marketing approaches.

Printed Materials

Whether you are printing holiday cards, ten-piece press kits, or product manuals, there are plenty of opportunities to green your print projects.

Ø **Use PDFs** for proofreading.

Ø **Integrate electronic communications.** Create electronic versions of materials such as media kits, press kits, reports, and other documents, then post them to your website and distribute them electronically. Include the Internet, email, blogs, mobile marketing, and intranets in your external and internal communications programs.

Ø **Drive people to your website.** Remember to include your URL on all printed materials including packaging. This will get your customers in the habit of using your website as their portal to your company and will help you build an email list. Every point of contact via the Internet is one less point of contact by mail.

†† **Reduce waste in design and production.** Instruct designers to reduce waste allowances and dimensions that require wasteful trimming when designing and printing materials. Test downsized pieces on different weights of paper. Lower acceptable print order overruns and require that overruns be recycled.

$ † **Consider recycled and other environmentally preferable paper for every print project.** Use recycled materials with as much post-consumer content as possible given your budget. Look into lightweight or PCW papers. Polypropylene papers might make sense if visibly labeled as recyclable. See Chapter 10 for a discussion of recycled paper.

$ **Use soy ink.** Although soy ink is commonly used, you still may have to specify it. For color printing, it's comparably priced with that of conventional color ink, but provides superior performance and is environmentally friendly. Black soy ink is about 25% more expensive than petroleum-based inks, but some printers report that they need less ink to produce the same amount of printed material.[4]

Direct Mail

Direct mail waste reduction is an area where environmental concerns and shareholder interests coincide.

—**Green Marketing:** *Leveraging Customer Data to Reduce Direct Mail Waste,* Aberdeen Group, February 2008

The problem with direct mail marketing is that it's inherently inefficient; 44% of all direct mail is thrown in the trash without ever being opened and read. According to the DMA, opened direct mail only yields an average of a 2.77% response. So, if you want to get 1,000 customers to respond to your direct mail piece, you have to mail, on average, 36,101 pieces of mail. Multiply that by millions of customers and millions of companies and you can see the problem.[5] But you may already know this. According to a March 2008 Aberdeen Group study, 40% of companies surveyed said direct mail waste reduction was one of the top two focus areas for improving eco-friendly business practices.[6]

The challenge for direct marketers is to reach the target audience with as much precision as possible, which means not sending out more mail than is necessary. By implementing these green practices, you'll increase the overall effectiveness of your direct mail campaigns, save money, and enhance customer satisfaction, which in turn improves customer loyalty, purchase behavior, and profitability.

🔗 The DMA has an excellent free web-based tool for identifying and generating a green direct marketing program, the Environmental Planning Tool and Policy & Vision Statement Generator. The user completes a best-practice, online checklist that includes over 100 strategies to make marketing practices more sustainable and then the system generates an environmental vision statement to use in the future. Go to www.the-dma.org/envgen.

✝ **Maintain good list hygiene.** List hygiene is the process of updating a mailing list to remove unwanted, duplicate, and undeliverable addresses. Cleaning mailing lists regularly and thoroughly is one of the cheapest, quickest, and most effective ways to green your marketing. There are several ways to verify mailing lists. It's a step any outside list manager is equipped to perform. But if you maintain your own mailing list, consider buying mailing verification software designed for small businesses (typically under 5,000 records). Verifying addresses will save you money and can also, under some circumstances, lower mailing rates. Consider offering incentives (such as the offer of a discount on their next purchase) for notification of duplicate mailings and incorrect addresses.

✝ **Don't mail to weak prospects.** By not mailing to customers who have not responded in the past six to twelve months, you can lower customer complaints and improve customer satisfaction. Go a step further and use software for segmentation, targeting, and predictive modeling to "select with care" customer names that should be mailed for differing promotions. (See "MSHC Partners: Greening Direct Mail" on page 206.)

 Segmentation is the practice of classifying customers into distinct groups (segments). For example, it might make sense to segment buyers by previous purchases, product category, age, or gender, and then mail targeted catalogs to each segment.

Targeting is a practice that involves evaluating various customer segments and deciding which ones you want to reach through direct marketing.

Predictive modeling is the practice of forecasting the likely future behavior of customers based on past history. Typically, software is used to assign customers scores or rankings that predict their anticipated actions.

✝ **Make it easy for customers to opt out of future solicitations**, an approach that not only saves you money, but also engenders lots of goodwill. Clearly label all marketing materials with an email or web address where customers can opt out. Then make it easy and automatic for them to do so.

✝ **Offer customers the option of receiving communications electronically.** Consider switching periodic mailings, such as invoices, reminders, and promotional pieces inserted into billing statements, to an electronic system to reduce the paper and postage you use. (See "Paper Reduction Strategies" in Chapter 10.)

✝ **Use environmentally preferable addressing and labeling techniques** on envelopes and boxes such as ink-jet technology and open address windows. Eliminate separate labels to save materials and money. Don't produce preprinted boxes so as not to create packaging that could become obsolete.

MSHC PARTNERS: GREENING DIRECT MAIL

MSHC Partners, a political communications firm with forty-five staffers and three U.S. offices, launched a small-scale green plan in mid-2008. A component of the initiative, described in greater detail in Chapter 2, involves providing green options for their client's print and direct mail jobs. The firm manages marketing through direct mail, microtargeting, and interactive services. They're also committed to environmental practices, which raises the question: Just how green can direct mail get?

By following industry best practices, MSHC's direct mail campaigns are inherently green in certain respects. For example, they work exclusively with union printers—the vast majority of whom use soy inks and have for the past few years. And targeting, segmentation, and predictive modeling is one of the firm's hallmarks—that is, figuring out precisely whom to mail to and making sure the mailing lists are in good shape. Says Joe Fuld, former MSHC partner and now president of the Campaign Workshop: "You can make the argument that good list hygiene is a green thing do to. But frankly, the reason to do good list hygiene is that it's incredibly cost-effective. If a client has 30,000 bad addresses on a list of 100,000, they're saving a ton of money by not mailing to those 30,000 bad addresses." In addition, the industry is moving away from print to reach those people who are online—a practice that conserves paper. Ultimately, the key to managing direct mail is targeting: "We see online communications as a way to use different tools to

$$ †† Test lists to improve response rates. Test purchased lists before mailing or marketing to the entire list. Test different versions of advertising and marketing offers, in mail and other media, to select those offers and media mixes that yield the highest response rates.

reach different people. There is still going to be an audience that's never going to be online and is only going to be reached by direct mail or telephone. Whereas, there are groups of people that are never going to read direct mail. So the idea is to segment your communication and figure out what is the best way to communicate to different groups." For now, using soy inks, practicing list hygiene, targeting, and segmentation are a reasonable green standard for direct mail, one that makes business sense.

What about paper? Even if you're on the leading edge in direct mail, at this writing, it may be hard to make a business case for using the greenest paper. For one thing, it could cost as much as 50% more to use chlorine-free, 100% PCW paper—but prices can vary dramatically. Says Fuld: "If the client is very interested in the environment, they're going to be more likely to want to pay the extra cost." But it's also a matter of education—and patience. "It's not just educating our clients. It's educating ourselves, so we know best how to convey it to the client—so we know what the easiest options are. The onus is on us." The good news: Higher-quality PCW paper, with higher levels of PCW content, are already more available at lower prices. And Fuld expects that trend to continue: "My bet is—it'll be just like soy inks. Because of the interest, you're going to see the price of PCW paper drop and then people will use more of it. And it will also have higher PCW content. You're already seeing it happen."

New Media

Given the high environmental cost of print marketing, not much attention gets paid to greening nonprint marketing. But all media activities generate greenhouse gases. Like any of your other business activities, an analysis of the sustainability of your media supply chain is important.

New Media

 Mobile media is advertising on mobile devices such as cell phones and PDAs via text messaging, video streams, podcasts, gaming, downloadable ring tones, and mobizines (mobile magazines).

Social media refers to Internet- and mobile-based technology through which users engage others and create user-generated content. These include social networking sites (LinkedIn, Facebook), social bookmarking sites (Stumble Upon), social news sites (Digg, Tip'd), microblogs (Twitter, Plurk), and other sites that are based on user interaction.

Viral marketing is a marketing strategy whereby email recipients forward messages on to others who in turn do the same, thereby quickly reaching exponential numbers of people.

Ø **Add Internet marketing to your media mix.** Whenever possible, use digital media to spread your marketing messages. Digital media, which became commonplace just a few years ago, is now known to have a growing and increasingly trusting online audience. Banner advertising, search engine advertising, classifieds, and lead generation activities are now common. Mobile media is also growing in popularity. Don't forget to use social media to engage those customers via Internet- and mobile-based technologies.

Although the use of digital advertising is not carbon neutral—the electricity necessary to run data centers is a significant source of greenhouse gases—media such as the Internet and mobile media, video-on-demand, and LED digital outdoor signs remain the least environmentally onerous types of advertising in terms of environmental cost per thousand people reached. Furthermore, the cost savings over traditional advertising can be significant. As an example, by posting its advertising for upcoming construction contracts exclusively on its website and eliminating newspaper ads, the State of Maine Department of Transportation estimates that it saves more than $100,000 a year.[7]

Ø **Check out your media vendors.** As an advertiser, you have tremendous leverage. Ask your media suppliers what they're doing to address the carbon output of their operations and to reduce emissions—just as you would any other vendor. If the newspaper or radio station where you advertise doesn't have an environmental program in place, you'll be nudging them to do so.

† **Use digital coupons.** Eliminate paper coupons. Use Internet and mobile media coupons instead. If you sell products online, you can register online coupon codes with an aggregator like RetailMeNot.com. If you're a member of an affiliate network such as Commission Junction, LinkShare, or Shareasale, you can often post online coupon codes through those networks. If you are not a member of a network, contact the aggregator directly.

Ø **Do your market research online.** While the days of printed questionnaires and in-store intercepts are not over yet, online questionnaires are proving to be just as effective in the vast majority of situations. In fact, there are many advantages to online surveys. They're more convenient for respondents (and therefore may yield better response rates) and less expensive to create and manage. Sign up for a no-cost account with a company like SurveyMonkey, Zoomerang, or QuestionPro that lets you create surveys using their web servers and then send them out over the Internet. You can use a template (some are free, some aren't) or you can easily create your own. If you've never written a survey, it will pay to take a quick online tutorial. And if you want to survey unrelated people, try Ask500People.com, a quick and inexpensive online tool for surveying groups of independent respondents.

Promotional Items

You may think of promotional items—also known as swag—as nothing more than useless and unnecessary giveaways. But in reality, promotional items can be an effective tool for promoting brand awareness. For example, a promotional item given away at a trade show can help draw traffic, create recall after the show, and provide contact information for prospects in a unique, memorable way. According to one study, event attendees are 52% more likely to stop by your exhibit if you have an appealing promotional item to give them.[8]

$ Give away eco-friendly alternatives for promotional items, many of which also promote environmentally friendly activities and practices. Look for items that are made of recycled or earth-friendly materials (products made of bamboo or repurposed materials), are reusable (reusable sport bottles, grocery totes), or have cradle-to-cradle design. Get creative. Say you want to give away printed marketing brochures at an upcoming trade show—consider giving away a promotional zip drive with the materials preloaded as PDFs instead.

Packaging

> We have all seen a great, eco-minded product wrapped in un-eco packaging, and inserted in an improperly sized un-eco box and filled with a very un-eco void fill.
>
> —**Dennis Salazar,** president of Salazar Packaging Inc., Sustainable Is Good blog, May 2008[9]

The way a product is packaged matters a lot environmentally. And thanks to Wal-Mart, it now matters a lot financially. In February 2008, Wal-Mart launched a Packaging Scorecard that rates product packaging based on its environmental friendliness. Scores and rankings are provided based on a variety of metrics—including greenhouse gas emissions, product-to-packaging ratio, space utilization, and innovation—for specific products offered by Wal-Mart suppliers. Given the immense purchasing power of Wal-Mart, it's changed the packaging industry. In one fell swoop, Wal-Mart made a product's packaging almost as important as the product itself when it comes to being stocked on Wal-Mart's shelves. And Wal-Mart-generated packaging improvements are only going to increase as the company continues to sharpen its metrics to place greater emphasis on greenhouse gas reductions and formulate more aggressive packaging weight-reduction goals. As of November 2008, more than 8,000 unique vendors had accessed the Packaging Scorecard website and more than 250,000 items had been entered into the scorecard. As a result, a wave of new sustainable packaging entered the market. As John Kalkowski, editorial director of *Packaging Digest*, wrote in an editorial: "No matter what Wal-Mart does, this sustainability program will become a de facto standard for the industry—the global muscle of this retail giant commands that much attention."[10]

$ † **Use packaging made from earth-friendly materials and designs.** When possible, use boxes, cases, mailers, and partitions made out of the highest post-consumer waste materials available. As examples, Globe Guard corrugated boxes and inflatable air pillow void fills are made from 100% post-consumer recycled content; and many types of resealable, plastic packaging are environmentally preferable to rigid packaging, because the production process typically uses fewer BTUs of energy, emits lower levels of greenhouse gases, and generates less waste.

$$ †† **Reduce package-to-product ratios.** Instruct designers to reduce the ratio of the weight of packaging compared to the weight or quantity of the product. (See the discussion of dematerialization on page 101.)

$$ †† **Think about cube utilization when designing packaging.** Cube utilization refers to how much space is used within a storage area, trailer, or container. Many package redesigns result in less packaging, thus allowing for more packages on every pallet. Fewer pallets enable efficient cube utilization that will reduce the transportation needs. (See also Chapter 12.)

14 GREEN BUSINESS TRAVEL

For most people in business, meetings are a
necessary evil.
—Diane Parker, TheEffectiveAdmin.com

For some companies, face-to-face contact with customers, clients, suppliers, and colleagues is an essential part of doing business. For others, conferences and conventions are essential. For some, off-site training is integral to operations. Whatever your business needs or company size, travel is likely a significant expense. Given technology and a competitive marketplace, it is quite possible to green business travel costs without spending more money, compromising the needs of the business, or losing the personal touch.

Defining the problem. All travel consumes energy and generates waste. In fact, airplane travel, lodging, and rental car usage can consume almost one-quarter of a business' carbon footprint and as much as 3% of its revenue. For most small businesses, implementing green travel policies will make it possible to reduce your carbon footprint, lower your expenses, and improve productivity.

Travel-intensive sectors. Almost all businesses require some travel. If you are a sales or client service business, participate in conferences and conventions regularly, or service businesses for their travel needs, you'll benefit significantly from this chapter. But the reality is this: If you or your employees travel for any of the following reasons, you should evaluate your travel practices:

- Conventions/conferences
- Customer/client meetings or events
- Exhibitions and sponsorships
- General business meetings or events
- Incentive events
- Management/executive meetings
- Recruiting
- Training programs/events

To put it in perspective. If every small business owner in the United States conducted one teleconference in lieu of a domestic business trip, it would save $25.4 billion in travel expenses and 10.5 million tons of CO_2. If every small business in the United States cut its business travel by a single domestic airline flight, it would save 4.9 million tons of CO_2—which would save 59,529 tanker trucks' worth of gasoline. And if every small business in the United States spent one less night in a hotel, it would save 1.6 billion gallons of water.[1]

Best practices. Although there are no industry guidelines for best practices in green business travel, the Aberdeen Group research brief, "Sustainable Travel: Reduce Your Carbon Footprint," which bases its information on key performance indicators from best-in-class companies, recommends three tactics:

- Measure your business' travel-related carbon footprint as a first step toward implementing policies that will help you reduce it.
- Encourage alternatives to travel such as web conferencing and teleconferencing.
- Travel more productively by taking fewer and longer trips.

Taking action. When it comes to business travel, employing a strategy that reduces the demand—also known as demand management—is a good place to start. Since airplane and car travel involve intensive greenhouse gas–emitting activities, the greenest practice you can employ is to find ways to reduce the need for travel—and to eliminate travel altogether.

The next best thing to reducing demand is to take a supplier's impact on the environment into consideration—such as whether they procure goods locally or sell goods made out of recycled materials or have green operating practices. You can establish travel policies that favor green providers, aggregating your travel purchases to leverage your buying power with them. The greater your travel needs, the more leverage you'll have.

Finally, purchasing offsets to mitigate the impact of your travel is an increasingly popular strategy that may make sense for your green program.

Green Travel Practices

No two ways around it: Reducing the number of business trips you take is the single best strategy for greening business travel. Not traveling for business means not having to postpone regular office work, saving the expenses of travel, and eliminating the carbon output from that travel. When you change your travel policies, be sure to communicate your goals and policies to everyone in your business.

Change the Way You Meet

For every meeting that involves travel, ask yourself: Can we accomplish our purposes without a face-to-face meeting? If the answer is yes, here are some alternatives:

Ø **Teleconference.** Companies can conduct meetings, training programs, demonstrations, and workshops involving multiple people in different locations. Everyone calls in to a central phone number and participates in a real-time audio conversation. A variety of free teleconferencing services allow you to schedule and manage telephone conference calls from any web browser at your convenience. With these free services, local and long-distance rates apply for callers. Low-cost alternatives, where toll-free numbers are supplied to teleconference participants, are also available.

Ø **Twitter chat.** If you want to have a real-time dialogue with several users, consider using a Twitter chat room. This can be done by simply creating a unique #hashtag and having participants follow the conversation in Twitter, or you can use a site like TweetChat.com or TinyChat.com.

$ **Web conference.** If your business involves meetings that require visual presentations or document sharing, consider an online web-conferencing service. These allow participants to communicate through text and video in addition to audio. The simplest web-conferencing methods use chat and instant messaging programs; more sophisticated approaches use webcams and streaming video or shared desktop presentations along with Voice over IP audio (VoIP), a computer application that enables the transmission of voice through the Internet. Other options include application and whiteboard sharing, Outlook integration, IM chat, multiple-party video, instant polling, and the ability to record a meeting for later playback. Cnet.com has reviews of all the major web-conferencing software at http://reviews.cnet.com/1990-6454_7-6212812-1.html.

Plan Ahead

Ø **Take fewer, longer trips.** Plan your trips carefully to make every trip more productive. Schedule more meetings per trip and include only those participants who are essential. *This is a key greening strategy.*

Ø **Make purchasing green travel easier.** Use one centralized travel agent or a technology system that directs employees to preferred vendors.

Ø **Schedule meetings on-site.** Next time you hold a meeting, select a site that's close to home for the majority of participants. If possible, host meetings at your offices to save time and money.

Ø **Choose hub cities for meetings that involve air travel.** If you have to get people from different locations together across great distances, find a meeting site near a major airline hub to reduce the need for connecting flights and rental cars. Or choose sites that minimize air travel.

Almost all the major airlines use a hub-and-spoke system for flight routes. The hub is a central airport where travelers change planes en route to destinations that are served by nonstop flights.[2] Go to http:// en.wikipedia.org/wiki/Airline_hub for a comprehensive list of hub airports.

† **Use preferred suppliers whenever possible.** If you, like many small businesses, have no preferred vendor relationships for travel, you may be able to achieve considerable cost savings by developing relationships with suppliers who will benefit from garnering a greater portion of your travel budget. If you have a small travel budget, your best savings may come from establishing a relationship with a particular travel agent. For bigger budgets, you may be able to achieve savings by going directly to the provider's corporate sales department.

† **Sign up for frequent-traveler programs** to promote the use of preferred vendors. If employees make their own travel arrangements, you might create a preferred supplier database that highlights preferred vendors and shows contracted rates and terms. Don't forget to market internal venues, such as conference rooms, in the preferred supplier database.

Hotels

$$ **Choose green hotels.** An average-size hotel purchases more products in one week than 100 families do in a year.[3] More and more hotels have begun greening their operations and facilities so in most cities

WEB CONFERENCING AT CARE2

CASE STUDY

Founded in 1998, Care2 is the largest online community for people interested in healthy, sustainable lifestyles—so the organization's business model is inherently green. "We connect individuals with organizations, opportunities and other caring individuals interested in making the world a better place," says Care2 Founder and President Randy Paynter. With more than 50 employees, 10 million members, and 400 nonprofit partners, the company has offices on the East and West Coasts, as well as employees scattered around the United States. And it's still growing. In order to enable face-to-face meetings among geographically dispersed staff members, Care2 introduced web conferencing in 2006 to facilitate internal meetings. "Human connections are so important to help an organization work efficiently and effectively," says Paynter. "And we find that literally seeing someone's face during a meeting builds these ties and helps people work together from remote locations." Paynter believes that connectedness builds a sense of commitment among team members that contributes to lower turnover and fewer mistakes. Without web conferencing, he says, "Over the long term, I think we'd start to see more problems, costs, and lost opportunities."

there are many facilities to choose from. Look for green corporate initiatives from major hotel companies as well as from independent hoteliers.

Ø **Opt out of daily sheet and towel service.** Let housekeeping know that you don't need clean sheets and towels every day to reduce energy and water use. As part of their environmental program, most hotels now give every guest this option.

Ø **Turn off the lights,** in-room HVAC systems, and electronics when you leave your room.

The firm uses a licensed web-conferencing solution with a video component that allows for shared access to spreadsheets, presentations, and other documents among meeting participants at different locations. "We have a big projector in our board room so everyone in the meeting can see it," says Paynter. Through web conferencing, Care2 has avoided the costs associated with extensive travel for internal meetings. "We don't feel the need to get staff physically connected as much as we used to," says Paynter. So the company is saving on travel expenses and reducing its carbon footprint.

In 2008, Care2 also began using webinars—online seminars available through its website at Care2.com—as a mechanism for reaching outside audiences and generating new sales leads. Care2's first three webinars drew several hundred attendees— people the organization otherwise could not have reached outside of a conference setting. Says Paynter, "We're gearing up for more as they've proven to be a good way to efficiently reach new clients."

Air Travel

There is just no easy way for [the aviation] industry to stay in the skies and keep them clean at the same time.

—**Kevin Klustner,** author of *Energy Efficiency: The Future Is Now*

The term "sustainable" is rarely seen in the same sentence as "airplane." An airplane's CO_2 emissions, per passenger and per mile, are almost as environmentally inefficient as driving a car with one passenger.[4] So, as a guiding principle: Use more environmentally friendly transportation

GREEN CERTIFICATION PROGRAMS FOR LODGING FACILITIES

There are dozens of certifying organizations for accommodations. The major ones in the United States include:

- ✓ EPA's ENERGY STAR for Hospitality Rating (www.energystar.gov).
- ✓ Green Globe Certification (www.greenglobecertification.com).
- ✓ Green Seal's Certification for Lodging Properties (www.greenseal.org).
- ✓ U.S. Green Building Council's LEED certification for new construction or existing buildings does not specifically identify lodging facilities, but the number of hotels planning to add LEED standards is growing and could be as high as one in five by 2009 (www.usgbc.org).[5]

such as trains, buses, and mass transit whenever possible. But when you must travel by plane, know that the economics of the airline industry—rising fuel prices and a global economic downturn—are leading all airlines to be more forward thinking about sustainability (even if they have a long way to go).

Ø **Fly Continental, Virgin Atlantic, or JetBlue.** In 2007, *Fortune* magazine named Continental Airlines as one of the "10 Green Giants" in America, citing the airline's $16 billion investment in efficient aircraft, fuel-saving winglets that reduce fuel emissions, their 75% reduction in the nitrogen oxide output from ground equipment at its Houston hub, its thirteen full-time staff environmentalists, and its corporate recycling practices. Virgin Atlantic is also considered a green leader in a brown industry. It has new fleets, innovative recycling programs, and has pledged to invest $3 billion in renewable energy technologies. JetBlue gets good reports because of their newer, more fuel-efficient aircraft and their in-flight recycling and waste management programs. Don't forget to become a frequent flyer on these airlines to encourage use. And there is a double bonus: The greener airlines typically receive—coincidentally or not—the highest ranks on customer satisfaction surveys.

$ Opt for nonstop flights. Takeoffs and landings are a major source of CO_2 emissions. *Note: Don't be fooled by so-called direct flights that involve stops without plane changes.*

Trains

$ Take a train. It's as simple as that. It's no wonder that record numbers of travelers are choosing trains over alternative transportation. In terms of how much energy it takes to move one person one mile, train travel is significantly more efficient than air and automobile travel,[6] and the price of a train ticket is often less than a flight and comparable to the cost of gas and tolls for auto travel.

Automobiles

Since a single occupant of a car uses more carbon per mile per person than any other mode of transportation, it makes sense that you should do anything you can to avoid putting a single passenger in a car.

$ Rent hybrid and alternative-fuel vehicles. The good news is that most of the major rental car companies offer these options. The bad news is that they often cost more to rent. As an alternative, consider any car that has a minimum 28 mpg EPA Highway Rating a viable option. Here are some tips to help you secure the most efficient rental car at the most economical cost:

- ■ Open a corporate account that does not charge you a premium rate for green cars. Your ability to do this will depend somewhat on your rental car volume, but check with the major companies to discuss options.

■ Rent small cars. Most small vehicles, other than small luxury cars, get better gas mileage. For example, 100% of Avis' economy, compact, intermediate, and standard cars meet EPA guidelines for fuel efficiency and are EPA SmartWay–certified. If not specified by the rental car agency in advance, simply ask for a fuel-efficient car at the rental desk.

■ Hire a taxi or car service that uses alternative-fuel vehicles, when available. Taxi and car services are going green across the country. More are sure to pop up every day, so see the Resources section for links to services in cities near you or use Google.

 The EPA SmartWay Transport program rates vehicles by assigning an Air Pollution Score and a Greenhouse Gas Score on a scale of 1-10. For the SmartWay designation, a vehicle must receive a score of 6 or better on both measures, and have a total score of at least 13. The SmartWay Elite designation is given to vehicles that score 9 or better on both measures. The complete guide is available at www.epa.gov/greenvehicles/Download.do, or look up a vehicle by make, model, type, or designation at www.epa.gov/greenvehicles/Index.do;jsessionid=8230bb3420316b523184.

Other Strategies for Greening Auto Travel

$ **Use mass transit.** When you're away on business, forgo the rental car and use mass transit or hotel shuttles whenever you can.

Ø **Carpool** when attending business meetings.

$ **Use electronic toll collection devices** (also called eToll devices) that allow you to skip cash payment lines and use automated toll collection lanes. Studies have shown that electronic toll collection reduces hydrocarbons and carbon monoxide emissions by 40–63% and reduces emissions of nitrogen oxides by 16%.[7] Some rental companies provide electronic toll collection devices for a fee.

$ Use GPS navigation to find the most direct and efficient route to your final destination.

Travel Agencies

If you prefer to use a travel agent for the convenience and service or to access their relationships with travel suppliers, the American Society of Travel Agents (ASTA) has a green certification program for qualifying travel agents. There are currently a few dozen ASTA green-certified travel agents in the United States. Ask your travel agent for a rundown of services and discounts available to your business.

To find a green-certified travel agent, go to www.travelsense .org/agents and select "green" from the ASTA Certified Specialist drop-down menu.

Green Meetings and Events

The waste associated with conferences, meetings, and events can be significant. Think about all the disposable utensils and paper—not to mention the promotional trinkets. Here are a number of greening strategies that won't diminish the impact of your meetings:

Ø **Don't serve bottled water.** By serving filtered tap water, you can save approximately $50 per attendee for a three-day meeting.

Ø **Eliminate disposable signs and dated materials.** Consider ways to create signage, badges, and other materials that can be saved and reused.

† **Donate leftover food.** Instead of throwing away unused food from an event, consider donating it to a local food bank or homeless shelter. Most cities and counties have at least one location where businesses can make food donations.

Go to Feeding America to locate a food bank near you at http:// feedingamerica.org/foodbank-results.aspx.

$$ Make sure you have a recycling plan in place. Having a sufficient number of well-marked recycling bins at events is a tangible way to show stakeholders your commitment to sustainability. Remember to make arrangements in advance to have materials transported to a recycling center following your meeting or event.

$$ Online registration from services like Eventbrite.com will save you time, money, and paper.

$$ Provide attendees with meeting handouts on a reusable flash drive. This tree-saving practice is also cheaper and easier than using paper handouts. There are a number of reasonably priced green and eco-friendly flash drives available. Another option is to use an online event service that can host meeting content digitally for download later.

$$ If you must use promotional giveaways, make them green. These days you can get a host of environmentally friendly promotional items ranging from customized aluminum water bottles to solar-powered laptop bags.

$–$$$ Source locally. Use local and sustainable produce, flowers, beverages, décor, and rentals.

$$–$$$ Carbon-balance your event. TerraPass will balance the environmental impact of your conference or company event with a carbon offset purchase. See "Offsetting Emissions" in Chapter 8 for a more in-depth discussion of carbon offsets.

TerraPass has an Event and Conference Carbon Footprint Calculator to determine an event's carbon output based on the number of people in attendance, and the number of flights and hotel rooms used at www.terrapass.com/event-carbon-calculator.

Eco-Tourism

Eco-tourism is travel to natural areas that conserve the environment and improve the well-being of local people.[8]

Does eco-tourism fit your business travel needs? It may make sense if there's a compelling reason to travel to a natural locale for team building, incentives, or a small conference. Keep in mind, however, that the carbon output of traveling to far-flung natural areas could quite possibly negate the benefits of choosing an eco-tourism destination. That said, there are a number of eco-lodges and eco-resorts in the United States. You can find a database of eco-tourism tour operators at www .ecotourism.org.

Offsets

$$$ Carbon offset your travel. Many of the major airlines, hotels chains, rental car agencies, and online travel agencies sell carbon offsets at the point of purchase.

15 GREEN PURCHASING

There is scarcely anything in the world that some man cannot make a little worse, and sell a little more cheaply. The person who buys on price alone is this man's lawful prey.

—John Ruskin, author, poet, and social critic

Whether your business is engaged in making something, selling something, or serving something, you use all kinds of materials and products in the process. Greening your purchasing involves thinking about your entire inbound supply chain with this overriding purpose in mind: to select and purchase goods and services that are affordable, *and* have the least possible environmental impact throughout the course of their life cycles—that is, during every phase including manufacturing, shipping/transportation, use, and recycling or disposal. Green purchasing does not always have to mean higher costs—although sometimes it will. By implementing some of the strategies described in this chapter—including a green procurement policy and green spend management—you can streamline your purchasing process, reduce overall costs, *and* improve your environmental footprint.

With any green purchasing program, the big question is this: How do you find and evaluate green alternatives to an endless list of everyday business products, such as paper goods, food products, raw materials, wholesale products, and construction materials? The answer depends on whether you're a manufacturer, retailer, or service provider. In fact, the definition of "environmentally preferable" varies from industry to industry, and from one business to another. Regardless of the type of business you operate, establishing environmental purchasing standards for *your* business—and invoking them in a purchasing policy—will take a lot of the guesswork out of your product and material choices.

 Environmentally preferable purchasing (EPP) is the practice of buying products and/or services that have a lesser or reduced impact on the environment and human health, when compared to competing products or services that serve the same purpose.

Defining the opportunity. Small businesses spend billions of dollars on goods and services each year. Every single one of those purchases has an impact on the environment. Whether you're buying copy paper or forklifts, that purchasing decision is an environmental decision. This is an area where small businesses can have an enormous impact. Given their tremendous collective purchasing power, small businesses can actually move the dial on the demand for environmentally friendly materials and products. If small businesses across the country increase demand for these products, it will promote innovation and expand the market for green products and materials; that, in turn, will reduce prices and allow a greater number of people to adopt environmentally friendly products and services. If that can happen, small business will be in a position to have an incredibly powerful, long-term impact on the environment. It will lead to an environmental paradigm shift in this country for which small businesses can take at least partial credit.

Best purchasing practices. There is no use in reinventing the wheel. When it comes to setting your green purchasing criteria, it can make sense to use or to follow established standards as guidelines—an approach that can save you time and provide you with a baseline for best practices. In general, the EPA's Environmentally Preferable Purchasing (EPP) standards are the most comprehensive green purchasing standards in the country. (See "EPP: Environmentally Preferable Purchasing" on page 230.)

🔗 Useful Internet links for setting standards:

- EPA and WaterSense efficiency standards and specifications for water-using fixtures and appliances at http://epa.gov/watersense/docs/matrix508.pdf.
- EPP efficiency standards and specifications for office products and furniture at www.epa.gov/epp/pubs/buying_green_online.pdf.
- Specifications for ENERGY STAR–rated products at www.energystar.gov/index.cfm?fuseaction=find_a_product.
- The EPA "WasteWi$e Tip Sheet on Buying or Manufacturing Recycled Products" at www.epa.gov/epawaste/partnerships/wastewise/pubs/buy.pdf.
- The Energy Information Administration's (EIA) Energy Efficiency "Appliance Standards and Labeling Related Links" at www.eia.doe.gov/emeu/efficiency/appliance_standards.html.
- Links to eighteen Greenseal "Choose Green" Reports at www.greenseal.org/resources/reports.cfm, covering eighteen purchasing categories from carpet to wood finishes and stains.
- EPEAT Purchaser Resources for Computer and Peripherals purchases at www.epeat.net/Procurement.aspx.
- WebBuyersGuide.com, free expert buying advice providing access to thousands of white papers, case studies, webcasts, and detailed listings for over 40,000 products and 17,000 companies.

Try to meet or exceed established standards such as these as much as you reasonably can. That being said, many represent the gold standard for sustainable purchasing. Meeting them may not always be financially feasible for a small business. Although you'll want to strive to achieve the highest possible level of sustainability, it may not always be possible to employ all the best practices set forth under the EPP or other established standards. At the very least, use them as a guide when establishing your purchasing criteria.

One reason to meet or exceed existing standards is because future efficiency standards are becoming—and will continue to become—more stringent. In a presidential memo issued in February 2009, President Obama called for new higher energy efficiency standards for an array of common appliances and more updated standards are sure to follow. So make sure the standards you use as guidelines are the most current.

EPP: ENVIRONMENTALLY PREFERABLE PURCHASING

On September 14, 1998, President Clinton signed Executive Order (EO)13101, titled "Greening the Government Through Waste Prevention, Recycling and Federal Acquisition," which led to the establishment of the current version of the EPA's Environmentally Preferable Purchasing program (EPP). It is the most comprehensive green purchasing program in the country. It provides guidance on how to identify and purchase environmentally preferable products and services so that government agencies can meet their executive order obligations. It details green criteria for hundreds of products and service categories.

✓ The EPA EPP site offers a tremendous amount of useful information on environmental purchasing in addition to specific information about product and service categories, environmental attributes within those categories, and methods for considering those attributes in purchasing decisions at www.epa.gov/epp.

> ✓ 🔗 The EPA EPP Green Purchasing Guides page includes general green purchasing guides and product- or service-specific guides at www.epa.gov/epp/pubs/green guides.htm.
> ✓ 🔗 Buying Green Online Report at www.epa.gov/epp/pubs/buying_green_online.pdf.

Taking action. The first step to greening your purchasing involves analyzing your spending. Once you have a clear idea of what you're buying, how much, and from what vendors, you can begin to look more closely at greening your spending practices. Ideally, you'll want to implement a green purchasing policy. Putting such a policy in place involves setting green purchasing priorities, establishing some environmental criteria for purchasing, and memorializing those standards in a formal policy. As soon as you've established a workable purchasing policy, be sure to communicate it to everyone on your staff who is authorized to make purchases. As part of the process of greening your purchasing, you'll also want to consider implementing spend management controls, an approach that allows you to manage and control spending more effectively. The steps involved in analyzing your spending and establishing a green purchasing policy, as well as the components of spend management, are outlined in this chapter.

Green Purchasing Practices

Green purchasing is something everyone can do. It's not an on-off switch. You can wade into it. You can identify key products that will make you green; you can often identify products that are going to save you money. You can change your purchasing patterns.

—Alex Szabo, CEO and cofounder, TheGreenOffice.com

Qualifying Green Materials: Basic Guidelines

There are certain attributes that distinguish green products and services from the alternatives. In general, greening opportunities fall into four basic categories:

1. Switching from toxic to nontoxic substances.
2. Reducing air emissions and hazardous waste.
3. Purchasing environmentally preferable materials and products.
4. Improving energy and water efficiency.

When making purchase decisions, look for these green attributes:

- Biobased content
- Energy efficient
- Eco-labels
- Nontoxic/reduced toxicity
- Rechargeable
- Recyclable
- Recycled content
- Remanufactured
- Reusable/Refillable
- Reduced/lightweight materials
- Locally sourced/near sourced
- Reduced packaging
- Recycled packaging

Green Materials

Biobased products are commercial or industrial products that are composed, in whole or in significant part, of biological products or renewable domestic agricultural or forestry materials.

Recycled content refers to the portion of a product, by weight or volume, that is composed of recovered materials.

Pre-consumer materials are recovered for recycling before a consumer uses them, such as fabric cuttings and scrap from paper manufacturing.

Post-consumer materials (also called post-consumer waste [PCW]) are recovered after having served the intended use as consumer items and have been diverted from solid waste for recycling such as used water bottles and old magazines.

Here are a few other basic guidelines for buying green products, greening your purchasing practices, and setting purchasing standards:

- Buy local. Sourcing products and materials locally is good for the environment and can often save you a lot of money. For example, most produce in the United States is shipped an average of 1,500 miles before being sold; as a result, more than 80% of the cost of food goes to shippers and other middlemen.[1]
- Use recycled content products everywhere you can. It is easy to source recycled content paper and products including consumables such as paper towels, napkins, toilet and facial tissue, trashcan liners, pens, and markers. Using reused and reclaimed materials is another option.
- Purchase remanufactured products whenever possible. Purchasing remanufactured products is a practical choice for products made out of interchangeable parts or for which replacement parts can be easily obtained. A wide variety of office products can be remanufactured. Ask your suppliers about the availability of everything from ink and toner cartridges to copiers and telephones to office furniture. Buying remanufactured products reduces the amount of material that goes to landfills. The downside is that remanufacturered

products are not equipped with the most current technology and may not be as efficient as new products.

■ Look for eco-labels—but choose carefully. Consider using reputable eco-labels when making purchasing decisions. For example, many companies require an EPEAT rating when buying new computers. The key is to only use eco-labels that are issued by independent third parties and recognized as legitimate.

■ Eliminate disposable items in the workplace. Use bagless vacuum cleaners. Provide customers with reusable shopping bags instead of plastic or paper. Ask customers if they need a bag or receipt instead of automatically providing one. Stock your break room or kitchen with reusable mugs, cups, plates, and cutlery. Provide cleaning cloths and sponges instead of paper towels. The list is endless.

■ Plan ahead to avoid expedited shipping. By planning ahead, you can eliminate shipping practices that are costly in terms of both dollars and the environmental impact.

■ Engage suppliers. Give preference to vendors that have environmental policies and initiatives in place. Also, task suppliers with helping you evaluate your current purchasing practices, and with helping you find cost-effective and environmentally preferable products and services. For example, when Princeton University asked their copy paper supplier, Boise Office Solutions, to provide purchasing data so that they could analyze their paper use, the supplier gave them essential information. It turned out that many departments were ordering a more expensive virgin paper instead of the less expensive 30% PCW paper.[2] Letting your suppliers do some of the homework not only will make your life easier, but also gives suppliers an economic incentive to provide greener offerings.

■ Buy cradle-to-cradle whenever possible. Try to purchase goods that are designed to be perpetually circulated in remanufacturing or recycling systems — not inevitably discarded. As John Ehrenfeld, executive director of the International Society for Industrial Ecology and former director of the MIT Program on Technology, Business, and Environment, says: "Reducing unsustainability (greening) is not the same as creating sustainability." This starts with, but is not limited to, using recycled content and biodegradable or recyclable products and materials everywhere you can economically do so. The highest order in purchasing is to buy only truly sustainable products and services.

Sourcing Suppliers

Once you've decided what products and services you can green, sourcing vendors and suppliers can be a challenge. If a product or service is hard to find, you may be able to find a consultant to help you — or you may have to be creative. Talk to other businesses in your area or your industry, and local business groups. Seek out community initiatives. For example, Project Green Fork, a nonprofit community initiative in Memphis, Tennessee, works with area restaurateurs to help them source everything from local produce to eco-friendly paper products to qualified recyclers. Trade association websites and trade magazines — with their supplier directories — can be an excellent place to start locating alternative suppliers.

Here are some insights into how to work with suppliers:

Fine-tune your supplier list. Once you've set some standards, start with your trusted and existing suppliers. Tell them of your new purchasing policies and give them the opportunity to continue to earn your business. And don't be shy about asking suppliers to improve their own environmental performance. It worked for Wal-Mart, and if enough customers ask, it will eventually have an impact. You may find, however, that you need new or additional vendors to meet your new needs. That will require you to do up-front research. How you go about this will depend on your purchasing needs, your geographic location, and your industry. For example, the construction industry has many excellent resources for finding green materials. Office supplies are another area where green products can easily be found. Again, talk to other businesses in your area and industry, and use local trade and business associations as resources.

Survey suppliers. Regardless of whether you use existing or new suppliers, develop a supplier questionnaire to help you compare vendors in terms of greenness, product availability, and price. (See Appendix B for a sample questionnaire.) You'll want to gather the following information:

- **Supplier greenness.** Ask about the supplier's environmental attributes, accreditations, and programs.
- **Product availability and shipping.** Are products available immediately and without expedited shipping? Are products available locally? Does the amount you need require a special order? If so, how long will it take to get it? Be sure to check for shipping charges or delivery surcharges.
- **Pricing.** Price breaks can be achieved at a variety of levels, depending on your needs. Ask for price per piece, unit pricing, and/or factory direct pricing. You may get the best price from a factory shipment, but if lead time is an issue, it may not be practical.
- **Specifications.** Be sure to include any supplier "spec" sheets that indicate compliance with the various criteria outlined in your purchasing policy.

Shop and search online. Certain product categories such as office supplies, office furniture, and electronics offer highly competitive pricing from conventional online retailers. In addition, online searches can yield valuable information about local suppliers with green credentials.

You'll want to join email lists to receive valuable online coupons and promotions.

👓 Sign up for Ebates.com, a free and automated rebate portal that lists thousands of online rebates, coupons, and cash-back offers as well as a "Shop Green" portal that takes you directly to the green section of retail web stores.

👓 Niche green office suppliers such TheGreenOffice.com are competitively priced and offer deep selections of green office supplies. The site's unique Green Screen feature helps shoppers quickly identify the relative greenness of specific products.

👓 Check out online coupon aggregators like RetailMeNot.com and FatWallet.com.

Don't Overlook Financial Incentives

When you're greening your purchasing practices, you'll be figuring costs into the equation. There are a number of financial incentives available to small businesses that invest in energy and other efficiency resources. Look into whether water or energy efficiency improvements are eligible for tax credits or rebates. Some jurisdictions offer tax credits or straight-out rebates for installing new, high-efficiency appliances, equipment, fixtures, and irrigation systems. There is also a federal deduction of up to $1.80 per square foot for energy efficiency upgrades to new and existing commercial buildings available for systems "placed in service" from January 1, 2006, through December 31, 2013. The 30% investment tax credits for solar energy and qualified fuel cell projects has also been extended to January 1, 2017.

👓 Check out these resources to determine if your project is eligible for incentives:

■ The Tax Incentives Assistance Project (TIAP) provides consumers and businesses with information about federal

CASE STUDY

FULL OF BEANS: FINDING RECYCLED AND ORGANIC MERCHANDISE

Mary Hutchens owns Full of Beans, an upscale children's clothing store in Washington, DC. When she started thinking about going green in 2008, purchasing was one of her biggest challenges. "It was one thing to recycle and start managing my energy efficiently, but finding suppliers for everything from recycled wrapping paper to organic clothing was a real challenge," she says. "At first, it was frustrating. None of my vendors offered recycled materials, and it was hard to find affordable clothing." By scouring the Internet, she discovered a cottage industry filled with new people who were producing organic cotton clothing—none of whom could afford to travel to New York for the major kids' retail show. "A lot of them are moms who are reentering the workforce," says Hutchens. "In the beginning, most of what they offered were small lines in infant sizes." Given the price, Hutchens changed her sales approach: "I'd tell my customers: It's made in the U.S. It's from a cottage industry. It's a really great product and we're trying to support

income tax incentives for energy-efficient products and technologies at www.energytaxincentives.org.
- U.S. Department of Energy consumer and business tax incentive information at www.energy.gov/taxbreaks.htm.
- U.S. Department of Energy: Energy Efficiency and Renewable Energy Tax Incentives for Energy Efficiency site at www1.eere.energy.gov/buildings/tax_incentives.html.
- The Database of State Incentives & Efficiency (DSIRE) is a comprehensive source of information on state, local, utility, and federal incentives that promote renewable energy and energy efficiency at www.dsireusa.org.

them." Her store's location, in a neighborhood where many of the residents are politically aware and concerned about the environment, made that strategy more effective.

By 2008, things had begun to change. "At the last show I went to, more of the larger vendors were finally adding a green part to their line. It seems they're just trying it out, so they're dedicating maybe 10% of their entire line to green offerings. It's a trial period—but at least the availability is increasing slightly," she says. In addition, some of her smaller vendors are adding toddler sizes. "I think everybody's going to get on this train," she says. "I'm just seeing more of it, for the first time."

As for the recycled packaging, major distributors are adding that as well. "Two years ago, it just wasn't available, but I think as more retailers express interest, the vendors are responding." All of which is good news for Hutchens, who caters to an upscale clientele and is dedicated to the idea of becoming more sustainable.

■ Incentives for ENERGY STAR purchases at www.energystar .gov/index.cfm?c=products.pr_tax_credits.

■ Incentives for water efficiency upgrades at www.epa.gov/ watersense/pp/find_rebate.htm.

■ The Fuel Efficient Vehicle Tax Incentives Information Center is available at www.fueleconomy.gov/Feg/taxcenter.shtml.

Private sector financing sources. Some private banks are starting to offer "green loans" for the financing of clean energy systems or energy efficiency improvements. Community banks often favor green loans. Check with your utility company, community bank, or commercial banker.

■Establishing a Green Purchasing Policy

While many companies have incorporated environmentally preferable purchasing principles into their operations, few have formal green purchasing programs in place. Even fewer attempt to collaborate with end-users, suppliers, and other supply chain partners. But going forward, if you choose to take these steps, you won't be alone. According to "Private Sector Pioneers," an EPA report on green procurement, more and more businesses are moving toward green purchasing practices, as well as the selection of like-minded vendors and suppliers. These businesses are motivated by four factors:

■ To satisfy customers
■ To distinguish a company from its competitors
■ To reduce costs
■ To participate in industry trends

Here are the basic steps for establishing a green procurement policy:

Step 1: Convene the green team. Developing green purchasing policies is one area where it really pays to have members of all areas of your company involved. Get input from end-users before you start setting new standards and policies, and enlist the support of your employees to research options and uncover opportunities. As the business owner, you may have the final say in purchasing decisions, but having your staff buy into the program will be the biggest factor in its success. For example, the decision to purchase reusable sponges may be yours, but if the cleaning staff believes that disposable cleaning cloths work better, those sponges will stay in the closet.

Step 2: Assess the opportunity. Enlist the support of your green team to help analyze your current purchasing practices by examining what you're spending, with which suppliers, and for what purpose. Then, use whatever resources you have at your disposal—including the EPA's EPP website; vendors and suppliers; local and national organizations and associations that serve your industry; and reputable green certification programs—to get ideas regarding environmentally preferable products and raw materials that might be appropriate for your business. Armed with that information, you can begin to set priorities for greening your purchasing policies. *Note: When you're developing purchasing policies, remember to include indirect expenses, such as office supplies and services, as well as direct expenses, such as materials needed in production and sales.*

Step 3: Set standards. Use the established government EPP standards for recycled paper and other products as guidelines when developing your own purchasing standards and use additional established industry standards for other product categories. Write these standards down as a formal policy. Establishing clear, written standards will eliminate confusion and facilitate on-the-spot decision making.

When setting standards for specific products, consider multiple environmental attributes, including:

- **Processing methods.** For example, bleaching is a key environmental difference among paper manufacturers.
- **Production certifications and eco-labels.** Do your homework. Find out what green certifications and eco-labels are attached to products and materials in your industry. Be wary of greenwashing. (See Chapter 4 for a discussion of eco-labels.)
- **Cost of transport and other supply chain issues.** Remember to incorporate the cost of transport—and associated sustainability issues—into your thinking. For example, a restaurant might make "buying local" a priority. A T-shirt manufacturer might require 100% organic cotton, but choose the supplier based on geography or shipping practices.

When formalizing your standards:

- Determine which attributes are requirements and which are preferences.

■ Create lists of approved products.

■ Establish environmental baselines for products. For example, define the minimum percentage of post-consumer recycled content for paper purchases, or require ENERGY STAR ratings for electronics and appliance purchases.

■ Create a list of all chemicals or processes to avoid.

Step 4: Take cost into account. In many cases, it will be possible to substitute environmentally preferable products without increasing cost. Regardless, as part of your standards, it is reasonable to require that green purchases be made at no more than a certain percentage premium cost parity. Talk to your vendors. Enlist their support in identifying savings opportunities that help meet your green goals. Before dismissing more expensive alternatives, investigate whether extra costs can be counteracted by higher efficiency, such as using high-yield ink, or by modest customer surcharges. Consider using the spend management approach outlined in this chapter to help you manage costs while going green. In addition, you'll want to figure financial incentives—such as rebates and tax credits into your analysis. (See "Don't Overlook Financial Incentives," page 237.)

Step 5: Phase in new products and materials. A phased approach allows you to test environmentally preferable products and materials to determine their efficacy before purchasing large quantities. This will allow you to maintain high quality standards. And don't forget the small stuff like greening basic office supplies or getting rid of the fax machine. When it comes to establishing green business practices, there's a difference between resources used in primary business activities and secondary ones. Green strategies involving the resources necessary for primary activities must be vetted more carefully than those related to secondary activities. For example, a restaurant has to think differently about whether to eliminate carryout cups compared to a real estate agency. Conversely, a real estate agency has to think differently than a restaurant about whether to use hybrid vehicles.

Green Spend Management

Remember Chip Rankin from EBC Carpet, whose effort to downsize his fleet was featured in a case study in Chapter 12? Motivated by the desire to increase fuel efficiency for the fleet of vans leased by his carpet cleaning franchise, Rankin asked his staff to conduct an eight-week analysis of the size of his cleaning crews relative to the size of the vans being used to transport them. As you may recall, he discovered that the company was using a lot of large vans to transport small crews. As a result, he began the transition to smaller vehicles, with an aim of moving his fleet to 50% small vehicles and 50% large vehicles. In the process, he significantly improved fuel efficiency and reduced leasing costs. That's the essence of spend management. It involves methodically analyzing, centralizing, and managing spending to increase efficiency. In Rankin's case, the analysis was done without the use of a computer model. And theoretically, any company that systematically examines its expenditures and spending patterns is engaged in spend management. But generally, spend management makes use of technology—in the form of spend management software—that enables you to control and monitor purchasing activities, and keep track of how much you're spending on what types of goods and services. The end result: more control over spending, greater efficiency, and lower overall costs. Spend management results in savings for a number of reasons—from getting better deals with suppliers and avoiding "maverick" or off-contract spending. An October 2008 Aberdeen Group analysis found that companies that leverage their spending information in purchasing save 67% more than companies that do not.

 Spend management refers to the systematic, sometimes technology-enabled, management of what you spend, with whom, and for what. The term encompasses processes and functions such as outsourcing, purchasing, e-procurement, and supply chain management.

Green spend management is a purchasing strategy for improving environmental performance, but it's also a viable approach to managing costs and creating long-term, sustainable value. Depending on the size and type of business you operate, it may or may not make sense to implement a technology-based spend management solution. If your expenditures on purchasing exceed $500,000 a year, then it might make sense for you to invest in an outsourced spend management system. Businesses that spend less might consider Staples Business Advantage spend management services for office products and services. Regardless, you'll want to start analyzing what you buy, from whom, and at what cost in aggregate—because it provides a way to categorize your purchasing, and identify current and potential suppliers by category. For example, in Rankin's case, he looked at the category of vehicle leasing and fuel efficiency relative to his actual needs.

Here are the basic steps involved in a conventional spend management program, many of which can be implemented without a dedicated or technology-enabled system:

- Analyze spending. Determine, in aggregate, what you're spending, with whom, and for what purpose. Use this information to categorize purchasing, and identify current and potential suppliers by category. Determine where you spend the most and what expenditures you might be able to eliminate or reduce, and where you might switch to environmentally preferable purchases.
- Centralize your purchasing. The fewer people with the authority to make purchases, the more likely you are to adhere to your purchasing policies, avoid redundant purchases, and earn contractual savings. If it's not possible to centralize, make sure purchasing policies are communicated to and understood by all staff members.
- Eliminate "maverick" spending. "Maverick" spending occurs when a staff member buys something that falls outside your

purchasing system. It can involve everything from not adhering to environmental criteria to shopping retail instead of using a preferred supplier with whom you've negotiated a contract at a discounted rate. When employees make impromptu purchases, they generally abandon purchasing standards. The result: increased costs and/or compromised standards. Centralized purchasing goes a long way to preventing maverick spending.

■ Consolidate suppliers. By combining purchases and directing them toward one or a few suppliers, you'll be in a better position to take advantage of volume discounts. You can also often save money on shipping and handling by making fewer and larger orders, which also leads to lower transportation emissions. If your current suppliers are not able to provide environmentally preferable products or volume discounts, consider replacing them. Initially, this might involve expanding the number of suppliers you use, and then reducing them once new ways to consolidate have been identified.

If you don't have the budget to finance a third-party spend management system, there are other approaches that can yield similar results. Even a well-designed Excel spreadsheet combined with a good working relationship with your accounting department can yield efficiencies and savings. Another approach: Link employee incentives to specific internal goals. For example, provide bonuses for meeting specific targets — such as achieving a 5–10% reduction in costs *and* increasing the amount of 100% PCW products by 20%. This will surely motivate staff to get costs down and meet your environmental goals.

If you already employ spend management practices in your business, you'll want to integrate your green purchasing policies into your overall program. If not, consider implementing a spend management program with a green spin on it — to maximize your cost savings while you green your business.

E-PROCUREMENT

E-procurement is a technology-enabled way to streamline purchasing by using Internet technology. It's a strategy for centralizing purchasing, controlling costs, sourcing vendors, and greening your purchasing. Think of eBay, which automates purchasing procedures and processes online. eBay is the consumer version of e-procurement in that it creates a marketplace for one buyer and many suppliers, or one supplier and many buyers. With e-procurement, you use an online marketplace to source products and services. You can list the type of product or materials you need, the specifications (including green specifications), how the bidding process will work, how suppliers will be scored, and other requirements. Suppliers are then invited to register online and "bidding" occurs for a set period of time. At the end, the contract award can be based on the criteria of your choosing. Once contracts are established, you can then create an online catalog for staff that includes only products and services that you have approved for purchase at the approved pricing. Using e-procurement is inherently green because it can reduce paper processes. But just as importantly, it can help you maintain green specifications—and manage costs.

Making It Work

Your green purchasing policy will only work if your employees comply with the standards you've set. As mentioned earlier, get employees to buy into the process from the very beginning. Just as importantly, once your purchasing policies have been established, communicate those standards—to avoid costly "maverick" spending and purchasing that falls outside your environmental guidelines.

Educate employees. Communicate your new policies in employee newsletters, intranets, and staff meetings. Also, improve the staff's green purchasing knowledge by providing the basic definitions and information for understanding your new environmental specifications.

Educate customers. Be sure to include statements on your product packaging about how much total and PCW recycled materials have been used, biodegradability, reduced chemical content, and third-party certifications. Include this information on your website and product literature.

For more information on communicating your green practices and objectives to employees and customers, see Chapter 6.

RESOURCES

1 WHAT DOES GOING GREEN MEAN?

General Green Sites

- Business.GOV's Green Business Guide at www.business.gov/guides/environment.
- Ecopreneurist.com, advice for eco-entrepreneurs.
- Environmental News Network featuring environmental headline news at www.enn.com.
- Environmental Protection Agency's Small Business Gateway at www.epa.gov/smallbusiness.
- Greenbiz.com, a leading green business site and portal.
- GreenBiz.com's State of Green Business 2009 at www.stateofgreenbusiness.com.
- *Harvard Business Review*'s Leading Green blog at http://blogs.harvardbusiness.org/leadinggreen.
- "The Practical Guide to Environmental Management for Small Business," a comprehensive guide from the EPA Small Business Division at www.smallbiz-enviroweb.org/html/pdf/EM_Guide0902.pdf.
- TreeHugger.com, the web's most popular green site.
- TriplePundit.com, business in the context of today's environmental and social challenges.
- Flex Your Power, California's statewide energy efficiency marketing and outreach campaign, includes best practice and purchasing guides at www.fypower.org.

Green Directories

- Best Green Blogs, a green blog directory, at www.bestgreenblogs.com.
- EcoBusinessLinks' Green Directory, a directory of green links

with more than 300 categories and 11,000 links at www
.ecobusinesslinks.com.

Climate Change

- The Environmental Defense Fund's Global Warming Myths and
  Facts at www.edf.org/page.cfm?tagID=1011.
- The Climate Change 2007 Report from the Intergovernmental
  Panel on Climate Change at www.ipcc.ch/ipccreports/ar4-syr
  .htm and Frequently Asked Questions at www.ipcc.ch/pdf/
  assessment-report/ar4/wg1/ar4-wg1-faqs.pdf.
- National Geographic's Global Warming Fast Facts at http://
  news.nationalgeographic.com/news/2004/12/1206_041206_
  global_warming.html.
- National Oceanic and Atmospheric Administration's (NOAA)
  Global Warming Frequently Asked Questions at www.ncdc
  .noaa.gov/oa/climate/globalwarming.html.
- The Nature Conservatory's Fast Facts About Climate Change
  from www.nature.org/initiatives/climatechange/activities/
  art19631.html.
- *New Scientist*'s Climate Change: A Guide for the Perplexed at
  www.newscientist.com/article/dn11462.
- Pew Center on Global Climate Change's Global Warming Facts
  and Figures at www.pewclimate.org/global-warming-basics/
  facts_and_figures.
- The Union of Concerned Scientists' Global Warming 101 at
  www.ucsusa.org/global_warming/global_warming_101/.
- World Business Council for Sustainable Development's
  Facts and Trends to 2050: Energy and Climate Change at
  www.wbcsd.org/includes/getTarget.asp?type=d&id=MTA2NDY.
- World Health Organization's 10 Facts on Climate Change and
  Health at www.who.int/features/factfiles/climate_change/en/
  index.html.

▓**2** GETTING STARTED

- ENERGY STAR for Small Business at www.energystar.gov/
  index.cfm?c=small_business.sb_index.
- "The Sustainable Office Toolkit," a set of resources and tools
  developed by P²AD to help offices of all types and sizes become
  more sustainable at www.p2ad.org/toolkit.

▓**3** GREEN OPPORTUNITIES

- "How to Write an Environmental Policy" at www.envirowise
  .gov.uk/page.aspx?o=Ref012.
- Wikipedia on SWOT analysis at http://en.wikipedia.org/wiki/
  SWOT_analysis.
- "Use SWOT to Kick-Start Your Planning" at www.entrepreneur
  .com/startingabusiness/businessplans/businessplancoachtim
  berry/article182034.html.
- "SWOT Analysis: A Peek Behind the Curtain" at http://
  entrepreneurs.about.com/od/businessplan/a/swotanalysis.htm.

▓**4** THINKING GREEN

General Thinking Green Resources
- "Practical Guide to Environmental Management for Small
  Business," by the EPA Small Business Division at www
  .smallbiz-enviroweb.org/html/pdf/EM_Guide0902.pdf.
- ENERGY STAR for Small Business at www.energystar.gov/
  index.cfm?c=small_business.sb_index.
- Center for Small Business and the Environment, information
  about how to invest in energy efficiency at www.aboutcsbe.org.

Advocacy
- National Small Business Association (NSBA). Although
  environmental issues are not a priority item for this national

advocacy group, they do important work in this area from time to time at www.nsba.biz.
- Small Business California, a small business organization with a strong interest in environmental issues at www.small businesscalifornia.org.
- The National Small Business Association's Action Network at www.capwiz.com/nsbaonline/mlm/signup.
- The Center for American Progress (CAP) has information on energy and environment policies that can be accessed by RSS feeds and issue alerts at www.americanprogress.org; CAP also runs political action campaigns at www .americanprogressaction.org.
- "Write to Congress" web stickers and a list of contact information for elected officials including the president, members of Congress, governors, state legislators, and local officials at www.capwiz.com/nsbaonline.
- *The Hill*'s White Papers Portal contains issue research on energy, the environment, and a variety of other topics at www .thehill.com/whitepapers.

Third-Party Certification
- Bcorporation.net certifies companies as having implemented social and environmental standards.
- Green America's Business Seal of Approval program certifies companies and lists them as green businesses in a National Green Pages directory at www.coopamerica.org/greenbusiness/ sealofapproval.cfm.
- OnePercentForThePlanet.org certifies that companies donate 1% of sales to environmental nonprofits.
- The Green Restaurant Association, a national certification program at www.dinegreen.com.
- GreenPlumbers, a national training and certification program at www.greenplumbersusa.com.

- The Association of Energy and Environmental Real Estate Professionals (AEEREP) awards the EcoBroker certification to commercial and residential real estate brokers at www.ecobroker.com.
- ASTA's (American Society of Travel Agents) Green Program consists of educational and promotional resources for member travel agents and suppliers at www.asta.org.

Eco-Labels

- GreenerChoices.org, a site by Consumers Union, the nonprofit publisher of *Consumer Reports*, has everything you need to know about eco-labels, including a searchable database, excellent information about what makes a good eco-label, and a glossary at www.greenerchoices.org/eco-labels/eco-home.cfm.
- An independent guide to hundreds of eco-labels is www.ecolabelling.org.

5 DEVELOPING YOUR PLAN

General Planning Resources

- Building Owners and Managers Association (BOMA) International and the "Guide to Writing a Commercial Real Estate Lease, Including Green Lease Language" (aka "The BOMA Green Lease Guide") at www.boma.org.

Calculators

- The EPA provides links to several key environmental calculators on one page at www.epa.gov/climatechange/wycd/waste/tools.html.
- An excellent energy use calculator for business can be found at www.energyguide.com.
- An excellent list of links to easy-to-use online conservation calculators at www.niagaraconservation.com/calculators.html.
- Generic ROI Calculator at www.solutionmatrix.com/download-center.html.

■ The Office Footprint Calculator uses information on employee transportation, facility construction, energy use, waste output, office supplies, and computers to calculate the "global acres" required to support activities and the carbon emissions that result at www.thegreenoffice.com/footprint.

■ The EPA's Greenhouse Gas Footprint Calculator provides a quick, rough estimate of your emissions, and information about easy ways to lower your footprint without buying offsets at www.epa.gov/climatechange/emissions/ind_calculator .html.

■ The Office of the Federal Environmental Executive's paper calculator compares the environmental impacts of papers made with different levels of post-consumer recycled content at www .ofee.gov/recycled/cal-index.asp.

■ The Federal Energy Management Program provides links to calculators that determine costs savings from buying a range of energy-efficient products. The site includes separate calculators for about thirty items, from lightbulbs to commercial air conditioners at www1.eere.energy.gov/femp/procurement/ eep_eccalculators.html.

■ ENERGY STAR's Financial Value Calculator at www.energystar .gov/ia/business/financial_value_calculator.xls.

■ ENERGY STAR's Cash Flow Opportunity Calculator at www .energystar.gov/ia/business/cfo_calculator.xls.

■ ScoreCard.org will generate a user-friendly web report about how clean your air and water is by zip code.

■ A clearinghouse for water conservation resources including the WaterWiser Drip calculator for measuring leakage is available at www.awwa.org/Resources/content.cfm?ItemNumber=29269 &navItemNumber=1561.

■ ENERGY STAR CFL bulb replacement ROI calculator at www.energystar.gov/ia/business/bulk_purchasing/bpsavings_ calc/CalculatorCFLs.xls.

■ GE Energy-Smart CFL ROI Calculator at www.gelighting.com/
na/home_lighting/products/pop_lighting_calc.htm.

6 COMMUNICATE. COMMUNICATE. COMMUNICATE.

General Resources

■ The Federal Trade Commission's guidelines for the use of
environmental marketing claims at www.ftc.gov/bcp/grnrule/
guides980427.htm.

■ The marketing agency BBMG issues free white papers,
webinars, and other valuable resources about green marketing
at www.bbmg.com.

Greenwash

■ TerraChoice's Six Sins of Greenwashing at www.terrachoice
.com/Home/Six_Sins_of_Greenwashing.

■ The Greenpeace greenwash criteria at www.stopgreenwash.org/
criteria.

Signs

■ www.recyclereminders.com/Recycling-Signs/Free-Recycling-
Signs.aspx has free customizable, downloadable recycling and
waste reduction signs.

■ The California Integrated Waste Management Board offers
colorful posters and stickers to download for free to
California businesses at www.ciwmb.ca.gov/BIZWASTE/
Posters.

Public Relations

■ Green Options Media at www.greenoptionsmedia.com.

■ Greener World Media at www.greenbiz.com.

■ Environmental News Network (ENN) at www.enn.com.

Social Media

■ Traffikd.com, a social media and Internet marketing blog.

- Care2.com, an online community for people interested in healthy, sustainable lifestyles.
- Change.org, a cause-driven online community.
- The event calendar at Greenbiz.com at www.greenbiz.com/ resources/view_calendar.
- The event calendar at SustainableIndustries.com at www .sustainableindustries.com/events/submissions.

7 REDUCING WASTE AND RECYCLING

General Resources
- The EPA FAQ database at http://waste.custhelp.com/cgi-bin/ waste.cfg/php/enduser/std_alp.php.
- WasteWi$e website at www.epa.gov/epawaste/partnerships/ wastewise.
- "Setting Up a Recycling Program at Your Small Business" at www.ct.gov/dep/cwp/view.asp?a=2714&q=324900&depNav_ GID=1645.
- WasteWi$e Helpline at 800-EPA-WISE (372-9473).
- Recycler's World at www.recycle.net.

Reducing Business Junk Mail
- Global Stewards junk mail reduction tips at www .globalstewards.org/junkmail.htm.
- More junk mail reduction tips at www.nativeforest.org/stop_ junk_mail/nfn_junk_mail_guide.htm.

Other Reuse Resources
- Redo.org, a nonprofit that promotes reuse, at www.redo.org.
- The Freecycle Network at Freecycle.org is made up of thousands of groups with millions of members who give and get stuff for free.

Other Recycling Resources

■ Earth911.org for good recycling information and a recycling search tool to locate waste collectors and drop-off sites.

■ Definitions of plastics resin codes at www.americanchemistry .com.

■ The Coca-Cola/NRC Recycling Bin Grant Program provides bins to selected grant recipients for the collection of beverage container recyclables in public settings at www .bingrant.org.

E-Waste and E-Cycling

■ Find a legitimate e-cycler—many of which provide convenient mail-in service from any state—at www.ban.org/pledge/ Locations.html.

■ For an interactive map of state e-waste legislation, go to www .electronicstakeback.com/legislation/state_legislation.htm.

■ A list of manufacturers with take-back programs at www .electronicstakeback.com/corporate/who_takes_back.htm.

■ An excellent list of manufacturer and retail programs and general information about the proper disposal and recycling of e-waste at www.earth911.com/electronics/proper-disposal-and-recycling-of-e-waste.

■ CollectiveGood.com is the mobile devices recycling resource for mobile phones, pagers or PDAs, and related accessories.

■ The Rechargeable Battery Recycling Corporation (RBRC) at www.rbrc.org is a nonprofit organization that collects old cell phones and rechargeable batteries. Their Call2Recycle program provides free collection boxes and plastic shipping envelopes.

■ The Federal Electronics Challenge has a variety of excellent resources including checklists, guidelines, and posters at www .federalelectronicschallenge.net/resources/eolmngt.htm.

■ The EPA's e-cycling site includes listings of donation and recycling programs for computers, cell phones, and other electronics at www.epa.gov/epawaste/conserve/materials/ecycling.

8 ENERGY MANAGEMENT

General Energy Conservation Resources

- U.S. Department of Energy Office of Energy Efficiency and Renewable Energy (EERE) at www.eere.energy.gov.
- U.S. Department of Energy ENERGY STAR program at www.energystar.gov.
- The DOE Office of Energy Efficiency and Renewable Energy's (EERE) Information Center Q&A at www1.eere.energy.gov/informationcenter.
- U.S. Department of Energy primer on insulation at www.ornl.gov/sci/roofs+walls/insulation/ins_01.html.
- www.DSIRE.org is a comprehensive source of information on state, local, utility, and federal incentives and policies that promote renewable energy and energy efficiency.

Clean Energy

- The Green Power Partnership provides green power advice, technical support, tools, and resources at www.epa.gov/greenpower.
- "PV vs. Solar Thermal" by Jonathan Lesser and Nicholas Puga at www.bateswhite.com/news/pdf/07012008_Business Money.pdf.
- Green-e.org, an independent consumer protection program for the sale of renewable energy and greenhouse gas reductions.

Energy Management Planning Resources

- Guidelines for Energy Management at www.energystar.gov/index.cfm?c=guidelines.guidelines_index.
- Climate Savers Computing Initiative at www.climatesavers

computing.org includes resources for greening IT and a Smart Computing product catalog.

- LocalCooling.com, a free application that automatically optimizes your PC's power consumption.
- "What's Better, Solar Thermal or Solar PV?" at www .solarpowerauthority.com/archives/lee-devlin/2008/07.

General/Green IT Resources

- *Green IT for Dummies* (John Wiley & Sons) is an excellent introductory resource. Also, HP sponsored a free, condensed, limited edition "Green IT for Dummies" guide for download at www.hp.com/hpinfo/globalcitizenship/environment/ productdesign/greenit4dummies.html.
- The Electronic Product Environmental Assessment Tool (EPEAT) at www.epeat.net.
- EU Standby Initiative's energy efficiency benchmarks for data centers at re.jrc.ec.europa.eu/energyefficiency/html/standby_ initiative.htm.
- Berkeley Lab Standby website provides information about how to reduce standby power at www.standby.lbl.gov.
- Infoworld.com, an excellent resource for general IT information.
- SmallBusinessComputing.com, an online magazine about small business IT needs.
- GreenerComputing.com, a resource for green IT information.
- InfoWorld Sustainable IT blog at http://weblog.infoworld.com/ sustainableit.

Online Shopping Resources

- An online store for power monitoring devices and solutions at www.powermeterstore.com.
- Manufacturers of EnergyMiser outlet plugs and products at www.usatech.com/energy_management/.

9 WATER CONSERVATION

General Water Conservation Resources

- EPA's water conservation site at www.epa.gov/oaintrnt/water/index.htm.
- EPA water conservation techniques at www.epa.gov/seahome/watcon.html.
- WaterSense, a partnership with the EPA, at www.epa.gov/watersense/index.htm.
- EPA Office of Water (OW) site at www.epa.gov/OW/index.html.

Planning Resources

- GreenPlumbersUSA.com lists plumbers across America who have been certified by participating in their training and accreditation program.
- Information about the EPA's GreenChill program at www.epa.gov/greenchill including a list of participating manufacturers at www.epa.gov/greenchill/gcpartners.html.
- A clearinghouse of water conservation resources including the WaterWiser Drip calculator for measuring leakage at www.awwa.org/Resources/content.cfm?ItemNumber=29269&navItemNumber=1561.

Parts and Products

- Weatherization, water, and energy conservation products at www.amconservationgroup.com and www.niagaraconservation.com.
- Reviews of low-flow toilets by plumber Terry Love at www.terrylove.com/crtoilet.htm.

Green Cleaning

- www.greencleaningfordummies.com, sponsored by the ISSA.
- www.ISSA.com/green is the Worldwide Cleaning Industry green cleaning portal.

■ CleanLink.com is the green cleaning portal for sanitary supply distributors, building service contractors, and in-house cleaning professionals.

Landscaping and Irrigation Resources

■ Water savings estimates and practices from the National Environmentally Sound Production Agriculture Laboratory (NESPAL) at the University of Georgia's College of Agricultural and Environmental Sciences at www.nespal.org/SIRP/IWC/Report/consprac.tbl980728.pdf.

■ Xeriscaping information at www.pubs.caes.uga.edu/caespubs/pubcd/B1073/B1073.htm.

■ Links to several states' greywater policies and laws at www.oasisdesign.net/greywater/law/index.htm.

■ A primer on cisterns and water catchment systems at www.greenbuilder.com/sourcebook/RainwaterGuide3.html.

■ A primer on harvesting rainwater for landscape use at www.ag.arizona.edu/pubs/water/az1052/harvest.html.

10 GREEN OFFICE SUPPLIES

Practical Resources

■ An excellent primer on copy paper choices at www.recycleworks.org/paper/copy_paper.html.

■ An excellent resource for help in making paper choices at www.conservatree.com.

General Parts and Products

■ CleanLink.com is an information resource for sanitary supply distributors, building service contractors, and in-house cleaning professionals.

■ TheGreenOffice.com is an online retailer with an excellent rating system as well as helpful webinars and an offset program.

■ www.ciwmb.ca.gov/WPIE/Electronics/InkAndToner.htm offers general information on computer and printer ink and toner cartridge reuse and recycling as well as a good list of cartridge reuse and recycling programs.

■ Visit www.cartridgeworldusa.com to locate a retail ink cartridge refiller near you.

Paperless Solutions

■ For electronic faxing services comparisons, go to www .faxcompare.com.

■ Two popular electronic signature services are www .echosign.com and www.docusign.com.

■ For a list of hosted CRM solutions, go to www.insidecrm.com/ whitepaper/hosted-crm-buyers-guide (free site registration required).

Remanufactured Office Products

■ The Business Products Industry Association (BPIA) report on Recycled Office Furniture at www.greenerbuildings.com/files/ document/O16F3340.pdf.

■ Greenseal's Choose Green Report on Office Products at www .greenseal.org/resources/reports/CGR_officesupplies.pdf.

11 GREEN HUMAN RESOURCES

General Green HR Resources

■ Valuable articles about all things HR at www.hreonline.com.

■ About.com HR provides information, links, tools, standard HR forms, and other HR-related material at www.humanresources .about.com.

■ HR.com touts itself as the largest social network and online community of HR executives.

■ An HR portal community with information about vendors and providers at www.hrvillage.com.

HR Technology

- HR and technology information, including an online buyers guide, at www.ihrim.org.
- HR World's list of key payroll providers and a comparison of the most important purchasing factors at www.hrworld.com/whitepaper/pdf/smb-payroll-comparison-guide_Mar08.pdf (free site registration necessary).

Benefits

- BenefitsLink.com offers information about benefits providers and more.
- "How to Go Green: Public Transportation" at www.planetgreen.discovery.com/go-green/public-transportation.
- Carticipate, a social network carpool application on the iPhone and Facebook, is available at www.carticipate.com.
- Avego, a rideshare application on the iPhone, at www.avego.com.
- Ecorio, a rideshare and carbon footprint calculator application, at www.ecorio.org.
- Google Transit at www.google.com/transit.

Telecommuting

- Tools for implementing a commuter benefits program at www.bestworkplaces.org/employ/index.htm.
- www.undress4success.com is a great telecommuting blog.
- Telecommuting resources including a step-by-step telecommuting program guide and forms for telecommuter assessments, policies, and agreements at http://egov.oregon.gov/ENERGY/TRANS/Telework/telehm.shtml.
- www.rideshare-directory.com, a list of national and local rideshare sites.
- www.goosenetworks.com, a free rideshare widget for websites.

Recruiting and Training

■ www.ere.net offers information and networking for recruiters and HR professionals.

■ *Training Magazine* at www.trainingmag.com.

12 GREEN TRANSPORTATION AND SHIPPING

General Resources

■ SmartWay partner list at www.epa.gov/smartway/transport/ partner-list/index.htm.

■ SmartWay Transport home page at www.epa.gov/smartway/ transport/index.htm.

■ www.eyefortransport.com, a leading provider of logistics and transportation information.

■ "The CFO's Guide to Transportation Spend Management" white paper at www.cfo.com/whitepapers/index.cfm/display whitepaper/11046312?f=search.

■ Online Buyer's Guide to Green Forklifts at www.buyerzone .com/industrial/forklifts/sst-forklift-trends.html.

■ Green ratings of popular shipping companies at www .climatecounts.org.

■ UPS fleet tips for improving gas mileage at www.pressroom.ups .com/mediakits/factsheet/0,1889,1314,00.html.

Trucking Resources

■ Backhaul load finder database at www.truck-loads.net/index.asp.

■ The Fleet Optimization Center, a service from the National Private Truck Council (NPTC) that helps private fleets find backhaul freight is available at www.chrwtrucks.com.

■ A backhaul matching resource at www.bestroutes.com/ truckstops.html.

■ Global coverage of shipping and the environment at www .sustainableshipping.com.

13 GREEN MARKETING AND COMMUNICATIONS

General Green Marketing and Communications Resources

- The Sustainable Advertising Partnership, a nonprofit organization with tools for promoting sustainability in the advertising industry at www.sustainableadvertisingpartnership .org.
- The Direct Marketing Association's Environmental Resource Center at www.dmaresponsibility.org/Environment.
- The Direct Marketing Association's Recycle Please Resources for Business at www.dmaresponsibility.org/Recycle/ Recycleplease_Resources.html.
- The Federal Trade Commission guidelines for the use of environmental marketing claims at www.ftc.gov/bcp/grnrule/ guides980427.htm.

Direct Mail

- Smart Addresser Lite mail verification software for small businesses at www.smartsoftusa.com/downloads/sa5/ SA5%20LT_Comparison_Chart.pdf.

Market Research

- www.surveymonkey.com, free online surveys.
- www.zoomerang.com, free online surveys.
- www.questionpro.com, free online surveys.
- www.ask500people.com, a quick and inexpensive online tool for surveying groups of independent respondents.

Packaging

- The Sustainable Packaging Coalition at www.sustainable packaging.org.

- Inside Sustainable Packaging, a well-respected blog by the makers of Globe Guard recycled packing materials at http://blog.salazarpackaging.com.
- From the producers of *Packaging World* magazine, an excellent resource for all things packaging-related at www.packworld.com.
- Packaging Digest, another excellent resource for all things packaging-related at www.packagingdigest.com.

Online Advertising

- Brickfish, the online social media advertising platform that employs user-generated content and social media to connect brands with consumers at www.brickfish.com.
- Genius Rocket, an online clearinghouse crowdsource that employs user-generated content and social media to connect marketers and creative people at www.genius rocket.com.
- Adwords, Google's advertising platform for advertisements served on Google.com and partner sites, at www.adwords .google.com.
- "Social Media Marketing Tactics" at www.seomoz.org/article/social-media-marketing-tactics.
- www.traffikd.com, a social media and Internet marketing blog, including a comprehensive list of social media and social networking sites, at www.traffikd.com/social-media -websites.
- B-2-B social communities at www.socialmediatoday.com.

Promotional Materials

- Proformagreen.com, a supplier of eco-friendly promotional products.
- Hallmark's Green Business holiday cards at www.hallmark .businessgreetings.com/7001-4600-3-0.

Coupons

- www.retailmenot.com, a coupon codes aggregator.
- Commission Junction, affiliate marketing and managed search services at www.cj.com.
- LinkShare, online marketing solutions at www.linkshare.com.
- Shareasale, affiliate marketing services at www.shareasale.com.

14 GREEN BUSINESS TRAVEL

General Resources

- "Taking Control of Travel Costs" white paper at www.cfo.com/whitepapers/index.cfm/displaywhitepaper/10339453?f=search.
- Information about the EPA SmartWay program at www.epa.gov/smartway/vehicles/smartway-certified.htm.
- A sustainable tourism information portal at http://destinet.ew.eea.europa.eu.
- MeetingStrategiesWorldwide.com has online resources for green meetings.
- Meeting Professionals International, the largest association of conference organizers, has lots of green meetings tips on MPIweb.org, including tips on how to hold a carbon-neutral event and Green Meetings encyclopedia.
- RezHub.com offers a green travel hub for booking green hotels and hybrid rental cars, and participating in carbon offsetting programs. The green hub features a Sort by Green Score and offers a unique profit-sharing/rebate program for businesses of all sizes at www.rezhub.com/GreenTravel/tabid/118/Default.aspx.
- Feeding America Food Bank Locator at www.feedingamerica.org/foodbank-results.aspx.
- The TerraPass Event and conference carbon footprint calculator at www.terrapass.com/event-carbon-calculator.

Teleconferencing and Web Conferencing

- Web-conferencing software reviews at http://reviews.cnet .com/1990-6454_7-6212812-1.html.
- www.conferzone.com for guidance on web conferencing including terminology, questions to ask when deciding on a web-conferencing solution site, and the latest web-conferencing research.
- www.webseminarian.com provides web-conferencing news, reviews, and opinions.

Green Travel Suppliers

- EPA's ENERGY STAR for Hospitality Rating at www .energystar.gov/index.cfm?c=hospitality.bus_hospitality and click through to the Hospitality Partners and Labeled Hotels links.
- Green Hotel Certification at www.greenhotelcertification.com/ hotels.html.
- Green Seal's Certification for Lodging Properties at www .greenseal.org/findaproduct/lodging_properties.cfm.
- DestiNet, a sustainable tourism information portal, has a comprehensive list of links to global travel certifying organizations at http://destinet.ew.eea.europa.eu/policies_ resources/fol954381/fol703514/fol442810.

Carbon Offset Programs

- Download "A Consumer's Guide to Retail Carbon Offset Providers" by Clean Air-Cool Planet (2006) at www.cleanair -coolplanet.org/ConsumersGuidetoCarbonOffsets.pdf.
- Guidance on setting up an offset program at www.smart aboutcarbon.com/businesses.php.

15 GREEN PURCHASING

General Green Purchasing Resources

- www.purchasing.com, an excellent trade magazine covering a variety of purchasing topics.

- TheGreenOffice.com has an excellent webinar on green purchasing basics (fee).

Green Purchasing Standards

- The EPA Environmentally Preferable Purchasing (EPP) home page at www.epa.gov/epp.
- The EPA Environmentally Preferable Purchasing (EPP) Green Purchasing Guides page includes general green purchasing guides and product- or service-specific guides at www.epa.gov/epp/pubs/greenguides.htm.
- Buying Green Online Report at www.epa.gov/epp/pubs/buying_green_online.pdf.
- The EPA and WaterSense efficiency standards and specifications for water-using fixtures and appliances at www.epa.gov/watersense/docs/matrix508.pdf.
- Specifications for more than fifty categories of ENERGY STAR–rated products at www.energystar.gov/index.cfm?fuseaction=find_a_product.
- The EPA "WasteWi$e Tip Sheet on Buying or Manufacturing Recycled Products" at www.epa.gov/epawaste/partnerships/wastewise/pubs/buy.pdf.
- Links to eighteen Greenseal "Choose Green" Reports at www.greenseal.org/resources/reports.cfm covering eighteen purchasing categories from carpet to wood finishes and stains.
- EPEAT Purchaser Resources for Computer and Peripherals purchases at www.epeat.net/Procurement.aspx.
- www.webbuyersguide.com, free expert buying advice providing access to thousands of white papers, case studies, and webcasts and detailed listings for over 40,000 products and 17,000 companies.
- The Energy Information Administration's (EIA) Energy Efficiency "Appliance Standards and Labeling Related Links" at www.eia.doe.gov/emeu/efficiency/appliance_standards.html.

Financial Incentives and Financing

■ The Tax Incentives Assistance Project (TIAP) provides consumers and businesses with information about federal income tax incentives for energy-efficient products and technologies at www.energytaxincentives.org.

■ U.S. Department of Energy consumer and business tax incentive information at www.energy.gov/taxbreaks.htm.

■ U.S. Department of Energy: Energy Efficiency and Renewable Energy Tax Incentives for Energy Efficiency site at www1.eere .energy.gov/buildings/tax_incentives.html.

■ The Database of State Incentives & Efficiency (DSIRE) is a comprehensive source of information on state, local, utility, and federal incentives that promote renewable energy and energy efficiency at www.dsireusa.org.

■ Incentives for ENERGY STAR purchases at www.energystar .gov/index.cfm?c=products.pr_tax_credits.

■ Incentives for water efficiency upgrades at www.epa.gov/ watersense/pp/find_rebate.htm.

■ The Fuel Efficient Vehicle Tax Incentives Information Center is available at www.fueleconomy.gov/Feg/taxcenter.shtml.

Online Purchasing

■ BuildingGreen.com, an independent company providing unbiased building-industry information including an online GreenSpec Directory of over 2,000 product descriptions for environmentally preferable products at www.buildinggreen .com/menus/index.cfm (subscription required for some content).

■ www.planetreuse.com, a free website for architects, designers, contractors, and material reclaimers to connect, find, and source reused building materials.

■ www.envirogadget.com, a great blog covering new eco-products.

APPENDIX A

GOING GREEN CHECKLIST

Use this checklist as a quick reference guide to the green practices outlined in the book, and a tool for keeping track of your progress. Refer back to the listed chapters for clarification when necessary.

REDUCING WASTE AND RECYCLING (from Chapter 7)

- ☐ Create a program to recycle as many of your office supplies as possible.
- ☐ Make recycling easy by providing clearly marked bins throughout the workplace.
- ☐ If your area doesn't provide recycling pickup for small businesses, appoint a recycling team to handle routine drops at a nearby facility.
- ☐ Find out more about WasteWi$e.
- ☐ Explore waste exchanges, if applicable.
- ☐ Look for material donation programs that serve your industry.
- ☐ Find ways to pool your resources.
- ☐ Recycling
  - ○ Know what can be recycled in your area.
  - ○ Check with the local government or public works department that is responsible for recycling
  - ○ Check with your landlord.
  - ○ Explore private recycling providers.
  - ○ Explore drop-off options.
- ☐ E-waste
  - ○ Reuse and recycle electronics (e-waste) instead of disposing of them.
  - ○ Locate end-of-life programs that take back and/or properly dispose of products once they have reached the end of their useful life.

- ○ Consider programs operated by reputable companies such as Dell, HP, Staples, OfficeMax, and Office Depot.
- ○ Look for e-cyclers that participate in the Basel Action Network's (BAN) Electronics Recycler's Pledge of True Stewardship, as well as e-cyclers that adhere to the EPA's R2 Responsible Recycling standards, which are in development and environmentally responsible, although far less stringent than BAN's.
- ☐ Encourage employee participation.
- ☐ Join TerraCycle.
- ☐ Make recycling easy.
  - ○ Provide clearly marked containers throughout the workplace; if you don't already have recycling bins in your office, purchase them.
  - ○ Locate bins in places where people need them, such as in copy, printing, and kitchen areas.
  - ○ Place paper recycling bins in individual offices.
- ☐ Explore opportunities to turn your recycling efforts into a profit center.

ENERGY MANAGEMENT (from Chapter 8)

- ☐ Create an energy management plan.
  - ○ Begin monitoring and collecting usage data.
  - ○ Determine which low-cost and no-cost energy-saving practices you can implement immediately to reduce costs and improve efficiency.
  - ○ Establish a set of policies to decrease energy consumption and eliminate energy waste.
- ☐ Easy energy conservation
  - ○ Get a free energy audit.
  - ○ Join ENERGY STAR for Small Business.
  - ○ Turn off lights (and other equipment) when not in use (i.e., at night).
  - ○ Turn off computers and monitors every night. Just shut them down!
  - ○ Use rechargeable batteries.
- ☐ Reduce standby or vampire power.
  - ○ Search for low standby products.
  - ○ Unplug infrequently used devices.
  - ○ Install Smart Strip Power Strips, Wattstopper Plug Load Controls, PlugMisers, and EnergyMiser plugs.
- ☐ Lighting
  - ○ Keep bulbs clean. Dirty bulbs can reduce light by as much as 50%.
  - ○ Replace existing or worn-out lightbulbs with high-efficiency lightbulbs.
  - ○ Upgrade to T8 (1" diameter) fluorescent lamp tubes, which are more efficient than older T12 (1.5" diameter) tubes.

O   Install ENERGY STAR–qualified exit signs.
☐   Maximize lighting efficiency.
   O   Use daylight to reduce artificial lighting needs during cold months; use solar screens or shades during hot months.
   O   Buy light-colored or translucent lampshades and consider painting your walls light colors to improve brightness, all of which reduce the need for lighting.
☐   Make use of lighting controls to reduce the amount of light used in your facility.
   O   Use timers to turn lights on and off automatically.
   O   Use bilevel switching to control groups of fixtures or lamps.
   O   Install switch plate occupancy/motion sensors in proper locations to automatically turn off lighting when no one is present and back on when people return.
☐   Temperature controls
   O   Install programmable thermostats and set goals to shift temperatures +/– 3 degrees.
   O   Use fans to delay or reduce the need for air conditioning—a temperature setting of up to 5 degrees higher can feel as comfortable with fans.
   O   When the temperature outside is more comfortable than inside, use fans to push air out and pull outside air in.
   O   Lower the hot water temperature controller on dishwashers and washing machines to reduce the amount of energy needed to heat the water you use.
☐   Weatherization
   O   Use weather stripping and caulking.
   O   Install chimney plugs, if applicable.
   O   Upgrade or install insulation in ceilings, walls, attics, floors, and windows.
   O   Install heavy curtains at windows and doors to keep drafts out.
   O   Install hot water tank blankets.
   O   When replacing windows, buy double or triple glazed.
☐   Heating and air conditioning
   O   Install a programmable thermostat.
   O   Change (or clean if reusable) HVAC filters.
   O   Use fans to delay or reduce the need for air conditioning.
   O   Take care of your heating, ventilating, and air-conditioning (HVAC) system with an annual maintenance contract.
☐   Food service equipment
   O   Lower the hot water temperature controller on dishwashers and washing machines.
   O   Clean refrigerator coils twice a year and replace door gaskets.

○   Have refrigeration systems serviced at least annually.
☐   Green information technology
☐   Power management
    ○   Turn off computers, monitors, and peripherals every night.
    ○   Set computers to enter sleep mode.
    ○   Set display monitors to enter sleep mode.
    ○   Set computers to put hard drives to sleep.
    ○   Turn computers off when not in use.
    ○   Keep computers plugged in when in use.
    ○   Change your energy settings on your laptop so that they are the same whether or not your laptop is plugged in.
    ○   Install eco-buttons.
    ○   Consider using software that allows the settings on a PC to be controlled centrally.
    ○   Unplug electronic device chargers when fully charged or install energy-saving power strips such as Smart Strips or Wattstoppers, which do it automatically.
☐   Switch to a green web host when your current contract is up.
☐   Use cloud computing.
☐   For larger IT departments, consider the following strategies:
    ○   Virtualization for servers and storage.
    ○   How your data center is designed in terms of energy loads, HVAC, and data consolidation.
☐   Consider technology-enabled energy management solutions.
☐   Renewable energy
    ○   Opt in to clean energy sources from your existing utility company.
    ○   Purchase green power from an alternative electricity supplier.
    ○   Buy renewable energy certificates (RECs) to offset your energy use.
    ○   Install solar thermal water heaters.
    ○   Install a solar electric system.
    ○   Install a small wind power device.
    ○   For new construction, install a geothermal heat pump.
☐   Consider carbon offsets after you've taken all possible measures to reduce emissions and when they are the best or only option available.

WATER CONSERVATION (from Chapter 9)

☐   Fix leaky toilets, faucets, and showerheads.
☐   Toilets
    ○   Insert water displacement devices in toilets.
    ○   Replace older, water-wasting toilets and urinals with newer models.

- O Install waterless urinals.
- ☐ Bathroom and kitchen sinks
  - O Install aerators on faucets.
  - O Install sensor-operated and self-closing faucets.
- ☐ Showers
  - O Use shower timers.
  - O Install low-flow showerheads.
  - O Install showerhead adaptors.
- ☐ Employ water efficiency technology.
  - O Install water-efficient appliances.
- ☐ Install a greywater system.
- ☐ Cleaning methods
  - O Do not overdilute cleaning chemicals.
  - O Revisit your maintenance schedules.
  - O Use entrance mats.
  - O Change to water-free or water-efficient cleaning methods.
- ☐ Irrigation and landscaping
  - O Water lawns and flower beds at night.
  - O Park cars and trucks in the grass when you wash them.
  - O Use mulch.
  - O Harvest rainwater.
  - O Install a drip irrigation system.
  - O When selecting new plants and grass to plant, choose drought-resistant varieties.
  - O Install inexpensive lawn and garden rain gauges.
  - O Use a water-saving hose nozzle.
  - O Use a hose timer.
  - O Install a smart irrigation system.
  - O Check with your building engineers to see if your water pressure can be reduced.
  - O Implement an outdoor landscape water conservation strategy.

PAPER REDUCTION STRATEGIES AND GREEN OFFICE SUPPLIES (from Chapter 10)

- ☐ Reduce paper use.
  - O Fax electronically.
  - O Whenever possible, use electronic forms for purchasing, employment applications, record keeping, etc.
  - O Have your payroll service issue paystubs via email.
  - O Send holiday cards and invitations electronically.

- O Use online banking to pay invoices, transfer money between accounts, and monitor your expenses.
- O Allow your customers to opt out of receipts.
- O Replace Post-it Notes with scrap paper.
- ☐ Change the way you print and copy.
  - O Don't print unless it's essential.
  - O Use scrap paper for notes instead of printing.
  - O Print and store documents in portable document format (PDF).
  - O Dedicate a copier or printer for draft documents.
  - O Switch to duplex printing and copying.
  - O Use multi-up printing when possible.
  - O Use Draft Mode or Fast Print as the default setting.
  - O Use Print Preview and Shrink to Fit functions.
  - O Use high-efficiency toner and ink.
  - O Install software that eliminates unnecessary printout pages.
- ☐ Send and store documents digitally.
  - O Store files electronically instead of on paper.
  - O Use a scanner to convert documents to a digital format.
  - O Use an online service for paperless faxing.
  - O Install a document management system.
- ☐ Office equipment
  - O Determine your copy volume before upgrading your copier.
  - O Install a multifunction device.
  - O Update your cash registers.
- ☐ Office furniture
  - O Send and receive faxes directly from your computer(s); if you fax the old-fashioned way, eliminate cover sheets by sticking a Post-it fax cover note on the first page.
  - O Send holiday cards and invitations electronically.
  - O Have your payroll service issue paystubs via email.
  - O Use online banking.
  - O For word processing, use the Arial Narrow font. It will reduce your printed page area by approximately 15%.
- ☐ Add this message to your email signature: *By not printing this email, you've helped save paper, ink, and trees.*
- ☐ Opt out of unnecessary catalogs and unwanted mailings. Whenever possible, provide only your company's name, phone, and email to other businesses—not your physical address.

GREEN HUMAN RESOURCES (from Chapter 11)

☐ Provide all employees with access to the green team.
☐ Commuting benefits
   ○ Promote public transportation.
   ○ Consider subsidizing employees' public transit costs with rebates, bonuses, or prepurchase of transit vouchers.
   ○ Promote walking and biking.
   ○ Support carpool programs.
   ○ Offer a shuttle or vanpool service.
   ○ Offer telecommuting.
   ○ Provide preferred parking for hybrid and high-efficiency vehicles.
   ○ Provide information about car insurance companies that give discounts to noncar commuters.
☐ Other green benefits
   ○ Give paid time to volunteer for environmental causes.
   ○ Give matching donations to green causes.
   ○ Encourage employees to conduct home energy audits.
☐ HR administration
   ○ Replace paper processes with online technologies.
   ○ Use an electronic signature service.
   ○ Offer direct deposit.
   ○ Convert company-specific, paper-based documents to online templates.
   ○ Use web-based employee self-service programs, which allow employees to request forms, submit changes, and receive approvals online.
☐ Outsource your HR functions.
☐ Training and recruiting
   ○ When hiring, prescreen candidates online or on the phone.
   ○ Accept résumés online.
   ○ Use blogs, wikis, and social networking tools to recruit or to communicate with staff.
   ○ Include eco-initiatives in internal newsletters along with information about programs and progress updates.
   ○ Set up an actual or virtual bulletin board where employees can post eco-information.
   ○ Hold training sessions on eco-issues.
   ○ Provide online training courses.

GREEN TRANSPORTATION AND SHIPPING (from Chapter 12)

☐ Review the Green Transportation Hierarchy.
☐ Find out more about the SmartWay Transport program.
☐ Green transport practices
    ○ Adopt technology to help manage the transportation process. Technologies such as transportation optimization and transportation management systems are software solutions for logistics management.
    ○ Balance daily deliveries so that you service clients in the same area on certain days.
    ○ Employ route optimization.
    ○ Plan ahead to reduce the number of empty or underutilized miles traveled.
    ○ Use wireless technology to make your mobile workforce more fuel efficient.
    ○ Transport 24/7—or as much as possible.
☐ Improve fuel efficiency.
    ○ Establish no-idling policies.
    ○ Use anti-idling technologies.
    ○ Establish anti-idling rules for receiving as well as deliveries.
    ○ Avoid left turns. Lower speed. Reducing highway speed by 5 mph can cut fuel use and greenhouse gas emissions by more than 7%.
    ○ Avoid rush hour. If you can, travel at off-peak times.
    ○ Travel light.
    ○ Provide driver training.
    ○ Make 100% on-time delivery your standard.
    ○ Use low-friction lubricants.
    ○ Make sure tires are properly filled.
    ○ Improve aerodynamics.
☐ Make your own fuel.
☐ Drive environmentally friendly company cars and trucks (and forklifts).
☐ Green shipping practices
    ○ For long-distance shipping, make ground transport your first preference.
    ○ Reuse packaging materials.
    ○ Use transportation contracts.
    ○ Use backhauling checks for backhaul rates first.
    ○ Avoid air freight whenever possible.
    ○ Avoid expedited shipping and delivery whenever possible.
    ○ Consolidate shipments.

○ Review and correct address labels.
○ Give preference to carriers and shippers that employ measurable environmental practices.

GREEN MARKETING AND COMMUNICATIONS (from Chapter 13)

☐ Reduce printed marketing materials.
  ○ Whenever possible, eliminate direct mail from your media mix. If you must send it, eliminate envelopes by using smaller mailers, postcards, and fold-and-mail forms.
  ○ Include your URL on all printed materials including packaging.
  ○ Reduce waste in design and production.
  ○ Create electronic versions of materials such as media kits, press kits, reports, and other documents, and then post them to your website.
☐ Maintain good list hygiene.
  ○ Update your company's mailing lists regularly to remove the undeliverable and duplicate addresses.
  ○ Don't mail to customers who have not responded in the past six to twelve months.
  ○ Make it easy for customers to opt out of mailings.
☐ Offer customers the option of receiving communications electronically.
☐ Test lists to improve response rates.
☐ Add Internet marketing to your media mix. Use Internet and mobile media coupons.
☐ Conduct market research using online surveys.
☐ Use the Direct Marketing Association's Environmental Planning Tool and Policy & Vision Statement Generator when planning print campaigns.
☐ Eliminate paper coupons.
☐ Packaging
  ○ Use packaging made from earth-friendly materials and designs.
  ○ Reduce package-to-product ratios.
  ○ Think about cube utilization when designing packaging.
☐ When conducting market research, use online surveys.
☐ Give away eco-friendly alternatives for promotional items.

GREEN BUSINESS TRAVEL
(from Chapter 14)

- ☐ Reduce the number of business trips you take.
- ☐ Take fewer, longer trips.
- ☐ Change the way you meet.
  - O Teleconference.
  - O Web conference.
  - O Schedule meetings on-site.
  - O Choose hub cities for meetings that involve air travel.
  - O Use preferred suppliers whenever possible.
  - O Sign up for frequent-traveler programs.
- ☐ Hotels
  - O Choose green hotels.
  - O Opt out of every-day sheet and towel service.
  - O Turn off the lights, in-room HVAC systems, and electronics when you leave your room.
- ☐ Air travel
  - O Fly Continental, Virgin Atlantic, or JetBlue.
  - O Choose an airline with fewer delays.
  - O Opt for nonstop flights.
- ☐ Take trains when possible.
- ☐ Automobiles
  - O Rent hybrid and alternative-fuel vehicles.
  - O Establish a corporate account where you are not charged a premium rate for green cars.
  - O Rent small cars.
  - O Hire a taxi or car service that uses alternative-fuel vehicles, when available.
- ☐ Promote mass transit when in town and for off-site travel.
- ☐ Carpool when attending business meetings.
- ☐ Use electronic toll collection devices.
- ☐ Use GPS navigation to find the most direct and efficient route to your final destination.
- ☐ Use a green-certified travel agent.
- ☐ Green meetings and events
  - O Don't serve bottled water.
  - O Eliminate disposable signs and dated materials.
  - O Use green transportation.
  - O Donate leftover food.
  - O Make sure you have a recycling plan in place.
  - O Register online, which will save you time, money, and lots of paper.
  - O Provide attendees with meeting handouts on a reusable flash drive.

- O Use eco-friendly promotional giveaways.
- O Use local and sustainable produce, flowers, beverages, décor, and rentals.
- O Carbon-balance your event.
- ☐ Walk or bike to meetings and for deliveries.
- ☐ Carpool to business meetings.
- ☐ Transportation
  - O Use electronic toll collector technology (like EZ Pass) to reduce emissions from idling.
  - O Use GPS navigation to find the most direct and efficient route to your final destination.
- ☐ Eliminate travel.
  - O Teleconference to conduct meetings, training programs, demonstrations, and workshops involving multiple people in different locations.
  - O Web conference if you need visual presentations or document sharing.
- ☐ Business travel
  - O Opt out of every-day sheet and towel service when staying in hotels.
  - O Turn off the lights, in-room HVAC systems, and electronics when you leave your hotel room. Whenever possible, host meetings at your offices or select a site that's close to home for most participants.
  - O Choose hub cities for meetings that involve air travel to reduce the need for fuel-inefficient connecting flights and rental cars.
  - O Choose an airline with fewer delays. Planes waste fuel while taxiing and idling at the gate.
  - O Opt for nonstop flights. Takeoffs and landings are a major source of CO_2 emissions.
  - O Take a train. Train travel is far more efficient than air or automobile travel.
  - O Rent small cars. Most small vehicles, other than small luxury cars, get better gas mileage.

GET INVOLVED (from Chapter 4)

- ☐ Join a green trade association and push for greater advocacy.
- ☐ Join or start a green task force within your trade association.
- ☐ Join a national or local small business organization that has a green agenda.
- ☐ Sign up for the National Small Business Association's Action Network advocacy email alerts that let you know how and when to send letters to your elected officials about important small business environmental issues. Then mobilize others to do the same.

- ☐ Sign up for the Center for American Progress' Energy & Environment RSS feeds and their issue alerts.
- ☐ Put a "Write to Congress" web sticker on your website so visitors can use the interactive banners to support small business issues or write letters to officials and the media.

■ GREEN PURCHASING (from Chapter 15)

- ☐ Create a purchasing policy.
  - ○ Step 1: Convene the green team.
  - ○ Step 2: Assess the opportunity.
  - ○ Step 3: Set standards.
  - ○ Step 4: Take cost into account.
  - ○ Step 5: Phase in new products and materials.
- ☐ Create policies to:
  - ○ Use less.
  - ○ Reuse instead of purchasing new.
  - ○ Reduce incoming and outgoing mail.
  - ○ Change the way you design, manufacture, or use products and materials to reduce product toxicity, waste, and the materials needed to get a product to market.
  - ○ Ship to point-of-use and near-sourcing
- ☐ Develop a supplier questionnaire.
- ☐ Shop and search online.
- ☐ Order supplies by phone or email.
- ☐ Look for financial incentives, tax credits, or rebates.
- ☐ See if on-bill financing (OBF) is available in your area.
- ☐ Implement green spend management.
  - ○ Analyze spending.
  - ○ Centralize purchasing.
  - ○ Eliminate "maverick" spending.
  - ○ Consolidate suppliers.
  - ○ Implement e-procurement.
- ☐ Communicate your new policies in employee newsletters, intranets, and staff meetings.
- ☐ Educate customers. Be sure to include statements on your product packaging about how much total and PCW recycled materials have been used, biodegradability, reduced chemical content, and third-party certifications.
- ☐ Institute a procurement policy favoring WaterSense-rated fixtures for future purchases.

COMMUNICATE. COMMUNICATE. COMMUNICATE. (from Chapter 6)

- ☐ Avoid greenwashing.
- ☐ Communicate with stakeholders.
- ☐ Communicate your green mission.
  - ○ Post it on your website on your main navigation bar.
  - ○ Post it in your offices or retail space.
  - ○ Include a link in emails, online newsletters, and all printed materials.
  - ○ Include an abridged version on all company press releases and in the About Us section of your website.
- ☐ Communicate your achievements.
- ☐ Make a business case with employees.
- ☐ Build awareness.
- ☐ Incorporate signage in the workplace.
  - ○ Use signs to promote internal programs.
  - ○ Use signs to post program reminders.
- ☐ Use newsletters and intranets.
- ☐ Remind your customers, your suppliers, and your staff about the importance of greening your operations with daily, weekly, or monthly communications via:
  - ○ Your website's home page.
  - ○ Email.
  - ○ Online newsletters.
- ☐ Promote your green program via:
  - ○ Events.
  - ○ Press announcements.
  - ○ Intranet posts.
  - ○ Bulletin board posts.
  - ○ Blog posts.
  - ○ Twitter.
  - ○ Holiday greetings.

APPENDIX B

■ SUPPLIER SUSTAINABILITY QUESTIONNAIRE

Company Name: Date:

The Supplier Sustainability Questionnaire must be completed and returned with your bid/proposal. This questionnaire is applicable to firms that provide services and/or goods.

1. What policies are in place to monitor and manage your supply chain regarding environmental issues? How does your company monitor and manage your supply chain regarding environmental issues?

_____

_____

2. What type of sustainable packaging/shipping materials do you use?

_____

_____

3. Does your company have a Green Transportation Plan for your operation?

_____

4. What does your company do to minimize the environmental costs associated with shipping?

_____

_____

5. Does your company have an environmental policy statement? Please provide link.

_____

6. Has your company ever been cited for noncompliance of an environmental or safety issue? If yes, state the reason, date, and outcome of the citation.

_____

_____

7. What programs do you have in place, or planned, for promoting resource efficiency?

_____

_____

8. Does your company have web-based materials available documenting your "green" initiatives? Please provide links.

_____

_____

9. If you are providing a product, does the manufacturer of the product that you are bidding/proposing have an environmental policy statement? If yes, please provide the manufacturer's environmental policy statement.

_____

_____

10. Have the product(s) that you are bidding/proposing been certified by a third-party organization, such as Green Seal or ENERGY STAR? If yes, which ones?

_____

_____

ENDNOTES

1

1. Mindy Fetterman, "Wal-Mart Grows 'Green Strategies,'" *USA Today*, September 25, 2006.
2. Nikki Johnson, "Thinking on the Outside of the Box," available at www.packworld.com/graphics/call/FoxjetWPdraft.pdf.
3. Peter Orszag, Congressional Budget Office, "Preparing for Our Common Future: Policy Choices and the Economics of Climate Change," available at www.cbo.gov/ftpdocs/99xx/doc9901/10-27-PresentationWellesley.pdf.
4. Jeffrey M. Jones, "In the U.S., 28% Report Major Changes to Live 'Green,'" available at www.gallup.com/poll/106624/US-28-Report-Major-Changes-Live-Green.aspx.
5. Environmental Leader, "Green Consumers Have Different Purchasing Motives," available at www.environmentalleader.com/2008/11/19/green-consumers-have-different-purchasing-motives/.
6. Experian Simmons, "Green Consumer Report: Digging Deeper into America's Green Mindset," Experian Information Solutions.
7. EcoAlign, "Banking the Green: Customer Incentives for EE and Renewables," available at www.ecoalign.com/news/ecopinion/banking-the-green.
8. Deloitte and Grocery Manufacturers Association, "Finding the Green in Today's Shoppers: Sustainability Trends and New Shopper Insights," available at www.deloitte.com/dtt/cda/doc/content/US_CP_GMADeloitteGreenShopperStudy_2009.pdf.
9. Havas Media, "Consumer Perception of Climate Change and Its Potential Impact on Business: Summary Conclusions," available at www.havasmedia.com/dynfiles/20080707155216_summary_conclusions.pdf.
10. Greener World Media, "State of Green Business 2009," available at www.stateofgreen business/com/.
11. Ibid.
12. PRWeb, "Study Identifies 4 Types of Green Consumers; 1 Group Most Likely to Respond to Green Marketing," available at www.prweb.com/releases/2007/11/prweb571361.htm.
13. Tompkins Associates, "'Greener' Companies Boost Image, Customer Satisfaction: Supply Chain Consortium Uncovers Added Benefits from Being Kind to Mother Earth," available at www.tompkinsinc.com/news/PR_2008/pr_091108.asp.
14. Aberdeen Group, "Getting from Green to Gold: Retail Success Factors and Outcomes," available at www.aberdeen.com/summary/report/benchmark/5213-RA-green-to-gold.asp.

3

1. J. Ottman, E. Stafford, and C. Hartman, "Green Marketing Myopia," *Environment* 48, 5 (2005): 22–36.
2. BBMG, "Conscious Consumer Report: Redefining Value in a New Economy" (2009).

4

1. Ben Elgin, "Little Green Lies," *Business Week*, October 29, 2007; Aspen/Snowmass, "Sustainability Report, 2006–2007," available at www.aspensnowmass.com/environment/programs/sustainreport.cfm.
2. Natural Marketing Institute, 2007 LOHAS Consumer Trends Database, www.nmisolutions.com/lohasd.html.

5

1. Glen L. Urban and John R. Hauser, *Design and Marketing of New Products*, 2nd edition (Upper Saddle River, NJ: Prentice Hall, 1993), 120–21; Jonas Matthing, Bodil Sandén, and Bo Edvardsson, "New Service Development: Learning from and with Customers," *International Journal of Service Industry Management* 15, 5 (2004): 479–98.
2. Allen Matkins, Attorneys at Law, "Green Building Update," September 17, 2008, available at www.jdsupra.com/documents/bf38b55d-6214-48b5-8f62-16701e7dc7a3.pdf.

6

1. J. A. Ottman, E. Stafford, and C. Hartman, "Green Marketing Myopia," *Environment* 48, 5 (2006): 22–36.
2. Ibid.
3. J. Austin, D. B. Hatfield, A. C. Grindle, and J. S. Bailey, "Increasing Recycling in Office Environments: The Effects of Specific, Informative Cues," *Journal of Applied Behavior Analysis* 26, 2 (1993): 247–53.

7

1. U.S. Environmental Protection Agency, "Municipal Solid Waste Generation, Recycling, and Disposal in the United States: Facts and Figures for 2006," available at www.epa.gov/epawaste/nonhaz/municipal/msw99.htm#links.
2. U.S. Environmental Protection Agency, "Sources and Emissions," available at www.epa.gov/methane/sources.html.
3. The Landfill Site, "Landfills: Environmental Problems," available at www.landfill-site.com/html/landfills_environmental_probl.php.
4. Larry Cummings, "Facts About Aluminum Recycling," April 2, 2007, available at http://earth911.com/blog/2007/04/02/facts-about-aluminum-recycling/. Calculated based on the following assumptions: Recycling one aluminum can saves the energy used to run one television for three hours; fifty workweeks in a year.
5. SKS Bottle & Packaging Inc., "Recycle Plastic Containers," available at www.sks-bottle.com/Recycle_Plastic.html.
6. Energy Information Administration, "Apples, Oranges and Btu," available at www.eia.doe.gov/neic/infosheets/apples.html.
7. U.S. Environmental Protection Agency, Design for the Environment, "Case Study 1: Managing Solvents and Wipes," available at www.epa.gov/dfe/pubs/lithography/case_studies/case1/lcasestudy1.html.

8

1.   Pure Energy Systems Network Inc., "Free Energy Quotes of Note," available at http://freeenergynews.com/Directory/Quotes/.

2.   ENERGY STAR, "Good Energy Management Is Good Business," available at www.energystar.gov/index.cfm?c=business.bus_good_business.

3.   Sir Stuart Rose, "Staying Green in a Tough Economic Climate," March 4, 2008, *Harvard Business Review Green*, available at www.hbrgreen.org/2008/03/the_hard_economics_of_green.html.

4.   ENERGY STAR, "Good Energy Management Is Good Business," available at www.energystar.gov/index.cfm?c=business.bus_good_business.

5.   ENERGY STAR, "Energy Strategy for the Future,"available at www.energystar.gov/index.cfm?c=business.bus_energy_strategy.

6.   TheBulb.com, "CFL Savings Calculator," available at www.thebulb.com/store/t-savings calculator.aspx. Calculated based on the following assumptions: Energy cost/kWh=$0.10; CFL life of 8,000 hours; 1.34 lbs of CO_2 emissions/kWh of electricity.

7.   ENERGY STAR, "Sure Enegy Savers," available at www.energystar.gov/index.cfm?c=sb_guidebook.sb_guidebook_sure_energy_savers_lighting.

8.   Byron Kennard, "How Small Business Can Slow Global Warming," CNNMoney.com, October 3, 2007, available at http://money.cnn.com/2007/10/02/smbusiness/global_warming.fsb/index.htm?postversion=2007100306.

9.   The International Energy Agency, "Fact Sheet: Standby Power Use and the IEA '1-Watt Plan,'" available at www.iea.org/Textbase/Papers/2008/cd_energy_efficiency_policy/3-Appliances%20and%20equipment/3-standby_fact.pdf.

10.   Richard Martin, "Can the Internet Save the Planet?" InformationWeek.com, available at www.informationweek.com/news/internet/showArticle.jhtml?articleID=205601559&pgno=1.

11.   Energy Information Administration, 2002 CBECS Detailed Tables, Table E4, available at www.eia.doe.gov/emeu/cbecs/cbecs2003/detailed_tables_2003/detailed_tables_2003.html#enduse03.

12.   Energy Information Administration, "Personal Computers and Computer Terminals in Commercial Buildings," available at www.eia.doe.gov/emeu/consumptionbriefs/cbecs/pcsterminals.html.

13.   Elena Varon, "Why Green IT Is Better IT," CIO.com, March 28, 2007, available at www.cio.com/article/100557/Why_Green_IT_is_Better_IT.

14.   Testimony of Joseph Romm, executive director of the Center for Energy and Climate Solutions, Washington, DC: September 21, 2000, before the Committee on Commerce, U.S. Senate, available at http://enduse.lbl.gov/Projects/rommtestimony000921.pdf.

15.   Ibid.

16.   Suzanne Foster and Chris Calwell, "Laptop Computers: How Much Energy Do They Use and How Much Can We Save?" Natural Resources Defense Council, August 2003.

17.   Ibid.

18.   Jacob Leibenluft, "Keep on Plugging: Should You Run Your Laptop Off Battery Power or Use a Charger?" *Slate*, December 2, 2008, available at www.slate.com/id/2205761.

19.   ENERGY STAR, available at www.eu-energystar.org/en/en_022p.shtml.

20.   Suzanne Foster and Chris Calwell, "Laptop Computers: How Much Energy Do They Use and How Much Can We Save?" Natural Resources Defense Council, August 2003.

21. Elena Varon, "Why Green IT Is Better IT," CIO.com, March 28, 2007, available at www.cio .com/article/100557/Why_Green_IT_is_Better_IT.

22. U.S. Department of Energy, Green Power Markets, "Green Power Markets," available at http://apps3.eere.energy.gov/greenpower/markets/index.shtml.

23. Ben Elgin, "Another Inconvenient Truth," *Business Week*, March 26, 2007, available at www .businessweek.com/magazine/content/07_13/b4027057.htm.

24. Swift, "Frequently Asked Questions," available at www.swiftwindturbine.com/frequently_ asked_questions.php.

25. American Wind Energy Association, "Annual Wind Industry Report," available at www.awea .org/publications/reports/AWEA-Annual-Wind-Report-2009.pdf.

26. National Renewable Energy Laboratory, "Geothermal Heat Pumps," available at www.nrel .gov/learning/re_geo_heat_pumps.html.

9

1. Calculated based on the following assumptions: Millions of gallons/day water use in Arizona = 6,730 (from "USGS Estimated Use of Water in the United States in 2000," available at http:// pubs.usgs.gov/circ/2004/circ1268/htdocs/table01.html).

2. Water Partners International, "Water Facts," available at www.water.org/waterpartners .aspx?pgID=916#Ref_1.

3. Steven Hanson, "Keep Your Floors Looking Great with Green Products," available at www .cleaningarticles.com/Article/Keeping-Your-Floors-Looking-Great-With-Green-Cleaning-Products/232.

4. Stephen Ashkin, "Water-Efficient Products and Techniques," CleanLink.com, March 2008, available at www.cleanlink.com/cp/article.asp?id=8461.

5. University of Minnesota, "Sparta Foods Saves Nearly $10,000 Through Water Conservation," Minnesota Technical Assistance Program, available at www.mntap.umn.edu/ intern/projects/spa-it13.htm.

10

1. Conservatree, "Trees into Paper," available at www.conservatree.com/learn/EnviroIssues/ TreeStats.shtml.

2. Depaul University, "Intelliprint," available at http://adminserv.depaul.edu/iprint/HTML/ impact.html.

3. Calculations based on the following assumptions: 266 workdays/year; 1 tree = 8,333.3 sheets of paper (Conserveatree, "Trees into Paper," www.conservatree.com/learn/EnviroIssues/ TreeStats.shtml).

4. Environmental Leader, "Xerox Says New Toner Cuts Digital Printing Devices' Power 15-30%," available at www.environmentalleader.com/2008/11/21/xerox-says-new-toner-cuts-digital-printing-devices-power-15-30.

5. National Resources Defense Council, "Green Living: Green Living Guides," available at www.nrdc.org/cities/living/chlorine.asp.

6. Cartridgeworld, "Recycling: Saving the World While Saving the Planet," available at www .cartridgeworldusa.com/section.aspx?id=6814.

7. BOMI Institute, "Furniture Refurbishing: Market Forces Are Making Refurbishing More Customer Friendly," *Today's Facility Manager*, August 2004.

11

1.   WorldatWork, "Is the 'Green' Movement in the Workplace Fact or Fiction?" available at www.worldatwork.org/waw/adimLink?id=25801.

2.   WorldatWork, "Four Out of Five College Students and Recent Grads Prefer Jobs at Green Companies," available at www.worldatwork.org/waw/adimComment?id=27793.

3.   World Business Council for Sustainable Development, "Driving Success: Human Resources and Sustainable Development," available at www.wbcsd.org/plugins/DocSearch/details.asp?type=DocDet&ObjectId=MTcxMDQ.

4.   Adrienne Fox, "Get in the Business of Being Green: Capitalize on Environmental Concerns Among Employees to Reap Benefits for Them—and Your Company," *HR Magazine*, June 2008.

5.   Calculated based on the following assumptions: 19,440,000 small businesses could allow one employee to telecommute = 26,400,000 small businesses *excluding* 6,960,000 small businesses that are identified as self-employed working from home (Department of Labor Statistics, "Work at Home 2004," September 22, 2005, Table 5, www.bls.gov/news.release/homey.t05.htm). Average person roundtrip miles to work = 30 miles and 30 minutes, medium car emissions = 1.1 pounds of CO_2/mile (Carbonify.com, "Carbon Dioxide Emissions Calculator," www.carbonify.com/carbon-calculator.htm).

6.   Envirowire, "It's Good to Share: Britain's Bosses Urged to Disclose Bills to Save Thousands," available at www.envirowise.gov.uk/uk/Press-Office/Press-Releases/UK-Press-Releases/Its-good-to-share-Britains-bosses-urged-to-disclose-bills-to-save-thousands.html.

7.   Planet Green, "How to Go Green: Public Transportation," available at http://planetgreen .discovery.com/go-green/public-transportation.

8.   Richard Week, "Can the Internet Save the Planet?" *InformationWeek*, January 12, 2008, available at www.informationweek.com/news/internet/showArticle.jhtml?articleID=205601559&pgno=1.

9.   *Entrepreneur*, "Human Resources Statistics," available at www.entrepreneur.com/encyclopedia/businessstatistics/article81978.html.

10.   The Telework Coalition, "Telework Facts," available at www.telcoa.org/id33.htm.

11.   Aberdeen Group, "Web 2.0, Talent Management, and Employee Engagement," available at www.aberdeen.com/c/report/research_briefs/5525-RB-talent-management-employee.pdf.

12.   Connected Ventures, available at http://viewit.cc/?r=AC42AE9A-F748-BAB6-86B9-1920773E4AE1.

12

1.   *Green Transportation Hierarchy: A Guide for Personal and Public Decision-Making*, prepared for Ottawalk and the Transportation Working Committee of the Ottawa-Carleton Round-table on the Environment, January 14, 1992.

2.   Kevin Klustner, "Transportation Is Moving—Slowly—Toward Sustainability," Greenbiz.com, October 1, 2007, available at www.greenbiz.com/feature/2007/10/02/transportation-moving-slowly-toward-sustainability.

3.   Greener World Media, "State of Green Business 2008," available at www.stateofgreen business.com/files/StateOfGreenBusiness2008.pdf.

4.   Joel Makower, "Ship It, Ship It Good: How Companies Are Driving Down the Impacts of Shipping," Grist.org, available at www.grist.org/biz/tp/2006/05/23/shipping/.

5.   InfinitePower.org, "Interactive Energy Calculators," available at www.infinitepower.org/calc_carbon.htm# (Total Contribution for CO_2 calculation); Frank Stodolsky, Linda Gaines, and

Anant Vyas, "Analysis of Technology Options to Reduce the Fuel Consumption of Idling Trucks," Transportation Technology R&D Center, available at www.transportation.anl.gov/pdfs/TA/15.pdf (supporting fact that diesel engine idling consumes about one gallon of diesel fuel per hour when the truck's heating or air-conditioning system is operated [for 5 brake horsepower load at 1,000 rpm; TMC 1999]).

6.   Richard Heinberg, "Oil and Politics," *Truthout*, May 14, 2008, available at www.truthout.org/article/oil-and-politics.

7.   Ibid.

8.   Ibid.

9.   Ibid.

10.   U.S. Environmental Protection Agency, SmartWay Transport Partnership, "The FLEET Model Short Version for Small Carriers," available at www.epa.gov/smartway/transport/index.htm.

11.   Ibid.

12.   Peter Ward, "10 Rules for Shippers," *Journal of Commerce*, December 6, 2004.

13.   Gary Petty, "Benefits of Fleet Optimization Center," available at http://fleetowner.com/management/privateline/benefits-fleet-optimization-center-0309/.

14.   Anthony Cola, "Going in Reverse: Obtaining Efficient Backhauling Services Presents a Number of Challenges, but the Cost Savings Are Worth the Effort," *Recycling Today*, May 2004.

15.   "Time Transportation Costs by Pre-Planning," *Mail: The Journal of Communication Distrubition*, March 2006, available at www.afms.com/files/MAILCOM%20Article%20-%2003-06.pdf.

13

1.   Spike Jones, "New Marketing Response Rate Study Published by DMA," Brains on Fire blog, December 30, 2005, available at http://brainsonfire.com/blog/index.php/2005/12/30/new-marketing-response-rate-study-published-by-dma/.

2.   Jim Ford, Borelaise Centre, and Climate for Ideas, "Climate Change Enclosed! Junk Mail's Impact on Global Warming," available at www.forestethics.org/downloads/ClimateReport.pdf.

3.   Remarks by Rupert Murdoch, chairman and chief executive officer, News Corporation, May 9, 2007, available at www.newscorp.com/energy/full_speech.html.

4.   Soya, "Information About Soy and Soy Products: Soy Ink," available at www.soya.be/soy-ink.php.

5.   Native Forest Network, "Guide to Stopping Junk Mail," available at www.nativeforest.org/stop_junk_mail/nfn_junk_mail_guide.htm.

6.   Aberdeen Group, "The Dirt on Direct Mail: Marketers Boost Revenues and Cut Costs While Reducing Environmental Waste," New Release, March 10, 2008, available at www.aberdeen.com/press/releases/press_release.asp?rid=275.

7.   Rebecca Pooler, "Electronic Advertising," Maine Is Technology 5, 7 (2002), available at www.state.me.us/newsletter/july2002/electronic_advertising.htm.

8.   Trade-Show-Advisor.com, "Enhance Results with a Trade Show Promotional Item," available at www.trade-show-advisor.com/trade-show-promotional-item.html.

9.   Dennis Salazar, "Globe Guard Post Consumer Recycled Boxes," Sustainable Is Good blog, May 5, 2008, available at www.sustainableisgood.com/blog/2008/05/globeguard.html.

10.   John Kalkowski, "Impact of Wal-Mart Scorecard Creates Concerns," PackagingDigest.com, March 1, 2008, available at www.packagingdigest.com/article/CA6536405.html.

14

1.   Costs calculated based on the following assumptions: Average domestic business trip = $1,054 (www.cnn.com/2007/TRAVEL/05/03/btravel.overview). An hour for a teleconference = $211 (www.wrplatinum.com/Downloads/8349.aspx). Average passenger miles/gallon = 33.4. A gallon of jet fuel = 21.095 lbs. of CO_2, one passenger mile = 0.63 lbs. of CO_2 (Transportation, Energy, and the Environment, Section A—U.S. Energy Consumption and Transportation Sector Energy Consumption, Table 4-21, www.eia.doe.gov). Overall (average) flight stage length = 632.5 miles (Air Carrier Traffic Statistics [Green Book]: June 2008).

2.   Dipasis Bhadra and Pamela Texter, "Airline Networks: An Econometric Framework to Analyze Domestic U.S. Air Travel," Research and Innovative Technology Administration, Bureau of Transportation Services, available at www.bts.gov/publications/journal_of_transportation_and_statistics/volume_07_number_01/html/paper_06/index.html.

3.   California Integrated Waste Management Board, "California Green Lodging Program," available at www.ciwmb.ca.gov/EPP/greenlodging/.

4.   Alan Durning, "Air Travel Heats Up the Planet," Sightline Institute, available at www.sightline.org/research/energy/res_pubs/rel_air_travel_aug04.

5.   Barbara E. Hernandez, "Hotels Queuing Up to LEED Sustainability," *BNET Travel*, October 1, 2008, available at http://industry.bnet.com/travel/1000245/hotels-queuing-up-to-leed-sustainability/.

6.   BTNOnline.com, "Business Travel News Webinar: Incorporate Environmentally Friendly Practices into Your Travel Management Program," August 13, 2008.

7.   Avis.com, "Avis Makes the World a Little Greener," available at www.avis.com/car-rental/content/display.ac?contentId=green-initiative-US_en-005366.

8.   The International Ecotourism Society (TIES), available at www.ecotourism.org/webmodules/webarticlesnet/templates/eco_template.aspx?articleid=95&zoneid=2.

15

1.   National Resources Defense Council, "Eat Local: Does Your Food Travel More Than You Do?" available at www.nrdc.org/health/foodmiles/.

2.   Princeton's Recycled Paper Campaign, "Greening Princeton," available at www.princeton.edu/-greening/paper.html.

INDEX

ABOUT THE AUTHOR

Jennifer Kaplan is a partner in Greenhance LLC; an adjunct faculty of marketing at Marymount University in Arlington, Virginia; a senior adviser to the Center for Small Business and the Environment (CSBE); and a regular contributor to Ecopreneurist.com. She lives with her family in Washington, DC.